PHILOSOPHICAL FOUNDATIONS
OF GERONTOLOGY

PHILOSOPHICAL FOUNDATIONS OF GERONTOLOGY

Patrick L. McKee, Ph.D.

Editor

Colorado State University

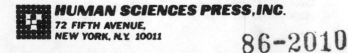

HUMAN SCIENCES PRESS, INC.
72 FIFTH AVENUE,
NEW YORK, N.Y. 10011

Printed in the United States of America
23456789   987654321

Library of Congress Cataloging in Publication Data

Main entry under title:

Philosophical foundations of gerontology.

  Includes bibliographies and index.
  Contents: On the types of human character / Aristotle — The Vedic ideal / Manu — On old age / Cicero — [etc.]
  1. Gerontology—Philosophy—Addresses, essays, lectures.   I. McKee, Patrick L.
HQ1061.p43   305.2′6′01   LC81-2922
                                    AACR2
ISBN 0-89885-040-1 (cloth)
ISBN 0-89885-041-X (paper)

CONTENTS

KEY TO ABBREVIATIONS

The following abbreviations are used throughout the bibliographies of this book:

AEHPG   Stuart Spicker, Kathleen Woodward and David VanTassel, *Aging and the Elderly: Humanistic Perspectives on Gerontology* (Atlantic Highlands, N.J.; Humanities Press, 1978)

E   *Ethics*

G   *The Gerontologist*

HD   *Human Development*

IJAHD   *The International Journal of Aging and Human Development*

JG   *Journal of Gerontology*

JMP   *Journal of Medicine and Philosophy*

JP   *Journal of Philosophy*

JVI   *Journal of Value Inquiry*

MAA   Bernice Neugarten, *Middle Age and Aging* (Chicago: University of Chicago Press, 1968)

O   *Omega*

PREFACE

Four aspects of old age have been repeatedly examined by philosophers. First, many philosophers have tried to define "successful" aging, in the sense of identifying the best way for people to live out the closing stages of their lives. They have agreed that the experiences of old age challenge the aging person to reevaluate his or her familiar pattern of life, and have tried to identify general moral principles for the guidance of life during old age. Three contrasting views have been developed. Representative statements of these, and the arguments used to support them, are included in the first part.

Second, philosophers have examined a variety of specific ethical problems that are created or intensified by old age. What is the rightful place of the old in society and culture? Do the aged infirm have a moral right to life's essentials even if they don't produce anything themselves? Does their claim to these things have a rational basis, and if so, what is it? Are the aged entitled to any special social status or privileges? What, with respect to the aged, is the rational basis for asserting or denying claims of this second kind? What ethical considerations bear on our desire to postpone or eliminate old age by extending the natural life span? Representative discussions of these specific ethical problems of old age are included in the second chapter.

A third philosophical issue of old age is found in the epistemological theory that people are capable of increasing degrees or levels of knowledge as they grow old. This idea is the basis of Plato's view that we should undertake the study of philosophy— commence the long struggle to overcome the illusions of life— only after we have reached the age of fifty. Other philosophers (Schopenhauer is an example) combine the idea of levels or degrees of knowledge with the view that as we age we develop through successive "stages of life," which give us an increasingly accurate understanding of life's meaning. The third part presents several variations on this important epistemological theme.

Besides helping to give perspective on the experience of aging itself, philosophers have an important contribution to make to the current development of gerontological theory. Many of the technical concepts of gerontology, including life satisfaction, alienation, disengagement, leisure, cognitive growth and decline, behavioral laws, theoretical explanation, and many others that are the staples of contemporary scientific thinking about aging, have a conspicuously philosophical dimension. In the fourth and final part, several of these gerontological concepts are examined from a philosophical perspective.

Part I

PHILOSOPHIES OF AGING

INTRODUCTION

Old age changes us. Some of the changes it brings, such as differences in physical appearances and minor shifts in emotional tone, are in themselves relatively insignificant. Others, including the achievement of perspective over life as a whole, retirement from one's life work, loss of loved ones and friends through death, and the approach of one's own death, are profound. Cumulatively, the whole process poses a broad, general question for the aging person that is essentially a question of personal philosophy: What is the best response, over all, to the radically changing conditions of life we experience in old age? Three answers to this question are presented in the selections included in this part.

According to the first view, the appropriate response to the onset of old age is a relatively complete withdrawal from the values, meanings, and relationships that inspire and direct life in the middle years. It advocates resignation to the inevitable loss of physical and mental powers that occurs in old age. Under conditions of decline that accompany old age, it is wrong, according to this view, for the aging person to persist in undertaking responsibilities, establish relationships, or actively pursue ideals appropriate for younger persons. Accordingly, the aging person should gradually forego the commitments and activities of earlier years and assume a relatively passive, acquiescent posture. Adopting a term that is well established in social gerontology, I will call this view the "philosophy of disengagement." Two versions of this position are represented here; the first in the selection from Aristotle's *Rhetoric* and the second in the Hindu classic text, *Laws of Manu*.

Aristotle's observation of the aged was surprisingly detailed and accurate. He noted the phenomenon of withdrawal from personal and social commitments observed also by many contemporary gerontologists, as well as the associated phenomenon of "normlessness,"[1] in which our normal concern about the approval of others is replaced by indifference. He also notes the phenomenon of "life review," to be explored in detail in Chapter 14. Finally, Aristotle observed how easy it is to misinterpret the external behavior of the elderly. He notes the fallacy of attributing to an old person the motives and intentions that explain behavior from the perspective of middle age, as when the moderation of old people is attributed to increased self-control, when it actually has a different basis.

Unquestionably, Aristotle's observations of the elderly were selectively negative. His view that the aged ought to respond to the losses experienced in growing old by withdrawing from active life is implicit in the contrasts he draws between the young, the old, and the middle-aged. Many of these contrasts are evident in the selection included here.

A more complex and less pessimistic expression of the philosophy of disengagement is found in the ancient Hindu text, *Laws of Manu*, containing the ethical teachings of the Hindu sage by that name. Manu's teaching prescribes organizing life into a pattern of four stages. First, there is the stage of Studenthood, devoted to study and development of self-control. Second, there is the stage of Householder, the time of marriage, career, and family responsibilities. Early old age corresponds to the stage of the Hermit, a period of gradual liberation of one's self from preoccupation with practical affairs and of gradually diminishing attachments to worldly objects and pleasures. Late old age constitutes the stage of the Ascetic, in which it is recommended that we restrict our attention to a daily regimen of inner and outer personal discipline, and strive for a final complete break with worldly ties. This process of withdrawal, if successful, has certain positive life-enhancing results, including "true insight into the nature of the world" (see section 74 of Manu's text) and achievement of the inner happiness and fulfillment that is appropriate in the final stages of life.

A second philosophy of aging, which I will call activism, is found in Cicero's *On Old Age* and Montaigne's essay "On Age." According to this view, the aging person should strive against decrement and loss, maintaining commitment to the values and pursuits of middle age for as long as possible. As Cicero puts it, ". . . old age, so far from being feeble and inactive, is even busy and is always doing and effecting something—that is to say, something of the same nature in each case as were the pursuits of earlier years" (*On Old Age;* see p. 29). This view represents the image of aging echoed in the popular tendency to admire old people who "stay active."

Activism does not necessarily rule out reduced levels of activity in old age. Even though it would be best for the aging person to continue pursuing the values and goals appropriate for middle age (there being no other values worth embracing), still, if advancing age makes this kind of activity less and less practicable, it is better overall to withdraw from the arena of active life before making an old fool of one's self. Even in such forced withdrawal, however, value commitments remain essentially those of earlier years.

A third philosophy of aging, found most notably in Plato, represents a middle ground between the first two. According to this view, the right response to the experience of growing old is neither resignation nor continuation of middle-age commitments, but the adoption of values and projects different from those appropriate for youth and middle age. Against activitism, this view affirms that old age makes possible discovery of values and meanings different in character from those accessible to us in youth and middle age; against asceticism, it affirms that the insights and values achievable in old age are related to worldly needs and interests and are of direct use to the world at large. In contrast to Aristotle's philosophy of disengagement, Plato advocates full participation of the old in governmental power and other positions of social responsibility.

In his essay "Death and Aging in Technopolis: Toward a Role Definition of Wisdom," Edmund Byrne views the elderly as the principal source of wisdom in society. Our rejection of the elderly from their role of sage in society derived, Byrne argues, from our society's excessively materialistic and economic conception of self-fulfillment. We tend to think of meaningful pursuit of self-fulfillment, Byrne believes, as appropriate only for the young and middle-aged, whose goals of self-fulfillment are heavily career- and work-related. But we seem to see the old, as we do the dying, as having no meaningful form of self-fulfillment left to pursue in the portion of life that remains to them. Byrne attempts to counter the prevailing ageist view of self-fulfillment by developing an alternative concept that is naturally and appropriately applied to the old. In doing so, he revives the idea that the old possess socially valuable wisdom that can be achieved only with age.

It is worth noting that the opposing view of Plato and Aristotle have a similar factual basis—observations about mental changes in old age. Aristotle, comparing the mental abilities of older people directly with those of younger people, found them weakened; Plato observed a developmental emergence of new and important powers of mind in old age. This selective perception of the facts of mental development in old age, which contributes so heavily to the differences between Plato's and Aristotle's philosophies of aging, continues in the empirical research of contemporary gerontologists. Some gerontologists, including Jack Botwinick,[2] David Guttman,[3] and Donald Hebb,[4] stress such decrements as decline in psychomotor reflexes, speeded learning tasks, objectivity, and short-term memory skills. Others, including Robert Butler,[5] Bernice Neugarten,[6] Robert Peck,[7] and Erik Erikson,[8] stress cognitive metamorphosis in old age. As with Plato and Aristotle, these different empirical orientations suggest different views about the appropriate conduct of life in old age and the proper place of the old in society. A major question for contemporary philosophy of aging concerns the logic of the process by which we are led to favor one of these empirical perspectives over the other.

The observations and opinions represented in part I force us to distinguish between factual and normative judgments concerning continued activity and disengagement. Factual judgments are judgments to the effect that as a matter of fact people do (or do not) lose ability to engage in meaningful active pursuits as they grow older. Normative judgments about disengagement are judgments about whether people ought to disengage as they grow older, whether that is a morally right thing for them to do. Obviously the two kinds of judgments may be related in various ways. Identifying the logical relations between them is an important part of a philosophy of aging. In the passages to follow, Aristotle seems to stress factual judgments of psychological decline, with a suggestion that ethical disengagement follows as a logical consequence. Montaigne seems to accept similar factual views, but does not think that these facts provide an ethical justification for disengagement. The *Manu* text places more direct stress on ethical considerations, suggesting that disengagement is a morally desirable life-style for the old independent of the physical or psychological changes accompanying it.

Plato's theory of aging requires a more complicated view of the facts and norms of aging. Certain declines in mind and body are recognized, but compensating gains are also recognized. What normative commitments are appropriate for the aged person, and what norms should guide society's treatment of the aged, will depend largely on which alleged losses and which alleged gains are or are not recognized as being relevant to these normative issues by a particular version of this view.

Finally, it will be clear in the following selections that philosophers sometimes deny popular beliefs to the effect that this or that change accompanying old age is a "loss" to the aging individual or to society. Two examples are Plato's denial that diminished capacity for sensory pleasure in old age is a loss, and Cicero's denial that changes in powers of memory accompanying old age are losses. When philosophers challenge popular interpretations of changes wrought by the aging process, the question they raise about the relevant change as a loss is normative, and can only be answered by the methods of normative enquiry.

Notes

[1]See especially E. Cumming and W. Henry, *Growing Old, The Process of Disengagement*. (New York: Basic Books, 1961, p. 46, p. 217).

[2]Jack Botwinick, *Cognitive Processes in Maturity and Old Age*. (New York: Springer, 1967, Chap. 8).

[3]David L. Guttmann, "Aging Among the Highland Maya: A Comparative Study," *Journal of Personality and Social Psychology*, Vol. 7, No. 1, 1967.

[4]Donald O. Hebb, "On Watching Myself Get Old," *Psychology Today*, Vol. 12, No. 6, 1978, pp. 15–23.

[5]Robert Butler, "The Life Review: An Interpretation of Reminiscence in the Aged," *Psychiatry, Journal for the Study of Interpersonal Processes*, Vol. 26, No. 1. (Reprinted in Part III, below.)

[6]Bernice L. Neugarten, "The Awareness of Middle Age." In *Middle Age*, ed. Roger Owen (London: British Broadcasting Corporation Publication, 1967. Reprinted in Bernice L. Neugarten, *Middle Age and Aging* (Chicago: University of Chicago Press, 1975).

[7]Robert C. Peck, "Psychological Developments in the Second Half of Life." In Bernice L. Neugarten, *Middle Age and Aging*. (Chicago: University of Chicago Press, 1975).

[8]Erik Erikson, *Childhood and Society*. (New York: Norton, 1963).

Chapter 1

ON THE TYPES OF HUMAN CHARACTER

Aristotle

Let us now consider the various types of human character, in relation to the emotions and moral qualities, showing how they correspond to our various ages and fortunes. By emotions I mean anger, desire, and the like; these we have discussed already. By moral qualities I mean virtues and vices; these also have been discussed already, as well as the various things that various types of men tend to will and to do. By ages I mean youth, the prime of life, and old age. By fortune I mean birth, wealth, power, and their opposites—in fact, good fortune and ill fortune.

To begin with the Youthful type of character. Young men have strong passions, and tend to gratify them indiscriminately. Of the bodily desires, it is the sexual by which they are most swayed and in which they show absence of self-control. They are change-

From Aristotle, *Rhetoric*, Book II, Chaps. 12–15, trans. W. Rhys Roberts, in *The Basic Works of Aristotle,* ed. Richard McKeon (New York: Random House, 1941). From *The Oxford Translation* of Aristotle. ed. W. D. Ross, Vol. II (1925). Reprinted by permission of Oxford University Press.

able and fickle in their desires, which are violent while they last, but quickly over: their impulses are keen but not deep-rooted, and are like sick people's attacks of hunger and thirst. They are hot-tempered and quick-tempered, and apt to give way to their anger; bad temper often gets the better of them, for owing to their love of honor they cannot bear being slighted, and are indignant if they imagine themselves unfairly treated. While they love honor, they love victory still more; for youth is eager for superiority over others, and victory is one form of this. They love both more than they love money, which indeed they love very little, not having yet learnt what it means to be without it—this is the point of Pittacus' remark about Amphiaraus. They look at the good side rather than the bad, not having yet witnessed many instances of wickedness. They trust others readily, because they have not yet often been cheated. They are sanguine; nature warms their blood as though with excess of wine; and besides that, they have as yet met with few disappointments. Their lives are mainly spent not in memory but in expectation; for expectation refers to the future, memory to the past, and youth has a long future before it and a short past behind it; on the first day of one's life one has nothing at all to remember, and can only look forward. They are easily cheated, owing to the sanguine disposition just mentioned. Their hot tempers and hopeful dispositions make them more courageous than older men are; the hot temper prevents fear, and the hopeful disposition creates confidence; we cannot feel fear so long as we are feeling angry, and any expectation of good makes us confident. They are shy, accepting the rules of society in which they have been trained, and not yet believing in any other standard of honor. They have exalted notions, because they have not yet been humbled by life or learned its necessary limitations; moreover, their hopeful disposition makes them think themselves equal to great things—and that means having exalted notions. They would always rather do noble deeds than useful ones: their lives are regulated more by moral feeling than by reasoning; and whereas reasoning leads us to choose what is useful, moral goodness leads us to choose what is noble. They are fonder of their friends, intimates, and companions than older men are, because they like spending their days in the company of others and have not yet come to value either their friends or anything else by their usefulness to themselves. All their mistakes are in the direction of doing things excessively and vehemently. They disobey Chilon's precepts by overdoing everything; they love too much and hate too much, and the same with everything else. They think they know everything, and are always quite sure about it; this, in fact, is why they overdo everything. If they do wrong to others, it is because they mean to insult them, not to do them actual harm. They are ready to pity others, because they think every one an honest man, or anyhow better than he is: they judge their neighbor by their own harmless natures, and so cannot think he deserves to be treated in that way. They are fond of fun and therefore witty, wit being well-bred insolence.

Such, then, is the character of the Young. The character of Elderly Men—who are past their prime—may be said to be formed for the most part of elements that are contrary of all these. They have lived many years; they have often been taken in and often made mistakes; and life on the whole is a bad business. The result is that they are sure about nothing and *under-do* everything. They "think," but they never "know"; and because of their hesitation they always add a "possibly" or a "perhaps," putting everything this way and nothing positively. They are cynical; that is, they tend to put the worse construction on everything. Further, their experience makes them distrustful and therefore suspicious of evil. Consequently, they neither love warmly nor hate bitterly but following the hint of Bias they love as though they will some day hate and hate as though they will some day love. They are smallminded, because they have been humbled by life: their desires are set upon nothing more exalted or unusual than what will help them to keep alive. They are not generous, because money is one of the things they must have, and at the same time their experience has taught them how hard it is to get and how easy to lose. They are cowardly, and are always anticipating danger; unlike that of the young, who are warm-blooded, their temperament is chilly; old age has paved the way for cowardice; fear is, in fact, a form of chill. They love life; and all the more when their last day has come, because the object of all desire is something we have not got, and also because we desire most strongly that which we need most urgently. They are too fond of themselves; this is one form that small-mindedness takes. Because of this, they guide their lives too much by considerations of what is useful and too little by what is noble—for the useful is what is good for oneself, and the noble what is good absolutely. They are not shy, but shameless rather; caring less for what is noble than for what is useful, they feel contempt for what people may think of them. They lack confidence in the future; partly through experience—for most things go wrong, or anyhow turn out worse than one expects; and partly because of their cowardice. They live by memory rather than by hope; for what is left to them of life is but little as compared with the long past; and hope is of the future, memory of the past. This, again, is the cause of their loquacity; they are continually talking of the past, because they enjoy remembering it. Their fits of anger are sudden but feeble. Their sensual passions have either altogether gone or have lost their vigor: consequently they do not feel their passions much, and their actions are inspired less by what they do feel than by love of gain. Hence men at this time of life are often supposed to have a self-controlled character; the fact is that their passions have slackened, and they are slaves of the love of gain. They guide their lives by reasoning more than by moral feeling; reasoning being directed to utility and moral feeling to moral goodness. If they wrong others, they mean to injure them, not to insult them. Old men may feel pity, as well as young men, but not for the same reason. Young men feel it out of kindness; old men out of weakness, imagining that anything that befalls any one else might easily happen to them, which, as we say, is thought that excites pity. Hence they are querulous, and not disposed to jesting or laughter—the love of laughter being the very opposite of querulousness.

　　Such are the characters of Young Men and Elderly Men. People always think well of speeches adapted to, and reflecting, their own character: and we can now see how to compose our speeches so as to adapt both them and ourselves to our audiences.

As for Men in their Prime, clearly we shall find that they have a character between that of the young and that of the old, free from the extremes of either. They have neither that excess of confidence which amounts to rashness, nor too much timidity, but the right amount of each. They neither trust everybody nor distrust everybody, but judge people correctly. Their lives will be guided not by the sole consideration either of what is noble or of what is useful, but by both; neither by parsimony nor by prodigality, but by what is fit and proper. So, too, in regard to anger and desire; they will be brave as well as temperate, and temperate as well as brave; these virtues are divided between the young and the old; the young are brave but intemperate, the old temperate but cowardly. To put it generally, all the valuable qualities that youth and age divide between them are united in the prime of life, while all their excesses or defects are replaced by moderation and fitness. The body is in its prime from thirty to five-and-thirty; the mind about forty-nine.

Chapter 2

THE VEDIC IDEAL: LAWS OF MANU

Manu

1. A twice-born Snâtaka, who has thus lived according to the law in the order of householders, may, taking a firm resolution and keeping his organs in subjection, dwell in the forest, duly observing the rules given below.
2. When a housholder sees his skin wrinkled, and his hair white, and the sons of his sons, then he may resort to the forest.
3. Abandoning all food raised by cultivation, and all his belongings, he may depart into the forest, either committing his wife to his sons, or accompanied by her.
4. Taking with him the sacred fire and the implements required for domestic sacrifices, he may go forth from the village into the forest and reside there, duly controlling his senses.

From F. Max Müller, ed., *The Sacred Books of the East,* Vol. XXV: *The Laws of Manu,* trans. G. Bühler (Delhi; Motilal Banarsidass, 1964). Reprinted by permission of the publishers.

5. Let him offer those five great sacrifices according to the rule, with various kinds of pure food fit for ascetics, or with herbs, roots, and fruit.

6. Let him wear a skin or a tattered garment; let him bathe in the evening or in the morning; and let him always wear his hair in braids, the hair on his body, his beard, and his nails being unclipped.

7. Let him perform the Bali-offering with such food as he eats, and give alms according to his ability; let him honor those who come to his hermitage with alms consisting of water, roots, and fruit.

8. Let him be always industrious in privately reciting the Veda; let him be patient of hardships, friendly towards all, of collected mind, ever liberal and never a receiver of gifts, and compassionate towards all living creatures.

9. Let him offer, according to the law, the Agnihotra with three sacred fires, never omitting the new-moon and full-moon sacrifices at the proper time.

10. Let him also offer the Nakshatreshri, the Âgrayana, and the Kâturmâsya sacrifices, as well as the Turâyana and likewise the Dâkshâyana, in due order.

11. White pure grains, fit for ascetics, which grow in spring and in autumn, and which he himself has collected, let him severally prepare the sacrificial cakes purodâsa and the boiled messes karu, as the law directs.

12. Having offered those most pure sacrificial viands, consisting of the produce of the forest, he may use the remainder for himself, mixed with salt prepared by himself.

13. Let him eat vegetables that grow on dry land or in water, flowers, roots, and fruits, the productions of pure trees, and oils extracted from forest-fruits.

14. Let him avoid honey, flesh, and mushrooms growing on the ground or elsewhere, the vegetables called Bhûstrina, and Sigruka, and the Sleshmântaka fruit.

15. Let him throw away in the month of Asvina the food of ascetics, which he formerly collected, likewise his worn-out clothes and his vegetables, roots, and fruit.

16. Let him not eat anything grown on ploughed land, though it may have been thrown away by somebody, nor roots and fruit grown in a village, though he may be tormented by hunger.

17. He may eat either what has been cooked with fire, or what has been ripened by time; he either may use a stone for grinding, or his teeth may be his mortar.

18. He may either at once after his daily meal cleanse his vessel for collecting food, or lay up a store sufficient for a month, or gather what suffices for six months or for a year.

19. Having collected food according to his ability, he may either eat at night only, or in the daytime only, or at every fourth mealtime, or at every eighth.

20. Or he may live according to the rule of the lunar penance Kândrâyana, daily diminishing the quantity of his food in the bright half of the month and increasing it in the dark half; or he may eat on the last days of each fortnight, once a day only, boiled barley-gruel.

21. Or he may constantly subsist on flowers, roots, and fruit alone, which have been ripened by time and have fallen spontaneously, following the rule of the Institutes of Vikhanas.

22. Let him either roll about on the ground, or stand during the day on tiptoe, or let him alternately stand and sit down; going at the Savanas at sunrise, at midday, and at sunset to water in the forest in order to bathe.

23. In summer let him expose himself to the heat of five fires, during the rainy season live under the open sky, and in winter be dressed in wet clothes, thus gradually increasing the rigour of his austerities.

24. When he bathes at the three Savanas, sunrise, midday,

and sunset, let him offer libations of water to the manes and the gods, and practicing harsher and harsher austerities, let him dry up his bodily frame.

25. Having reposited the three sacred fires in himself, according to the prescribed rule, let him live without a fire, without a house, wholly silent, subsisting on roots and fruit,

26. Making no effort to procure things that give pleasure, chaste, sleeping on the bare ground, not caring for any shelter, dwelling at the roots of trees.

27. From Brâhma*n*as who live as ascetics, let him receive alms, barely sufficient to support life, and from other householders of the twice-born castes who reside in the forest.

28. Or the hermit who dwells in the forest may bring food from a village, receiving it either in a hollow dish of leaves, in his naked hand, or in a broken earthen dish, and may eat eight mouthfuls.

29. These and other observances must a Brâhma*n*a who dwells in the forest diligently practice, and in order to attain complete union with the supreme Soul, he must study the various sacred texts contained in the Upanishads,

30. As well as those rites and texts which have been practiced and studied by the sages R*i*shis, and by Brâhma*n*a householders, in order to increase their knowledge of Brahman, and their austerity, and in order to sanctify their bodies;

31. Or let him walk, fully determined and going straight on, in a northeasterly direction, subsisting on water and air, until his body sinks to rest.

32. A Brâhma*n*a, having got rid of his body by one of those modes practiced by the great sages, is exalted in the world of Brahman, free from sorrow and fear.

33. But having thus passed the third part of a man's natural

term of life in the forest, he may live as an ascetic during the fourth part of his existence, after abandoning all attachment to worldly objects.

34. He who after passing from order to order, after offering sacrifices and subduing his senses, becomes tired with giving alms and offerings of food, an ascetic, gains bliss after death.

35. When he has paid the three debts, let him apply his mind to the attainment of final liberation; he who seeks it without having paid his debts sinks downwards.

36. Having studied the Vedas in accordance with the rule, having begat sons according to the sacred law, and having offered sacrifices according to his ability, he may direct his mind to the attainment of final liberation.

37. A twice-born man who seeks final liberation, without having studied the Vedas, without having begotten sons, and without having offered sacrifices, sinks downwards.

38. Having performed the Ishti, sacred to the Lord of creatures Pragâpati, where he gives all his property as the sacrificial fee, having reposited the sacred fires in himself, a Brâhmana may depart from his house as an ascetic.

39. Worlds, radiant in brilliancy, become the portion of him who recites the texts regarding Brahman and departs from his house as an ascetic, after giving a promise of safety to all created beings.

40. For that twice-born man, by whom not the smallest danger even is caused to created beings, there will be no danger from any quarter, after he is freed from his body.

41. Departing from his house fully provided with the means of purification Pavitra, let him wander about absolutely silent, and caring nothing for enjoyments that may be offered to him.

42. Let him always wander alone, without any companion,

in order to attain final liberation, fully understanding that the solitary man, who neither forsakes nor is forsaken, gains his end.

43. He shall neither possess a fire, nor a dwelling, he may go to a village for his food, he shall be indifferent to everything, firm of purpose, meditating, and concentrating his mind on Brahman.

44. A potsherd instead of an alms-bowl, the roots of trees for a dwelling, coarse worn-out garments, life in solitude and indifference towards everything, are the marks of one who has attained liberation.

45. Let him not desire to die, let him not desire to live; let him wait for his appointed time, as a servant waits for the payment of his wages.

46. Let him put down his foot purified by his sight, let him drink water purified by straining with a cloth, let him utter speech purified by truth, let him keep his heart pure.

47. Let him patiently bear hard words, let him not insult anybody, and let him not become anybody's enemy for the sake of this perishable body.

48. Against an angry man let him not in return show anger, let him bless when he is cursed, and let him not utter speech, devoid of truth, scattered at the seven gates.

49. Delighting in what refers to the Soul, sitting in the postures prescribed by the Yoga, independent of external help, entirely abstaining from sensual enjoyments, with himself for his only companion, he shall live in this world, desiring the bliss of final liberation.

50. Neither by explaining prodigies and omens, nor by skill in astrology and palmistry, nor by giving advice and by the exposition of the Sâstras, let him ever seek to obtain alms.

51. Let him not in order to get go near a house filled with hermits, Brâhmanas, birds, dogs, or other mendicants.

52. His hair, nails, and beard being clipped, carrying an

alms-bowl, a staff, and a water-pot, let him continually wander about, controlling himself, and not hurting any creature.

53. His vessels shall not be made of metal, they shall be free from fractures; it is ordained that they shall by cleansed with water, like the cups, called *K*amasa, at a sacrifice.

54. A gourd, a wooden bowl, an earthen dish, or one made of split cane, Manu, the son of Svayambhu, has declared to be vessels suitable for an ascetic.

55. Let him go to beg once a day, let him not be eager to obtain a large quantity of alms; for an ascetic who eagerly seeks alms, attaches himself also to sensual enjoyments.

56. When no smoke ascends from the kitchen, when the pestle lies motionless, when the embers have been extinguished, when the people have finished their meal, when the remnants in the dishes have been removed, let the ascetic always go to beg.

57. Let him not be sorry when he obtains nothing, nor rejoice when he obtains something, let him accept so much only as will sustain life, let him not care about the quality of his utensils.

58. Let him disdain all food obtained in consequence of humble salutations, for even an ascetic who has attained final liberation, is bound with the fetters of the Sa*m*sâra by accepting food given in consequence of humble salutations.

59. By eating little, and by standing and sitting in solitude, let him restrain his senses, if they are attracted by sensual objects.

60. By the restraint of his senses, by the destruction of love and hatred, and by the abstention from injuring the creatures, he becomes fit for immortality.

61. Let him reflect on the transmigration of men, caused by their sinful deeds, on their falling into hell, and on the torments in the world of Yama:

62. On the separation from their dear ones, on their union with hated men, on their being overpowered by age and being tormented with diseases,

63. On the departure of the individual soul from this body and its new birth in another womb, and on its wanderings through ten thousand millions of existences,

64. On the infliction of pain on embodied spirits, which is caused by demerit, and the gain of eternal bliss, which is caused by the attainment of their highest aim, gained through spiritual merit.

65. By deep meditation let him recognize the subtile nature of the supreme Soul, and its presence in all organisms, both the highest and the lowest.

66. To whatever order he may be attached, let him, though blemished by a want of the external marks, fulfil his duty, equal-minded towards all creatures; for the external mark of the order is not the cause of the acquisition of merit.

67. Though the fruit of the Kataka tree the clearing-nut makes water clear, yet the latter does not become limpid in consequence of the mention of the fruit's name.

68. In order to preserve living creatures, let him always by day and by night, even with pain to his body, walk, carefully scanning the ground.

69. In order to expiate the death of those creatures which he unintentionally injured by day or by night, an ascetic shall bathe and perform six suppressions of the breath.

70. Three suppressions of the breath even, performed according to the rule, and accompanied with the recitation of the Vyâhritis and of the syllable Om, one must know to be the highest form of austerity for every Brâhmana.

71. For as the impurities of metallic ores, melted in the blast of a furnace, are consumed, even so the taints of the organs are destroyed through the suppression of the breath.

72. Let him destroy the taints through suppressions of the breath, the production of sin by fixed attention, all sensual attachments by restraining his senses and organs, and all qualities that are not lordly by meditation.

73. Let him recognize by the practice of meditation the progress of the individual soul through beings of various kinds, a progress hard to understand for unregenerate men.

74. He who possesses the true insight into the nature of the world, is not fettered by his deeds; but he who is destitute of that insight, is drawn into the circle of births and deaths.

75. By not injuring any creatures, by detaching the senses from objects of enjoyment, by the rites prescribed in the Veda, and by rigorously practicing austerities, men gain that state even in this world.

76 – Let him quit this dwelling, composed of the five
77. elements, where the bones are the beams, which is held together by tendons instead of cords, where the flesh and the blood are the mortar, which is thatched with the skin, which is foul-smelling, filled with urine and ordure, infested by old age and sorrow, the seat of disease, harassed by pain, gloomy with passion, and perishable.

78. He who leaves this body, be it by necessity as a tree that is torn from the river-bank, or freely like a bird that quits a tree, is freed from the misery of this world, dreadful like a shark.

79. Making over the merit of his own good actions to his friends and the guilt of his evil deeds to his enemies, he attains the eternal Brahman by the practice of meditation.

80. When by the disposition of his heart he becomes indifferent to all objects, he obtains eternal happiness both in this world and after death.

81. He who has in this manner gradually given up all

attachments and is freed from all the pairs of opposites, reposes in Brahman alone.

82. All that has been declared above depends on meditation; for he who is not proficient in the knowledge of that which refers to the Soul reaps not the full reward of the performance of rites.

83. Let him constantly recite those texts of the Veda which refer to the sacrifice, those referring to the deities, and those which treat of the Soul and are contained in the concluding portions of the Veda Vedânta.

84. That is the refuge of the ignorant, and even that the refuge of those who know the meaning of the Veda; that is the protection of those who seek bliss in heaven and of those who seek endless beatitude.

85. A twice-born man who becomes an ascetic, after the successive performance of the above-mentioned acts, shakes off sin here below and reaches the highest Brahman.

86. Thus the law valid for self-restrained ascetics has been explained to you; now listen to the particular duties of those who give up the rites prescribed by the Veda:

87. The student, the householder, the hermit, and the ascetic, these constitute four separate orders, which all spring from the order of householders.

88. But all or even any of these orders, assumed successively in accordance with the Institutes of the sacred law, lead the Brâhma*n*a who acts by the preceding rules to the highest state.

89. And in accordance with the precepts of the Veda and of the Sm*r*iti, the housekeeper is declared to be superior to all of them; for he supports the other three.

90. As all rivers, both great and small, find a resting-place in the ocean, even so men of all orders find protection with householders.

91. By twice-born men belonging to any of these four orders, the tenfold law must be ever carefully obeyed.

92. Contentment, forgiveness, self-control, abstention

from unrighteously appropriating anything, obedience to the rules of purification, coercion of the organs, wisdom, knowledge of the supreme Soul, truthfulness, and abstention from anger, form the tenfold law.

93. Those Brâhma*n*as who thoroughly study the tenfold law, and after studying obey it, enter the highest state.

94. A twice-born man who, with collected mind, follows the tenfold law and has paid his three debts, may, after learning the Vedânta according to the prescribed rule, become an ascetic.

95. Having given up the performance of all rites, throwing off the guilt of his sinful acts, subduing his organs and having studied the Veda, he may live at his ease under the protection of his son.

96. He who has thus given up the performance of all rites, who is solely intent on his own particular object, and free from desires, destroys his guilt by his renunciation and obtains the highest state.

97. Thus the fourfold holy law of Brâhma*n*as, which after death yields imperishable rewards, has been declared to you . . .

Chapter 3

ON OLD AGE

Cicero

Cato: "Old age withdraws us from active pursuits." From what pursuits? Is it not from those which are followed because of youth and vigor? Are there, then, no intellectual employments in which aged men may engage, even though their bodies are infirm? Was there, then, no employment for Quintus Maximus? And none, Scipio, for your father, Lucius Paulus, the father-in-law of that best of men, my son? And those other old men, like Fabricius, Curius, and Coruncanius—were they doing nothing, when by their wisdom and influence they were preserving the state?

To the old age of Appius Claudius was also added blindness; yet when the sentiment of the senate was inclining towards peace

From Cicero, *On Old Age,* trans. W. A. Falconer (Cambridge, Mass.: Harvard University Press, 1923). This work is in the form of a dialogue between Cato, age 84, Scipio, age 35, and Laelius, age 36. In this passage, Cato expresses the main elements in his philosophy of old age. Reprinted with permission of Loeb Classical Library.

and alliance with Pyrrhus, he did not hesitate to say what Ennius has thus put into verse:

> Your minds that once did stand erect and strong,
> What madness swerves them from their wonted course?

—and so on, in most impressive style. But you are familiar with the poem, and, after all, the actual speech of Appius is still extant. It was delivered seventeen years after his second consulship, although ten years had intervened between the two consulships and he had been censor before he was consul. Hence, it is known that he was undoubtedly an old man at the time of the war with Pyrrhus, and yet such is the story as we have it by tradition.

Those, therefore, who allege that old age is devoid of useful activity adduce nothing to the purpose, and are like those who would say that the pilot does nothing in the sailing of the ship, because, while others are climbing the masts, or running about the gangways, or working at the pumps, he sits quietly in the stern and simply holds the tiller. He may not be doing what younger members of the crew are doing, but what he does is better and much more important. It is not by muscle, speed, or physical dexterity that great things are achieved, but by reflection, force of character and judgment; in these qualities old age is usually not only not poorer, but is even richer.

But perhaps it seems to you that I who engaged in various kinds of warfare as private, captain, general, and commander-in-chief, am unemployed now that I do not go to war. And yet I direct the senate as to what wars should be waged and how; at the present time, far in advance of hostilities, I am declaring war on Carthage, for she has long been plotting mischief; and I shall not cease to fear her until I know that she has been utterly destroyed. And I pray the immortal gods to reserve for you, Scipio, the glory of completing the work which your grandfather left unfinished. Thirty-three years have passed since that hero's death, but each succeeding year will receive his memory and pass it on. He died in the year before I was censor, nine years after I was consul; and while I was holding the latter office he was elected consul for the second time. If, then, he had lived to his hundredth year, would he be repenting of his old age? No, for he would not be employing his time in running and in leaping, or in long-distance throwing of the spear or in hand-to-hand sword play, but he would be engaged in using reflection, reason, and judgment. If these mental qualities were not character-istic of old men, our fathers would not have called their highest deliberate body the "senate." Among the Lacedaemonians, for example, those who fill their chief magistracies are called "elders," as they are in fact. And indeed, if you care to read or hear foreign history, you will find that the greatest states have been overthrown by the young and sustained and restored by the old.

> How lost you, pray, your mighty state so soon?

for such is the question put in a play entitled *The Wolf* by the poet Naevius. Several answers are given, but the one chiefly in point is this: Through swarms of green, declaiming, silly lads. True enough, for rashness is the product of the budding-time of youth, prudence of the harvest-time of age.

But, it is alleged, the memory is impaired. Of course, if you do not exercise it, or also if you are by nature somewhat dull. Themistocles had learned the names of all the citizens of Athens by heart; do you think, then, that after he became old he was wont to address as Lysimachus one who in fact was Aristides? I, for instance, know not only the people who are living, but I recall their fathers and grandfathers, too; and as I read their epitaphs I am not afraid of the superstition that, in so doing, I shall lose my memory; for by reading them I refresh my recollection of the dead. I certainly never heard of any old man forgetting where he had hidden his money! The aged remember everything that interests them, their appointments to appear in course, and who are their creditors and who their debtors.

And how is it with aged lawyers, pontiffs, augurs, and philo-sophers? What a multitude of things they remember! Old men retain their mental faculties, provided their interest and application continue; and this is true, not only of men in exalted public station, but likewise of those in the quiet of private life. Sophocles composed tragedies to extreme old age; and when, because of his absorption in literary work, he was thought to be neglecting his business affairs, his sons haled him into court in order to secure a verdict removing him from the control of his property on the ground of imbecility, under a law similar to ours, whereby it is customary to restrain heads of families from wasting their estates. Thereupon, it is said, the old man read to the jury his play, *Oedipus at Colonus,* which he had just written and was revising, and inquired: "Does that poem seem to you to be the work of an imbecile?" When he had finished he was acquitted by the verdict of the jury. Think you, then, that old age forced him to abandon his calling, or that it silenced Homer, Hesiod, Simonides, Stesichorus, or Isocrates, and Gorgias (whom I have mentioned already), or any of those princes of philosophy Pythagoras, Democritus, Plato, and Xenocrates, or Zeno and Cleanthes of a later time, or Diogenes the Stoic, whom you both have seen at Rome? Rather, did not activity in their several pursuits continue with all of them as long as life itself?

But come now—to pass over these divine pursuits—I can point out to you Roman Farmers in the Sabine country, friends and neighbors of mine, who are scarecely ever absent from the field while the more important operations of husbandry, as sowing, reaping, and storing the crops, are going on. Although this interest of theirs is less remarkable in the case of annual crops,—for no one is so old as to think that he cannot live one more year—yet these same men labor at things which they know will not profit them in the least.

He plants the trees to serve another age, as our Caecilius Statius says in his *Young Comrades.* And if you ask a farmer, however old, for whom he is planting, he will unhesitatingly reply, "For the immortal gods, who have willed not only that I should receive these blessings from my ancestors, but also that I should hand them on to posterity."

And the same Caecilius, in writing of the old man making

provision for a future generation, spoke to better purpose than he did in the following lines:

> In truth, Old Age, if you did bring no bane
> but this alone, 'twould me suffice: that one,
> By living long, sees much he hates to see.

Possibly, also, many things he likes; and as for things one does not wish to see, even youth often encounters them. However, this other sentiment from the same Caecilius is worse:

> But saddest bane of age, I think, is this:
> That old men feel their years a bore to youth.

A pleasure, rather than a bore, say I. For just as wise men, when they are old, take delight in the society of youths endowed with sprightly wit, and the burdens of age are rendered lighter to those who are courted and highly esteemed by the young, so young men find pleasure in their elders, by whose precepts they are led into virtue's paths; nor indeed do I feel that I am any less of a pleasure to you than you are to me. But you see how old age, so far from being feeble and inactive, is even busy and is always doing and effecting something—that is to say, something of the same nature in each case as were the pursuits of earlier years. And what of those who even go on adding to their store of knowledge? Such was the case with Solon, whom we see boasting in his verses that he grows old learning something every day. And I have done the same, for in my old age I have learned Greek, which I seized upon as eagerly as if I had been desirous of satisfying a long-continued thirst, with the result that I have acquired firsthand the information which you see me using in this discussion by way of illustration. And when I read what Socrates had done in the case of the lyre, an instrument much cultivated by the ancients, I should have liked to do that too, if I could; but in literature I have certainly labored hard.

I do not now feel the need of the strength of youth—for that was the second head under the faults of old age—any more than when a young man I felt the need of the strength of the bull or of the elephant. Such strength as a man has he should use, and whatever he does should be done in proportion to his strength. For what utterance can be more pitiable than that of Milo of Crotana? After he was already an old man and was watching the athletes training in the racecourse, it is related that, as he looked upon his shrunken muscles, he wept and said, "Yes, but they now are dead." But not as dead as you, you babbler! For you never gained renown from your real self, but from brute strength of lungs and limb. Of a far different stamp were Sextus Aelius and Titus Coruncanius of ancient times, and Publius Crassus of a later date, by whom instruction in jurisprudence was given to their fellow-citizens, and whose skill in law continued to the very last gasp.

The orator, I fear, does lose in efficiency on account of old age, because his success depends not only upon his intellect, but also upon his lungs and bodily strength. In old age, no doubt, the voice actually gains (I know not how) that magnificent resonance which even I have not lost, and you see my years; and yet the style of speech that graces the old man is subdued and gentle, and very often sedate and mild speaking of an eloquent old man wins itself a hearing. And although one cannot himself engage in oratory, still, he may be able to give instruction to a Scipio or a Laelius! For what is more agreeable than an old age surrounded by the enthusiasm of youth? Or do we not concede to old age even strength enough to instruct and train young men and equip them for every function and duty? And what more exalted service can there be than this? For my part, Scipio, I used to consider Gnaeus and Publius Scipio and your two grandfathers, Lucius Aemilius and Publius Africanus, fortunate in being attended by throngs of noble youths; and no teachers of the liberal arts should be considered unhappy, even though their bodily vigor may have waned and failed.

And yet, even that very loss of strength is more often chargeable to the dissipations of youth than to any fault of old age; for an intemperate and indulgent youth delivers to old age a body all worn out. For example, Cyrus, in Xenophon, in that discourse which he delivered when he was very old and on his death-bed, says that he had never felt that his old age was any less vigorous than his youth had been. I remember that in my boyhood I saw Lucius Metellus, who, four years after his second consulship became Chief Pontiff and held that sacred office for twenty-two years, and I recall that he enjoyed such great vigor of body to the end of his days that he did not feel the loss of youth. I need say nothing of myself in this connexion, though to do so is an old man's privilege and permitted of one of my age.

But, grant that old age is devoid of strength; none is even expected of it. Hence both by law and by custom men of my age are exempt from those public services which cannot be rendered without strength of body. Therefore, we are not only not required to do what we cannot perform, but we are not required to do even as much as we can. Yet, it may be urged, many old men are so feeble that they can perform no function that duty or indeed any position in life demands. True, but that is not peculiar to old age; generally it is a characteristic of ill-health. Note how weak, Scipio, was our adoptive father, the son of Publius Africanus! What feeble health he had, or rather no health at all! But for this he would have shone forth as the second luminary of the state; for to his father's greatness of intellect he had added a more abundant learning. What wonder then, that the aged are sometimes weak, when even the young cannot escape the same fate?

But it is our duty, my young friends, to resist old age; to compensate for its defects by a watchful care; to fight against it as we would fight against disease; to adopt a regimen of health; to practice moderate exercise; and to take just enough of food and drink to restore our strength and not to overburden it. Nor, indeed, are we to give our attention solely to the body; much greater care is due to the mind and soul; for they, too, like lamps, grow dim with time, unless we keep them supplied with oil. Moreover, exercise causes the body to become heavy with fatigue, but intellectual activity gives buoyancy to the mind. For when Caecilius speaks of "the old fools of the cosmic stage," he has in mind old men characterized by credulity, forgetfulness, and carelessness, which are faults, not of old age generally, but only of an old age that is drowsy, slothful, and inert. Just as waywardness and lust are more often found in the young man than in the old, yet not in all who are young, but only in those naturally base, so that senile debility, usually called "dotage," is a characteristic, not of all old men, but only of those who are weak in mind and will.

Appius, though he was both blind and old, managed four sturdy sons, five daughters, a great household, and many dependents; for he did not languidly succumb to old age, but kept his mind ever taut, like a well-strung bow. He maintained not mere authority, but absolute command over his household; his slaves feared him, his children revered him, all loved him, and the customs and discipline of his forefathers flourished beneath his roof. For old age is honored only on condition that it defends itself, maintains its rights, is subservient to no one, and to the last breath rules over its own domain. For just as I approve of the young man in whom there is a touch of age, so I approve of the old man in whom there is some of the flavor of youth. He who strives thus to mingle youthfulness and age may grow old in body, but old in spirit he will never be.

I am now at work on the seventh volume of my *Antiquities*. I am collecting all the records of our ancient history, and at the present moment am revising all the speeches made by me in the notable causes which I conducted. I am investigating the augural, pontifical, and secular law; I also devote much of my time to Greek literature; and, in order to exercise my memory, I follow the practice of the Pythagoreans and run over in my mind every evening all that I have said, heard, or done during the day. These employments are my intellectual gymnastics; these the race-courses of my mind; and while I sweat and toil with them I do not greatly feel the loss of bodily strength; I act as counsel for my friends; I frequently attend the senate, where, on my own motion, I propose subjects for discussion after having pondered over them seriously and long and there I maintain my views in debate, not with strength of body, but with force of mind. But even if I could not perform these services, nevertheless, my couch would afford me delight while reflecting on the very things that I lacked the strength to do. However, the fact that I can do them is due to the life that I have led. For the man who lives always amid such studies and pursuits as mine is not aware of the stealthy approach of age. Thus employed his life gradually and imperceptibly glides into old age, and succumbs, not to a quick assault, but to a long-continued siege.

We come now to another ground for abusing old age, and that is, that it is devoid of sensual pleasures. O glorious boon of age, if it does indeed free us from youth's most vicious fault! Now listen, most noble young men, to what that remarkably great and distinguished man, Archytas of Tarentum, said in an ancient speech repeated to me when I was a young man serving with Quintus Maximus at Tarentum: "No more deadly curse," said he, "has been given by nature to man than carnal pleasure, through eagerness for which the passions are driven recklessly and uncontrollably to its gratification. From it come treason and the overthrow of states; and from it spring secret and corrupt conferences with public foes. In short, there is no criminal purpose and no evil deed which the lust for pleasure will not drive men to undertake. Indeed, rape, adultery, and every like offense are sent in motion by the enticements of pleasure and by nothing else; and since nature—or some god, perhaps—has given to man nothing more excellent than his intellect, therefore this divine gift has no deadlier foe than pleasure; for where lust holds despotic sway, self-control has no place, and in pleasure's realm there is not a single spot where virtue can put her foot.

"Imagine," he begged, to make his meaning clearer, "imagine a person enjoying the most exquisite bodily pleasure to be had. No one will doubt, I think, that such a man, while in the midst of this enjoyment, is incapable of any mental action, and can accomplish nothing requiring reason and reflection. Hence there is nothing so hateful and so pernicious as pleasure, since, if indulged in too much and too long, it turns the light of the soul into utter darkness." My Tarentine host Nearchus, who remained steadfast in his friendship to the Roman people, told me that, according to tradition, Archytas uttered these words while conversing with

Pontius the Samnite, father of the man who defeated the consuls Spurius Postuminus and Titus Veturius at the Caudine Forks. Indeed he further told me that Plato the Athenian was present and heard Archytas deliver this discourse, and, upon investigation, I find that Plato did come to Tarentum in the consulship of Lucius Camillus and Appius Cladius.

Now, why did I quote Archytas? To make you realize that if reason and wisdom did not enable us to reject pleasure, we should be very grateful to old age for taking away the desire to do what we ought not to do. For carnal pleasure hinders deliberation, is at war with reason, blindfolds the eyes of the mind, so to speak, and has no fellowship with virtue.

It was a disagreeable duty that I performed in expelling Lucius Flaminus from the senate, for he was a brother of that most valiant man, Titus Falminius, and had been consul seven years before; but I thought that lust merited the brand of infamy. For, when in Gaul during his consulship, at the solicitation of a courtesan at a banquet, he beheaded a prisoner then under condemnation for some capital offense. While his brother, my immediate predecessor, was censor, Lucius escaped punishment, but Flaccus and I could by no means approve of conduct so flagrant and abandoned, especially when to his crime against an individual he added dishonor to the state.

I often heard from my elders—who, in turn, said they, when boys, had heard it from old men—that Gaius Fabricius used to marvel at the story told him, while an envoy at the headquarters of King Pyrrhus, by Cineas of Thessaly, that there was a man at Athens who professed himself "wise" and used to say that everything we do should be judged by the standard of pleasure. Now when Manius Curius and Tiberius Coruncanius learned of this from Fabricius they expressed the wish that the Samnites and Pyrrhus himself would become converts to it, because, when given up to pleasure, they would be much easier to overcome. Manius Curius had lived on intimate terms with Publius Decius who, in his fourth consulship, and five years before Curius held that office, had offered up his life for his country's safety; Fabricius and

Coruncanius also knew him, and they all were firmly persuaded, both by their own experience and especially by the heroic deed of Decius, that assuredly there are ends, inherently pure and noble, which are sought for their own sake, and which will be pursued by all good men who look on self-gratification with loathing and contempt.

Why then, do I dwell at such length on pleasure? Because that fact that old age feels little longing for sensual pleasure not only is no cause for reproach, but rather is ground for the highest praise. Old age lacks the heavy banquet, the loaded table, and the oft-filled cup; therefore, it also lacks drunkeness, indigestion, and loss of sleep. But if some concession must be made to pleasure, since her allurements are difficult to resist, and she is, as Plato happily says, "the bait of sin,"—evidently because men are caught therewith like fish—then I admit that old age, though it lacks immoderate banquets, may find delight in temperate repasts. Gaius Duellius, son of Marcus, and the first Roman to win a naval victory over the Carthaginians, was often seen by me in my childhood, when he was an old man, returning home from dining out, attended, as was his delight, by a torch bearer and flute player— an ostenation which as a private citizen he had assumed, though without precedent: but that much license did glory give him.

But why speak of others. Let me now return to myself. In the first place I have always had my club companions. Moreover, it was in my quaestorship that clubs in honour of Cybele were organized, when the Idaean worship was introduced at Rome, and therefore I used to dine with these companions—in an altogether moderate way, yet with a certain ardour appropriate to my age, which, as time goes on, daily mitigates my zest for every pleasure. Nor, indeed, did I measure my delight in these social gatherings more by physical pleasure than by the pleasure of meeting and conversing with my friends. For our fathers did well in calling the reclining of friends at feasts a convivium, because it implies a communion of life, which is a better designation than that of the Greeks, who call it sometimes a "drinking together" and sometimes an "eating together," thereby apparently exalting what is of least value in these associations above that which gives them their greatest charm.

For my own part, because of my love of conversation, I enjoy even "afternoon banquets," not with my contemporaries only, very few of whom now remain, but also with you and with those of your age; and I am profoundly grateful to old age, which has increased my eagerness for conversation and taken away that for food and drink. But if there are any who find delight in such things (that I may by no means seem to have declared war on every kind of pleasure, when, perhaps, a certain amount of it is justified by nature), then I may say that I am not aware that old age is altogether wanting in appreciation even of these very pleasures. Indeed I find delight in the custom established by our forefathers of appointing presidents at such gatherings; and in the talk, which, after that ancestral custom, begins at the head of the table when the wine comes in; and I enjoy cups, like those described in Xenophon's *Symposium,* that are small in size, filled with dewlike drops, cooled in summer, and, again, in winter, warmed by the heat of sun or fire. Even when among the Sabines I keep up the practice of frequenting such gatherings, and every day I join my neighbors in a social meal which we protract as late as we can into the night with talk on varying themes.

But it may be urged that, in old men, "pleasure's tingling," if I may so call it, is not so great. True, but neither is their yearning for pleasures so great, and moreover, nothing troubles you for which you do not yearn. It was an excellent reply that Sophocles made to a certain man who asked him, when he was already old, if he still indulged in the delights of love. "Heaven forbid!" he said. "Indeed I have fled from them as from a harsh and cruel master." For to those who eagerly desire such things the want of them is perhaps an annoyance and a trouble; but to those who are sated and cloyed with them it is more pleasant to be in want of them than to possess them; though, indeed, a man cannot "want" that for which he has no longing, and therefore I assert that the absence of longing is more pleasant.

But granting that youth enjoys pleasure of that kind with a

keener relish, then, in the first place, as I have said, they are petty things which it enjoys; and, in the next place, although old age does not possess these pleasures in abundance, yet it is by no means wanting in them. Just as Ambivius Turpio gives greater delight to the spectators in the front row at the theatre, and yet gives some delight even to those in the last row, so youth, looking on pleasures at closer range, perhaps enjoys them more, while old age, on the other hand, finds delight enough in a more distant view.

Chapter 4

ON AGE

Montaigne

I cannot accept the way in which we establish the duration of our life. I see that the sages, as compared with popular opinion, make it a great deal shorter. "What," said the younger Cato to those who wanted to keep him from killing himself, "am I now at an age where I can be reproached for abandoning life too soon?" Yet he was only forty-eight. He regarded that age as quite ripe and quite advanced, considering how few men reach it. And those who delude themselves with the idea that some course or other which they call natural promises a few years beyond, might do so properly if they had a privilege to exempt them from the many accidents to which we are all naturally subject, and which can interrupt this course that they promise themselves.

What an idle fancy it is to expect to die of a decay of powers

From *The Complete Works of Montaigne: Essays, Travel Journal, Letters,* trans. Donald M. Frame (Stanford: Stanford University Press, 1943). Reprinted by permission of the publishers.

brought on by extreme old age, and to set ourselves this term for our duration, since that is the rarest of all deaths and the least customary! We call it alone natural, as if it were contrary to nature to see a man break his neck by a fall, be drowned in a shipwreck, or be snatched away by the plague or a pleurisy, and as if our ordinary condition did not expose us to all these mishaps. Let us not flatter ourselves with these fine words: we ought perhaps rather to call natural what is general, common, and universal.

Death of old age is a rare, singular, and extraordinary death, and hence less natural than the others; it is the last and ultimate sort of death; the further it is from us, the less it is to be hoped for. It is indeed the bourn beyond which we shall not go, and which the law of nature has prescribed as not to be passed; but it is a very rare privilege of hers to make us last that long. It is an exemption which she grants by special favor to a single person in the space of two or three centuries, relieving him of the misfortunes and difficulties that she has cast in the way of others during this long period.

Thus my idea is to consider the age we have reached as one few people reach. Since in the ordinary course of things men do not come thus far, it is a sign that we are well along. And since we have passed the customary limits which are the true measure of our life, we must not hope to go much further. Having escaped so many occasions of dying, at which we see everyone stumble, we must recognize that an extraordinary fortune, and one out of the usual, like the one that is keeping us going, is not due to last much longer.

It is a defect in the very laws to hold this false idea: they have it that a man is not capable of the management of his estate until he is twenty-five, whereas he will hardly keep the management of his life that long. Augustus cut off five years from the ancient Roman ordinances, and declared that it was enough for those assuming the office of judge to be thirty. Servius Tullius released the knights who had passed forty-seven from service in war; Augustus set this back to forty-five. To send men back into retirement before the age of fifty-five or sixty seems not very reasonable to me. I should be of the opinion that our employment and occupation should be extended as far as possible, for the public welfare; I find the fault in the other direction, that of not putting us to work soon enough. Augustus had been universal judge of the world at nineteen, and yet would have a man be thirty in order to pass judgment on the position of a gutter.

As for me, I think our souls are as developed at twenty as they are ever to be, and give the promise of all they ever can do. No soul which at that age has not given very evident earnest of its strength has given proof of it later. The natural qualities and virtues give notice within that term, or never, of whatever vigor or beauty they possess:

> If the thorn will not prick at birth,
> It never will prick on earth,

they say in Dauphiné.

If I were to enumerate all the beautiful human actions, of whatever kind, that have come to my knowledge, I should think I would find that the greater part were performed, both in ancient times and in our own, before the age of thirty, rather than after. Yes, often even in the lives of the same men.

May I not say that with all assurance about those of Hannibal and of Scipio, his great adversary? They lived a good half of their life on the glory acquired in their youth: great men afterward in comparison with all others, but by no means in comparison with themselves.

As for me, I hold it as certain that since that age my mind and my body have rather shrunk than grown, and gone backward rather than forward. It is possible that in those who employ their time well, knowledge and experience grow with living; but vivacity, quickness, firmness, and other qualities much more our own, more important and essential, wither and languish.

> When age has crushed the body with its might,
> The limbs collapse with weakness and decay,
> The judgment limps, and mind and speech give way.
>   Lucretius

Sometimes it is the body that first surrenders to age, sometimes, too, it is the mind; and I have seen enough whose brains were enfeebled before their stomach and lets; and inasmuch as this is a malady hardly perceptible to the sufferer and obscure in its symptoms, it is all the more dangerous. For the time, I complain of the laws, not that they leave us at work too long, but that they set us to work too late. It seems to me that considering the frailty of our life and how many ordinary natural reefs it is exposed to, we should not allot so great a part of it to birth, idleness, and apprenticeship.

Chapter 5

THE MYTH OF THE CAVE

Plato

Next, said I, compare our nature in respect of education and its lack to such an experience as this. Picture men dwelling in a sort of subterranean cavern with a long entrance open to the light on its entire width. Conceive them as having their legs and necks fettered from childhood, so that they remain in the same spot, able to look forward only, and prevented by the fetters from turning their heads. Picture further the light from a fire burning higher up and at a distance behind them, and between the fire and the prisoners and above them a road along which a low wall has been built, as the exhibitors of puppet shows have partitions before the men themselves, above which they show the puppets.

All that I see, he said.

See also, then, men carrying past the wall implements of all

From Plato, *Republic:* VII, trans. Paul Shorey, (Cambridge, Mass: Harvard University Press, 1953). Reprinted by permission of the publishers and the Loeb Classical Library. This work is in the form of a dialogue in which Socrates is the principle speaker.

kinds that rise above the wall, and human images and shapes of animals as well, wrought in stone and wood and every material, some of these bearers presumably speaking and others silent.

A strange image you speak of, he said, and strange prisoners.

Like to us, I said. For, to begin with, tell me do you think that these men would have seen anything of themselves or of one another except the shadows cast from the fire on the wall of the cave that fronted them?

How could they, he said, if they were compelled to hold their heads unmoved through life?

And again, would not the same be true of the objects carried past them?

Surely.

If then they were able to talk to one another, do you not think that they would suppose that in naming the things that they saw they were naming the passing objects?

Necessarily.

And if their prison had an echo from the wall opposite them, when one of the passers-by uttered a sound, do you think they would suppose anything else than the passing shadow to be the speaker?

By Zeus, I do not, said he.

Then in every way such prisoners would deem reality to be nothing else than the shadows of the artificial objects.

Quite inevitably, he said.

Consider, then, what would be the manner of the release and healing from these bonds and this folly if in the course of nature something of this sort should happen to them. When one was freed from his fetters and compelled to stand up suddenly and turn his head around and walk and to lift up his eyes to the light, and in doing all this felt pain and, because of the dazzle and glitter of the light, was unable to discern the objects whose shadows he formerly saw, what do you suppose would be his answer if someone told him that what he had seen before was all a cheat and an illusion, but that now, being nearer to reality and turned toward more real things, he saw more truly? And if also one should point out to him each of the passing objects and constrain him by questions to say what it is, do you not think that he would be at a loss and that he would regard what he formerly saw as more real than the things now pointed out to him?

Far more real, he said.

And if he were compelled to look at the light itself, would not that pain his eyes, and would he not turn away and flee to those things which he is able to discern and regard them as in very deed more clear and exact than the objects pointed out?

It is so, he said.

And if, said I, someone should drag him thence by force up the ascent which is rough and steep, and not let him go before he had drawn him out into the light of the sun, do you not think that he would find it painful to be so haled along, and would chafe at it, and when he came out into the light, that his eyes would be filled with its beams so that he would not be able to see even one of the things that we call real?

Why, no, not immediately, he said.

Then there would be need of habituation, I take it, to enable him to see the things higher up. And at first he would most easily discern the shadows and, after that, the likenesses or reflections in water of men and other things, and later, the things themselves, and from these he would go on to contemplate the appearances in the heavens and heaven itself, more easily by night, looking at the light of the stars and the moon, than by day the sun and the sun's light.

Of course.

And so, finally, I suppose, he would be able to look upon the sun itself and see its true nature, not by reflections in water or phantasms of it in an alien setting, but in and by itself in its own place.

Necessarily, he said.

And at this point he would infer and conclude that this it is that provides the seasons and the courses of the year and presides over all things in the visible region, and is in some sort the cause of all these things that they had seen.

Obviously, he said, that would be the next step.

Well then, if he recalled to mind his first habitation and what passed for wisdom there, and his fellow bondsmen, do you not think that he would count himself happy in the change and pity them?

He would indeed.

And if there had been honors and commendations among them which they bestowed on one another and prizes for the man who is quickest to make out the shadows as they pass and best able to remember their customary precedences, sequences, and coexistences, and so most successful in guessing at what was to come, do you think he would be very keen about such rewards, and that he would envy and emulate those who were honored by these prisoners and lorded it among them, or that he would feel with Homer and greatly prefer while living on earth to be serf of another, a landless man, and endure anything rather than opine with them and live that life?

Yes, he said, I think that he would choose to endure anything rather than such a life.

And consider this also, said I. If such a one should go down again and take his old place would he not get his eyes full of darkness, thus suddenly coming out of the sunlight?

He would indeed.

Now if he should be required to contend with these perpetual prisoners in "evaluating" these shadows while his vision was still dim and before his eyes were accustomed to the dark—and this time required for habituation would not be very short—would he not provoke laughter, and would it not be said of him that he had returned from his journey aloft with his eyes ruined and that it was not worthwhile even to attempt the ascent? And if it were possible to lay hands on and to kill the man who tried to release them and lead them up, would they not kill him?

They certainly would, he said.

This image then, dear Glaucon, we must apply as a whole to all that has been said, likening the region revealed through sight to the habitation of the prison, and the light of the fire in it to the power of the sun. And if you assume that the ascent and the contemplation of the things above is the soul's ascension to the intelligible region, you will not miss my surmise, since that is what you desire to hear. But God knows whether it is true. But, at any rate, my dream as it appears to me is that in the region of the known the last thing to be seen and hardly seen is the idea of good, and that when seen it must needs point us to the conclusion that this is indeed the cause for all things of all that is right and beautiful, giving birth in the visible world to light, and the author of light and itself in the intelligible world being the authentic source of truth and reason, and that anyone who is to act wisely in private or public must have caught sight of this.

I concur, he said, so far as I am able.

Come then, I said, and join me in this further thought, and do not be surprised that those who have attained to this height are not willing to occupy themselves with the affairs of men, but their souls ever feel the upward urge and the yearning for that sojourn above. For this, I take it, is likely if in this point too the likeness of our image holds.

Yes, it is likely.

And again, do you think it at all strange, said I, if a man returning from divine contemplations to the petty miseries of men cuts a sorry figure and appears most ridiculous, if, while still blinking through the gloom, and before he has become sufficiently accustomed to the environing darkness, he is compelled in court-rooms or elsewhere to contend about the shadows of justice or the images that cast the shadows and to wrangle in debate about the notions of these things in the minds of those who have never seen justice itself?

It would be by no means strange, he said.

But a sensible man, I said, would remember that there are two distinct disturbances of the eyes arising from two causes, according as the shift is from light to darkness or from darkness to light, and, believing that the same thing happens to the soul, too, whenever he saw a soul perturbed and unable to discern something, he would not laugh unthinkingly, but would observe whether coming from a brighter life its vision was obscured by the unfamiliar darkness, or whether the passage from the deeper dark of ignorance into a more luminous world and the greater brightness had dazzled its vision. And so he would deem the one happy in its experience and way of life and pity the other, and if it pleased him to laugh at it, his laughter would be less laughable than that at the expense of the soul that had come down from the light above.

That is a very fair statement, he said.

Then, if this is true, our view of these matters must be this, that education is not in reality what some people proclaim it to be in their professions. What they aver is that they can put true knowledge into a soul that does not possess it, as if they were inserting vision into blind eyes.

They do indeed, he said.

But our present argument indicates, said I, that the true analogy for this indwelling power in the soul and the instrument whereby each of us apprehends is that of an eye that could not be converted to the light from the darkness except by turning the whole body. Even so, this organ of knowledge must be turned around from the world of becoming together with the entire soul, like the scene-shifting periactus in the theater, until the soul is able to endure the contemplation of essence and the brightest region of being. And this, we say, is the good, do we not?

Yes.

Of this very thing, then, I said, there might be an art, an art of the speediest and most effective shifting or conversion of the soul, not an art of producing vision in it, but on the assumption that it possesses vision but does not rightly direct it and does not look where it should, an art of bringing this about.

Yes, that seems likely, he said.

Then the other so-called virtues of the soul do seem akin to those of the body. For it is true that where they do not preexist, they are afterward created by habit and practice. But the excellence of thought, it seems, is certainly of a more divine quality, a thing that never loses its potency, but, according to the direction of its conversion, becomes useful and beneficient, or, again, useless and harmful. Have you never observed in those who are popularly spoken of as bad, but smart, men how keen is the vision of the little soul, how quick it is to discern the things that interest it, a proof that it is not a poor vision which it has, but one forcibly enlisted in the service of evil, so that the sharper its sight the more mischief it accomplishes?

I certainly have, he said.

Observe then, said I, that this part of such a soul, if it had been hammered from childhood, and had thus been struck free of the leaden weights, so to speak, of our birth and becoming, which attaching themselves to it by food and similar pleasures and gluttonies turn downward the vision of the soul—if, I say, freed from these, it had suffered a conversion toward the things that are real and true, that same faculty of the same men would have been most keen in its vision of the higher things, just as it is for the things toward which it is now turned.

It is likely, he said.

Well, then, said I, is not this also likely and a necessary consequence of what has been said, that neither could men who are uneducated and inexperienced in truth ever adequately preside over a state, nor could those who had been permitted to linger on to the end in the pursuit of culture—the one because they have no single aim and purpose in life to which all their actions, public and private, must be directed, and the others, because they will not voluntarily engage in action, believing that while still living they have been transported to the Islands of the Blessed?

True, he said.

It is the duty of us, the founders, then, said I, to compel the best natures to attain the knowledge which we pronounced the greatest, and to win to the vision of the good, to scale that ascent, and when they have reached the heights and taken an adequate view, we must not allow what is now permitted.

What is that?

That they should linger there, I said, and refuse to go down again among those bondsmen and share their labors and honors, whether they are of less or of greater worth.

Do you mean to say that we must do them this wrong, and compel them to live an inferior life when the better is in their power?

You have again forgotten, my friend, said I, that the law is not concerned with the special happiness of any class in the state, but is trying to produce this condition in the city as a whole, harmonizing and adapting the citizens to one another by persuasion and compulsion, and requiring them to impart to one another any benefit which they are severally able to bestow upon the community, and that it itself creates such men in the state, not that it may allow each to take what course pleases him, but with a view to using them for the binding together of the commonwealth.

(Socrates next discusses the elements of correct education in the first twenty years of life. A good education in this period will include study of a number of arts and sciences, which are, however, learned in piecemeal fashion, not unified in relation to each other by a single integrating perspective. We next pick up the discussion to follow the emergence of "dialectic"—the unifying or integrating power of mind—in later development.) Ed.

After this period, I said, those who are given preference from the twenty-year class will receive greater honors than the others, and they will be required to gather the studies which they disconnectedly pursued as children in their former education into a comprehensive survey of their affinities with one another and with the nature of things.

That, at any rate, he said, is the only instruction that abides with those who receive it.

And it is also, said I, the chief test of the dialectic nature and its opposite. For he who can view things in their connection is a dialectician; he who cannot, is not.

I concur, he said.

With these qualities in mind, I said, it will be your task to make a selection of those who manifest them best from the group who are steadfast in their studies and in war and in all lawful requirements, and when they have passed the thirtieth year to promote them, by a second selection from those preferred in the first, to still greater honors, and to prove and test them by the power of dialectic to see which of them is able to disregard the eyes and other senses and go on to being itself in company with truth. And at this point, my friend, the greatest care is requisite.

How so? he said.

Do you not note, said I, how great is the harm caused by our present treatment of dialectic?

What is that? he said.

Its practitioners are infected with lawlessness.

They are indeed.

Do you suppose, I said, that there is anything surprising in this state of mind, and do you not think it pardonable?

In what way, pray? he said.

Their case, said I, resembles that of a supposititious son reared in abundant wealth and a great and numerous family amid many flatterers, who on arriving at manhood should become aware that he is not the child of those who call themselves his parents, and should not be able to find his true father and mother. Can you divine what would be his feelings toward the flatterers and his supposed parents in the time when he did not know the truth about his adoption, and, again, when he knew it? Or would you like to hear my surmise?

I would.

Well, then, my surmise, is, I said, that he would be more likely to honor his reputed father and mother and other kind than the flatterers, and that there would be less likelihood of his allowing them to lack for anything, and that he would be less inclined to do or say to them anything unlawful, and less liable to disobey them in great matters than to disobey the flatterers—during the time when he did not know the truth.

It is probable, he said.

But when he found out the truth, I surmise that he would grow more remiss in honor and devotion to them and pay more regard to the flatterers, whom he would heed more than before, and would henceforth live by their rule, associating with them openly, while for that former father and his adoptive kin he would not care at all, unless he was naturally of a very good disposition.

All that you say, he replied, would be likely to happen. But what is the pertinency of this comparison to the novices of dialectic?

It is this. We have, I take it, certain convictions from childhood about the just and the honorable, in which, in obedience and honor to them, we have been bred as children under their parents.

Yes, we have.

And are there not other practices going counter to these, that have pleasures attached to them and that flatter and solicit our souls, but do not win over men of any decency; but they continue to hold in honor the teachings of their fathers and obey them?

It is so.

Well, then, said I, when a man of this kind is met by the question, What is the honorable? and on his giving the answer which he learned from the lawgiver, the argument confutes him, and by many and various refutations upsets his faith and makes him believe that this thing is no more honorable than it is base, and when he has had the same experience about the just and the good and everything that he chiefly held in esteem, how do you suppose that he will conduct himself thereafter in the matter of respect and obedience to this traditional morality?

It is inevitable, he said, that he will not continue to honor and obey as before.

And then, said I, when he ceases to honor these principles and to think that they are binding on him, and cannot discover the true principles, will he be likely to adopt any other way of life than that which flatters his desires?

He will not, he said.

He will, then, seem to have become a rebel to law and convention instead of the conformer that he was.

Necessarily.

And is not this experience of those who take up dialectic in the fashion to be expected and, as I just now said, deserving of much leniency?

Yes, and of pity too, he said.

Then that we may not have to pity thus your thirty-year-old disciples, must you not take every precaution when you introduce them to the study of dialectic?

Yes, indeed, he said.

And is it not one chief safeguard not to suffer them to taste of it while young? For I fancy you have not failed to observe that lads, when they first get a taste of disputation, misuse it as a form of sport, always employing it contentiously, and, imitating confuters, they themselves confute others. They delight like puppies in pulling about and tearing with words all who approach them.

Exceedingly so, he said.

And when they have themselves confuted many and been confuted by many, they quickly fall into a violent distrust of all that they formerly held true, and the outcome is that they themselves and the whole business of philosophy are discredited with other men.

Most true, he said.

But an older man will not share this craze, said I, but will rather choose to imitate the one who consents to examine truth dialectically than the one who makes a jest and a sport of mere contradiction, and so he will himself be more reasonable and moderate, and bring credit rather than discredit upon his pursuit.

Right, he said.

And were not all our preceding statements made with a view to this precaution; our requirement that those permitted to take part in such discussions must have orderly and stable natures, instead of the present practice of admitting to it any chance and unsuitable applicant?

By all means, he said.

Is it enough, then, to devote to the continuous and strenuous study of dialectic undisturbed by anything else, as in the corresponding discipline in bodily exercises, twice as many years as were allotted to that?

Do you mean six or four? he said.

Well, I said, set it down as five. For after that you will have to send them down into the cave again, and compel them to hold commands in war and the other offices suitable to youth, so that they may not fall short of the other type in experience either. And in these offices, too, they are to be tested to see whether they will remain steadfast under diverse solicitations or whether they will flinch and swerve.

How much time do you allow for that? he said.

Fifteen years, said I, and at the age of fifty those who have survived the tests and approved themselves altogether the best in every task and form of knowledge must be brought at last to the goal. We shall require them to turn upward the vision of their souls and fix their gaze on that which sheds light on all, and when they have thus beheld the good itself they shall use it as a pattern for the right ordering of the state and the citizens and themselves throughout the remainder of their lives, each in his turn, devoting the greater part of their time to the study of philosophy, but when the turn comes for each, toiling in the service of the state and holding office for the city's sake, regarding the task not as a fine thing but a necessity. And so, when each generation has educated others like themselves to take their place as guardians of the state, they shall depart to the Islands of the Blessed and there dwell. And the state shall establish public memorials and sacrifices for them as to divinities if the Pythian oracle approves or, if not, as to divine and godlike men.

A most beautiful finish, Socrates, you have put upon your rulers, as if you were a statuary.

And on the women too, Glaucon, said I, for you must not suppose that my words apply to the men more than to all women who arise among them endowed with the requisite qualities.

That is right, he said, if they are to share equally in all things with the men as we laid it down.

Chapter 6

DEATH AND AGING IN TECHNOPOLIS: TOWARD A ROLE DEFINITION OF WISDOM

Edmund Byrne

The way a society treats its elder members depends to a large degree on the value it attributes to old age. The value of old age to a society depends in turn upon its views about the meaning or purpose of life. And a society's views about the meaning or purpose of life are formulated primarily to help make sense out of the inevitability of death. Thus, it is apparent that in any given society there is a close connection between its treatment of the elderly and its philosophy of death and dying.

Now it is well known from anthropological studies that the elderly are treated quite differently in different societies. In some cases, they are shown great respect. In other cases, they tend to be resented like guests who have overstayed their welcome.[1] The factors that determine these and other differences in attitude towards the elderly are numerous, and include among others the ratio

From Edmund Byrne, "Death and Aging In Technopolis: Towards a Role Definition of Wisdom," *The Journal of Value Inquiry*, X, Fall, 1976. Reprinted by permission of the author and publisher.

between population and resources, the availability of housing, employment and services, the system of owning and distributing property both on the part of individuals and collectively, the average life expectancy, and so on. In other words, it is the total human ecology of a society and its environment that determines how that society will think about and deal with its older members. Accordingly, it can be argued that any favorable attitude towards the old that disregards perceived ecological constraints is probably some form of self-serving hypocrisy. But this argument fails if in fact it can be shown that a truly human ecology must include at least some concerns that go beyond the confines of the spatiotemporal world of immediate and mediated perception. And this, I would contend, is certainly the case with regard to people's attempts to assay the very meaning of human life in the face of imminent death.[2] For, what people conclude about primordial concern can and does affect just about every aspect of their behavior towards the natural and social environment in which they live. And in particular it would seem to have a pronounced effect upon how they deal with old age, whether in themselves or in others.

In this paper, I will argue that our own society's philosophy of death and dying has a largely negative effect on public policies towards the elderly, and that these policies will be changed for the better when and if we come to appreciate our elderly as the principal sources of our collective wisdom. Toward these ends, I shall consider in turn some basic types of theories about death, some basic attitudes towards dying and the duration of dying, some models of aging as they affect and/or embody attitudes toward old age, and finally the place of creative expansion in one's advanced years.

THEORIES OF DEATH

People die of many different causes, and sometimes it is important medically or legally to determine with some accuracy

the physical causes of a person's death. This, of course, is especially the case if there is some reason to suspect that the person has
not died of so-called natural causes. What is meant by natural
causes, presumably, is a set of organic conditions which, without
any external interference, become so deleterious that the organism
can no longer function. When this point is reached is a matter that
is decided partly by the current standards of medical technology.
Sufficiently continuous absence of brain waves is now the basis for
determining death; but the absence of pulse or of breath were once
taken to be adequate signs of death. Given the capabilities of
modern medicine, the earlier signs of death would no longer be
considered adequate; and, to think futuristically for a moment, it
may be that not even the cessation of brain functioning will forever
remain a definitive sign of death.[3] The point here, however, is that
whenever and however death comes to the organism, it marks the
end of that organism's existence as a viable functioning entity; and
accordingly, it also marks the limits of medical responsibility.[4]
Social responsibility extends to disposition of the now lifeless
body; and legal responsibility extends to settling the affairs of the
person who has died. These various responsibilities having been
duly carried out, there remains only the most difficult task of all: to
make some sense out of the event that has taken place.

The task of making some sense out of death has, of course,
resulted in a rich and varied profusion of cultural responses. But it
is sufficient for my purposes to reduce all of these responses to
essentially two: one that is satisfied to see death as a termination of
life, and one that prefers to see death as some sort of transition
from one mode of life to another. Thus, we may for short speak of
a termination theory or a transition theory of death. Either theory
may be predominantly individualistic or predominantly holistic in
orientation. A termination theory, for example, might stress the
finality of the individual or it might stress the continuity and/or
priority of the group. A transition theory might emphasize the
continuation of the deceased as a distinct individual ("personal
immortality"), as a familiar or tribal ancestor, or simply as sub-
sumed under some all-encompassing spiritual personality. Transi-

tion theories may be further divided into those that recognize only one condition or status after departure from this earthly life (call them "arrival theories"), and those that recognize any number of stages or phases hereafter, sometimes including reincarnation, but usually providing for an eventual attainment of some permanent status (call these "stage theories").

Which of these theories of death would strike the reader as being most acceptable depends upon a variety of factors, the most salient being those of personal need and cultural availability. The latter determines whether a given theory qualifies as what William James spoke of as a "live option," but cultural interpenetration has so intensified since the nineteenth century, when James was writing, that every option with regard to a theory of death must be considered as being at least potentially live for any individual regardless of his or her formative culture. Thus, personal need, or preference, assumes a greater importance than ever before. On the other hand, there are arguments to the effect that each and every one of these theories, however metaphysical or supernatural its mode of expression, is essentially just one more manifestation of a given society's need for self-maintenance and perpetuation. These arguments, especially as articulated in structural anthropology, sociology of knowledge and phenomenology of religion, are in my judgment persuasive.[5] And accordingly I see no need to make any clearcut distinction between a supernatural transition theory, which I would reject, and a natural transition theory, one form of which I find empirically defensible and personally appealing.

This particular transition theory of death, which underlies all that follows, takes a group-oriented and even species-oriented view of death as one's transition from being an agent (or efficient cause) to being a model (or exemplary cause) of human advancement. On this evolutionary and vitalist theory of death, an individual lives first in his or her own works and then in the effect of those works on others who will live after. The quasi-immortality thus suggested is, of course, not automatic, but is rather an opportunity for a kind of organismic apotheosis, whether among a few survivors or among millions. In either case, we thus achieve what

Clarence Darrow sought when he said, "The emotion to live makes most of us seek to project our personality a short distance beyond the waiting grave."[6]

ATTITUDES TOWARD DYING

Given the fact of death as what Paul Tillich called "the end, the last moment of our future,"[7] both society as a whole and each of us as individuals do adopt some stance or attitude with regard to death. In the abstract, of course, it is easy enough to recite the syllogism which concludes from the mortality of man and the humanness of John that John is mortal. It is, however, in the concrete that John experiences that mortality; and if I happen to be John, the mortality in question is not just a statistic but perhaps a constant pain that I must continually acknowledge in some appropriate way.[8] In other words, my death will be a problem not for me but for others; it is my dying, my approach to death, that is a problem for me existentially. The range of reactions that I may take toward my own dying has been articulated by many writers, including John Donne, André Malraux, and Thomas Mann.[9] It has been portrayed by Ingmar Bergman in such films as *Wild Straw-berries, The Seventh Seal,* and *Cries and Whispers,* and by John Boorman in his brilliant film, *Zardoz.*[10] To clinicians, probably the most authoritative analysis of attitudinal stages in the dying process is the justly famous work of Elisabeth Kubler-Ross.[11]

What all these studies tend to show is that on the level of lived experience one can distinguish a number of different attitudes, or mindsets, toward dying and that in many cases these distinct attitudes occur successively in the same person who is dying. It would be of considerable interest to determine to what extent the accounts of the different studies on attitudes toward dying are consistent (in some ways they seem not to be). But my object here is simply to develop a framework for discussing old age; so it will suffice to assert that no matter how many different attitudes toward dying can be experienced existentially, they can all be divided analytically into four basic modes: neutral, negative, affirmative, and mixed (or conflicted).

The neutral attitude, first of all, has had some staunch defenders shown through history, especially in military circles. If thought of as absolute fearlessness, it is perhaps best illustrated by the old maxim, "Cowards die a thousand deaths; brave men die but once." If thought of as an absence of all emotion and even of any willful preference, it calls to mind the ancient Stoic ideal of *apathia* towards all pain and suffering, including dying, which amounted to a kind of equanimity that one maintains, in the words of Marcus Aurelius, "whether in chains or on the throne." This extremely rationalist approach seems not to have been an entirely successful censor of affect in time of stress, since the suicide rate among the Stoics was notoriously high.

The negative attitude, which may range from simple disapproval through intense opposition, is usually thought to be the most prevalent of all attitudes towards dying. In its most gentle form it has been poignantly articulated by Lewis Carroll:

We are but older children, dear,
Who fret to find our bedtime near.[12]

The sentiment here expressed is, to be sure, exceptionally gracious, and is no doubt exemplified in individual cases. But even in the face of Freud's assurances that we are as strongly motivated by a death-wish as we are by a will to pleasure, even those of us who have suicidal tendencies would be prepared to accept the old maxim that "where there's life, there's hope." And thus has the average person's reluctance to die been used against him so often by those whose quest for power is undaunted by any ordinary scruples about the sanctity of life. Almost always understandable and sometimes even commendable, this will to live can in exceptional circumstances simply point up the mediocrity of our values, as an anonymous "A" reminds us in his poem about the Hungarian Revolution of 1956:

As long as the fighter breathes
The world holds its breath.
As long as he cries and calls
People hold their silence around him.
As long as he lives
The world plays dead.
When he gives up and dies
The world begins to live again,
Selling cotton, river cruises, good meals.[13]

The affirmative attitude towards dying is often recommended as being most appropriate for anyone who is in fact going to die. And at first glance this seems to make very good sense. In particular, it would seem to be eminently appropriate for a person with a terminal illness, provided only, as Kubler-Ross has shown, that that person shall have first gone through such other stages as denial and rebellion. But apart from this special clinical situation, there is reason to question the applicability of Kubler-Ross's recommendations. For the very claim that someone is going to die is itself problematic: granting that each of us is indeed *going* to die, who of us is in fact *about* to die? Who of us should feel required to say, with the gladiators of old, "Nos morituri salutamus"? These questions invite us to expand our discussion of attitudes towards dying to take into account such factors as one's expectations and preferences as to the time and cause of death and as to the duration of the dying process, and the effect of age on these expectations and preferences. And by so doing we will prepare a context for describing the mixed, or conflicted, attitude with regard to dying.

Viewed simplistically as a straightfoward matter of actuarial statistics, one's expectations as to time of death vary inversely with age: the older one is, the sooner one expects to die. But if the unexpected or atypical be taken into account, as in the case of an impending head-on collision, this expectation might well be revised downward rather precipitously. If one's preferences in the matter also be taken into account, the ratio between expectation and preference can vary quite markedly over the course of one's lifetime; and the resulting attitudinal pattern will be unique for each individual. Thus, if one tried to construct a graph of a person's attitudes towards life and death over time, it might look something like an irregular cardiogram, with the most dramatic shifts towards preference for death occurring on the occasion of an adolescent trauma, a divorce, the death of a loved one, a professional failure, a painful illness or injury, and so on.

In short, my personal expectations and preferences with regard to living and dying are different at different times in my life, and the resulting graph of my attitudinal shifts over time is uniquely mine. In a similar fashion, the way in which I measure the duration of my dying might be unique to me as an individual. Considerably less unique to the individual, and perhaps most readily associated with the duration of dying, is the often dramatized situation in which the patient is informed by his physician that he has only *N* units of time left to live.

Still more generalized models of the duration of dying are found in the diversified repertoire of our cultural heritage. There is a tendency on the part of some Christian sects, for example, to view the whole of life as a preparation for death; and the corollary to this view, which is traceable to St. Augustine among others, is that we begin to die the moment we begin to live—a kind of personalized law of entropy.[14] A much more common view is the one that encourages us to think about our lifespan as ascending and descending a hill, with all the resulting talk about being "at the peak" or "over the hill" or "on the decline" or whatever. Take, for example, these few lines from Sara Teasdale's poem, *The Long Hill*:

> I must have passed the crest a while ago
>   And now I am going down—
> Strange to have crossed the crest and not to know,
> But the brambles were always catching the hem of my gown.[15]

To show that this downhill or denouement view of the duration of dying has been responsible for a great deal of mischievous public policy toward the elderly would require a separate paper;

but I shall return to it below when I take up the parabolic curve model of aging. For the moment, it is enough just to note that, happily, this view is not universally accepted. For example, when Oliver Wendell Holmes addressed the nation by radio on his ninety-first birthday he compared all the years that went before to a horse race, and then went on to remind his listening audience that "The riders in a race do not stop short when they reach the goal. There is a little finishing canter before coming to a standstill."[16] An even stronger statement along these lines is contained in a note which George Bernard Shaw wrote at the age of ninety-four, on the day before an accident that led to his death:

> The will to live is wholly inexplicable. Rationally, I ought to blow my brains out, but I don't and I won't . . . Most people hold on to the last moment and die a "Natural Death" as I mean to, though at 94 I ought to clear out, my bolt being shot and overshot.[17]

How different was Shaw's approach to dying from that of a prominent Indianapolis attorney who submitted his own obituary to the local newspaper in 1943, when he was sixty, and then proceeded to live another thirty years! Indeed, Shaw almost seems to be saying that it is cowards, and not "brave men," who die but once. His final statement is most important, however, for the distinction it makes between dying a natural death and dying a violent death (examples of which are mentioned in the full text). For it is this distinction that forces us to modify clinically based recommendations about the need for a terminally ill person to arrive eventually at an attitude of resignation. Studies show, for example, that children as a group only gradually come to accept the finality of death around the ninth or tenth year.[18] And Herbert Marcuse even sees libertarian reasons for not accepting death too readily. As he puts it, "Compliance with death is compliance with the master over death: the polis, the state, nature, or the god."[19]

What is at issue in all these instances is the survival value of a will to live in the face of apparently imminent death. Such a will to live is medically significant in certain kinds of cases; and it is of quite universal significance when the threat to one's life is external rather than internal to the organism, as when one is confronted by an assailant, or by an imminent traffic accident, or by any of an uncounted variety of wartime situations. In such instances, generally speaking, the greater the likelihood of death, the greater the survival value of an unwillingness to die.[20]

Such, then, are the factors that come into play in the mixed or conflicted attitude towards dying, which is probably the most common of all. In this mode, one's attitude is a kind of stressed neutrality, in that it includes both affirmative and negative attitudes toward dying. More specifically, the mixed mode takes so many factors into consideration that it makes the distinction between affirmative and negative seem somewhat simplistic. What are these factors? They include, among others, health, life expectancy, threats to life, status, lifestyle, self-image, human relationships, cultural heritage, values, goals and ideals.

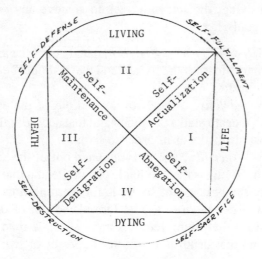

Figure 6–1. Attitude systems with regard to life and death, living and dying.

It is perhaps impossible to construct an adequate representation of such a complex configuration. But one can at least suggest how the various factors are interrelated by considering the dynamics of the self in terms of: (1) its reality-context; (2) its goals; (3) its behavior preferences tending toward these goals; (4) its culturally established priorities; and (5) the situational demands made upon all of the foregoing. Each of these factors, to be considered in order, is represented in the model in Figure 6–1.

The *reality-context* may be thought of as consisting of two polarities: life and death; living and dying. The first polarity is exclusive, i.e., one or the other but not both obtains in any given case. The second polarity is inclusive, i.e., both not only may be co-present but in most instances are. Life is a precondition for living, but it is also a precondition for dying. Death is the termination both of life and of living, and is always preceded by a period of dying, however brief.

In response to the reality-context of life and death and of living and dying, the self may seek to achieve any or all of the following goals:

a. *Self-fulfillment,* a goal formulated out of the assumptions that "life is for the living" and that it should be lived to the fullest;

b. *Self-defense,* a goal formulated out of the assumptions that death stalks the living and that accordingly one must ward off death in order to live;

c. *Self-sacrifice,* a goal formulated out of the assumptions that dying is the inevitable end of life and that accordingly the best use of living is for learning how to die;

d. *Self-destruction,* a goal formulated out of the assumptions that living requires more struggle than it is worth and that death is therefore the lesser of two evils.

Even if the goals just enumerated are not ordinarily achieved, each of them is approached by a specific set of *behavior preferences*. The first of these, self-actualization, tends toward the goal of self-fulfillment. Self-maintenance tends toward the goal of self-defense; self-abnegation tends toward the goal of self-sacrifice; and self-denigration is directed toward the goal of self-destruction.

Each of these goals and each of these behavior-preferences is operative to one degree or another, at one time or another, in each and every one of us. Some of them, moreover, tend to be correlated in more or less stable configurations, especially under the influence of a given cultural setting or cultural heritage.

Self-actualization and self-denigration (and their respective goals) appear to be logically and diagrammatically opposed to one another, and so presumably would not often be adopted simultaneously. But the sight of a bonze immolating himself in the streets of Saigon warns us to be mindful of a widespread belief that the self is fulfilled only insofar as it is dissipated into an absolute Self. Similarly, it would seem at first glance that self-maintenance and self-abnegation (and their respective goals) are both logically and diagrammatically opposed to one another. But here again the logically inconsistent proves to be psychologically compatible; for, there are many people, especially but not exclusively among the elderly, whose entire strategy for self-maintenance depends upon a meticulous attention to the bidding of others—in short, self-abnegation. The first set of diametric opposites is also reminiscent of Freud's dichotomy between Eros and Thanatos; and the second set calls to mind a long tradition of erudite debate over the relative merits of egoism and altruism.

Turning from the diametric opposites to each of the four triangles in Figure 6-1, we can represent certain preferences for combinations of goals taken two at a time. The respective configurations are identified by Roman numerals, and can be briefly described as follows:

Configuration I: The chief value is life itself, which must be maintained at any cost and which, paradoxically, can be brought to fulfillment only through self-abnegation and self-sacrifice. (Although perhaps somewhat a caricature of Christianity, this caricature is accurate enough to have been accepted by Friedrich Nietzsche and others as the reality.)

Configuration II: The chief value is living, which one should seek to the fullest, directly through self-actualizing endeavors and indirectly, when necessary, through self-maintaining behavior. (This predominantly humanist view, which may or may not be egocentric depending on how "self" is defined, probably represents mainstream thinking at least in the developed countries of the world. It is not easily distinguished from hedonism, but as formulated in humanistic psychology it is a very responsible and at times altruistic point of view.)

Configuration III: The chief value consists of dealing with and dealing out death, especially insofar as it is precisely by means of such dealing that one maintains oneself, unless and until one loses the gamble in this zero-sum game and is destroyed. (Though perhaps most readily associated with the ethos of the underworld, this view is in its essentials shared by many adventurers and by career military personnel all around the world.)

Configuration IV: At first glance, it would not seem that there could be any widespread preference for an attitude configuration that combines self-abnegation and self-denigration, except in a pathological way. Thus, the morbid tendency towards self-sacrifice and self-destruction would be expected in a case of chronic depression; and, as was shown in Bergman's *The Seventh Seal,* people doomed to death by bubonic plague might well take to flailing themselves in reparation for their sins. What is less readily recognized is that the whole thrust of what we call modern civilization tends to maneuver the elderly as a group into this configuration.[21] But, as Albert Camus has suggested in *The Plague,* there are other and nobler ways to respond to the inevitable.

In light of the foregoing, we may note finally that one configuration is more likely to be adopted in a given situation than others, but the more likely configuration might not be the most appropriate. As the studies of Elisabeth Kubler-Ross seem to show, for example, self-fulfillment is the most appropriate goal even for one who is terminally ill; but the clinical setting has not tended to foster that goal or the attitudes inclining thereto. In the case of old age, a whole variety of factors has conspired to encourage attitudes that favor dying more than living, death rather than life. And not the least of these factors is the prevailing model of the human lifespan, that of the parabolic curve.

MODELS OF AGING

The standard model of the human lifespan is one that assumes that power or energy is the measure of life and that accordingly one's lifespan follows a curve that rises and then falls, parabolically.[22] Commonly viewed as a hill that one ascends and descends, as already noted, this standard model is only described more eloquently by the erudite. Note, for example, the words of Carl Jung:

> With the same intensity and irresistibility with which it strove upward before middle age, life now descends; for the goal no longer lies on the summit, but in the valley where the ascent began. The curve of life is like the parabola of a projectile which, disturbed from its initial state of rest, rises and then returns to a state of repose.[23]

Noting next that "the psychological curve of life . . . refuses to conform to this law of nature," Jung then goes on to find some justification for this psychic recalcitrance in parapsychological phenomena.[24] But his willingness to consider life after death an open question for science is not typical of the scientific community, current popular interest in the occult notwithstanding. Against a cosmological backdrop of universal death (the law of entropy), living species on the planet earth are seen to rise and fall in accordance with their ability to cope (survival of the fittest); and the same applies to the history of the human species as well. So why should it be any different for individual human beings? Such, at least, is the effect of much public policy, especially as it pertains to the elderly.

Committed as it is to the parabolic model of life, society generally has even less use for the old than it does for the young. And just as it deals with the young as those who are preparing to live, so does it deal with the old as those who have already lived or at least had their chance for life. It is by no means self-evident that this is the most desirable distribution of status and meaning in a society; but it is certainly the most prevalent in a modern industrial nation such as ours. Victor Frankl once noted that if one's life has any meaning, it should have meaning even when one has little to look forward to but death.[25] But how difficult this becomes when the society in which one lives makes all of the sources of meaning practically off-limits to all but those who are riding the crest! For, not only power but also pleasure and wealth and knowledge and even the opportunity for service are most readily available to the middle-aged monopolizers of our society.

About the only significant source of meaning that is not monopolized by the middle-aged managerial class is wisdom. Wisdom, long understood as a holistic understanding of some complex process: a skill or craft, the sciences, the universe as a whole, or most especially the way to live one's life as a human being. Thus understood, the ancient ideal of wisdom is in some respects comparable to today's systems approaches to problem-solving in areas as diverse as traffic control, courtroom litigation, or cancer research. Indeed, these latter approaches, especially when linked to the computer, seem so sophisticated in their technological meticulosity as to make mere human wisdom seem pre-historic at best.[26] Nonetheless, many people—with or without access to a computer—are manifestly incapable of building meaningful lives for themselves in today's technopolis. So they look for guidance to rock music, astrology, psychotherapy, psychocybernetics, gurus, and any of a hundred other more or less fallible revelations. Does this not indicate that for all our technological prowess, we are just as much in need of human wisdom as any of our preindustrial forebears?[27] Our forebears, however, looked to their elders for such wisdom, whereas we in general do not. Why is it that we have so little respect for the wisdom of our elders? The underlying reason, I believe, is to be found in the very structure of a highly technological society.

In the low-technological society, tools are still selected and valued according as they fit in to the needs of the people. In the high-technological society, by contrast, it is people who are selected and valued according as they fit into the needs of society's tools. Much is gained, of course, by this willingness to sacrifice the organic to the mechanistic way of life. But the values lost in the process are, in the judgment of many observers, far more precious.

These values, generically identified as humanistic, include all that Tonnies found worthwhile in the community *(Gemeinschaft)* of old: a preference for the interpersonal, the familial, the organic. The modern way of doing things requires people to live more anonymously, contractually, and impersonally as they go about what tasks remain to humans in a world that thrives on making, selling, servicing, and using machines.[28] As society replaces one kind of machine with another, it in effect shifts its values from those who served the old to those who serve the new. Thus, the man who knows everything about vacuum tubes is soon displaced by a man who knows something about transistors—or about printed circuits, or. . . .

In a society such as this, wisdom tends to be left in the attic of discarded mementos, as people search for more modern ways to ward off the villainy of "future shock." Talk of "retraining" people is no more efficacious than talk of recycling bottles. For neither is considered necessary to keep the wheels of production turning. (It is only when one stops to wonder who will *buy* all the products turned out that people acquire value as "consumers" and unemployment becomes an *economic* problem.) So it is preferred that people, like bottles, be conveniently disposable. If only the pattern of life today remained somewhat constant from one generation to the next, the young could learn much of value from their elders, as was once the case in the preindustrial world. But if the only constant is change itself, then the future is god and the young are its priests. This, at least, is what Margaret Mead seems to be saying when she characterizes ours as a postfigurative rather than a prefigurative society.[29]

In short, the traditional value of the elderly to a society was their claim to a wisdom that comes precisely with age. But today, if there is any interest in wisdom, it is more likely to be sought from the middle-aged or the young, if not from some nonhuman source like the computer. The elderly, of course, are still free to contend that they are of some value to our society; but the burden of proof is on them. Unfortunately, few of our elders contend anything of the kind. Most tend instead, however reluctantly, to accept the myth of rugged individualism that requires them either to "make it" on their own or else move over to make room for those who purportedly can.

What is especially noxious about this system-serving ostracism of the old is that it commits us all to the Malthusian zero-sum game that makes the rise of some require the demise of others. This way of dealing with the elderly further assumes that the evolution of the human species is to be measured only in terms of external or material growth, to the total neglect of internal or spiritual growth. What does it matter, we seem to be saying, that some of our greatest musicians, writers, statesmen and philosophers are also among our most long-lived members? These few, we like to believe, are but exceptions that prove the rule. And yet the rule itself is of our own making.[30] Our oppression of the old is so effective that the few who thrive in spite of it must be truly outstanding—much like children who escape the ghetto. What magnificent and ennobling contributions might we therefore expect of our senior citizens if we once would recognize that what they can best offer is not worthless but truly priceless?

Maybe we have not yet suffered enough as a people from social alienation, political corruption, economic crisis and personal disillusionment to really concern ourselves seriously with the possibility that we have bought society at the price of community. But if the day ever comes when our hunger for community is intense enough to make us ask basic questions about where we are really going as a people, we may then remember what simple folk have never forgotten: if one must go where one has never been, it can do no harm to ask directions of another who is already there. Thus might one yet hear, as Carlos Castenada heard from an Indian "man of knowledge":

> (Old age) is the cruelest (enemy) of all, the one (a man) won't be able to defeat completely, but only fight away . . . But if the man sloughs off his tiredness, and lives his fate through, he can then be called a man of knowledge, if only for the brief moment when he succeeds in fighting off his last, invincible enemy. That moment of clarity, power, and knowledge is enough.[31]

Such a recommendation would not have been surprising to the science fiction writer, Ray Bradbury, who once said:

> My books are victories against darkness, if only for a small while. Each story I write is a candle lit for my own burial plot which it may take some few years to blow out. More than many writers, I have known this fact about myself since I was a child. It puts me to work each day with a special sad-sweet-happy urgency.[32]

Bradury's notion of working against time and almost against death is a fine example of the individualistic quest for quasi-immortality through one's work. What this view lacks, at least in its explicit statement, is an awareness of the species-specific significance of an individual's work and how this can help to aggrandize an elderly person's view of his or her continuing role in the scheme of things. This latter view is nowhere stated more eloquently than it was by Bertrand Russell in his *New Hopes for a Changing World:*

> An individual human existence should be like a river—small at first, narrowly contained within its banks, and rushing passionately past boulders and over waterfalls. Gradually the river grows wider, the banks recede, the waters flow more quietly, and in the end, without any visible break, they become merged in the sea, and painlessly lose their individual being. The man who, in old age, can see his life in this way, will not suffer from the fear of death, since the things he cares for will continue. And if, with the decay of vitality, weariness increases, the thought of rest will not be unwelcome. The wise man should wish to die while still at work, knowing that others will carry on what he can no longer do, and content in the thought that what was possible has been done.[33]

Thus does Bertrand Russell formulate a model for a wise old age by combining the work ethic of the West with the often repeated image of the flowing river so dear to the philosophy of the East.[34] And by so doing he implicitly aligns the intellectualist tradition of a community of scholars with such evolutionistic models as those of Friedrich Nietzsche and Nikos Kazantzakis, each of whom views the individual as a bridge over which mankind walks to a richer and more meaningful life.[35]

What all of this suggests is that we need to work towards a society in which the elderly would play a sapiential role that can be represented by the model in Figure 6–2.

Imagine an inverted cone the point of which is on the plane of action and the base of which is on the plane of human (or species specific) aspiration. Imagine further that a second circle is formed by a plane of personal concerns (see Fig. 6–1) that transects the cone between its point and its base. The cone as a whole moves horizontally in various directions, and as it dies it traces out on the plane of action a pattern that represents the unique life span of this one particular human being. This human being's attention, represented by the entire cone, is free to move up toward the fullness of human aspiration or down toward the concrete particularity of action in the real world. But actions performed in the concrete attain the fullness of human aspiration only as filtered through the plane of personal concerns; and so it is inversely with any attempt to express such aspirations in one's concrete actions. There are

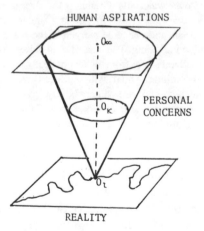

HUMAN ASPIRATIONS

0_∞

0_K

PERSONAL CONCERNS

0_L

REALITY

Figure 6–2.   Sapiential Model of Individual Life Span.

degrees of accomplishment, however, depending upon how closely the plane of one's personal concerns comes to approximate the plane of human aspiration. The more one's personal concerns recede from that high plane to the level of reality as given, the more the pattern traced in reality will resemble the pattern of every other person in one's immediate environment. But the more one's personal concerns approach the plane of human aspirations, the more one's actions in reality will trace out a new and different pattern that can be of service as a guide and inspiration to others.

Thus, for example, the black woman portrayed by Cecily Tyson in *The Autobiography of Jane Pittman* accepted every racist evil that came into her centenary life, until in her advanced old age she at long last defied segregationist constraints, drank from a forbidden drinking fountain, and by that act enlarged the scope of possibilities toward which her people could thereafter aspire because of her. So it can be with every human being whose personal concerns rise through time to become one with human aspirations and then produce creative actions that change the pattern of human life. We are, for better or worse, what we do, both as individuals and as a species. But what we do is of value only to the extent that it helps all of us learn something more about how to be fully human. It is in this sense that I choose to interpret what Oliver Wendell Holmes wrote in his poem, "The Chambered Nautilus":

> Build thee more stately mansions, O my soul,
>   As the swift seasons roll!
>   Leave thy low-vaulted past!
> Let each new temple, nobler than the last,
> Shut thee from heaven with a dome more vast,
>   Till thou at length art free,
> Leaving thine outgrown shell by life's
>   Unresting sea!

NOTES

[1]Compare, for example, the following: Lucy Mair, *An Introduction to Social Anthropology*, (Oxford: Clarendon Press, 1965, pp. 50–52, 106–11); A. P. Elkin, *The Australian Aborigines* (Garden City, N. Y.: Anchor, 1964, p. 87);

William Graham Sumner, *Folkways* (1906; New York: Dover, 1959), nn. 12 and 547; Claude Lévi-Strauss, *The Elementary Structures of Kinship*, rev. ed. (Boston: Beacon Press, 1969, pp. 329–45); Clyde Kluckhohn and Dorothea Leighton, *The Navaho*, rev. ed. (Garden City, N. Y.: Anchor, 1962, pp. 117–9).

²The issue here presented is strikingly illustrated by Elkin, *op. cit.*, pp. 311–38. See also G. Van Der Leeuw, *Religion in Essence and Manifestation* (New York: Harper Torchbooks, 1963, Vol. I, pp. 212–3.)

³It should not be concluded from these remarks that artificial maintenance of life is necessarily desirable or even justifiable. Religious, ethical, and financial considerations enter in now as ever. And to these must now be added the exceptional burden placed on the medical definition of death by the new and ever expanding field of organ transplantation. See Christian Barnard and Curtis Bill Pepper, *One Life* (New York: Bantam, 1971, pp. 353–402); David W. Louisell, "Transplantation: Existing Legal Constraints," in *Law and Ethics of Transplantation* ed. Gordon Wolstenholme and Maeve O'Connor, (London: J. A. Churchill, 1968, pp. 91–4); Catherine Lyons, *Organ Transplants: The Moral Issues* (Philadelphia: Westminster, 1970, pp. 75–89); Robert S. Morison, "Dying," *Scientific American*, Vol. 229, n. 3 (September 1973) p. 59.

⁴In a different vein, to say that medical responsibility extends even as far as organic death presupposes a somewhat idealized—or at least legally sensitive—interpretation of the Hippocratic oath. In a complex situation, however defined, some criteria of selection are often operative in order to focus available personnel and material on those deemed most likely to benefit from immediate treatment. These criteria may be overt, e.g., in the case of transplant recipient decisions or in the case of "truage" decisions in a war zone military hospital; or they may be tacit, as in the case of socioeconomic constraints that make medical treatment of any kind a privilege of opportunity which the poor of the world enjoy only minimally.

⁵See Peter L. Berger and Thomas Luckmann, *The Social Construction of Reality*. (Garden City, N. Y.: Anchor, 1967); Claude Lévi-Strauss, *The Savage Mind*. (Chicago: University of Chicago Press, 1966); Vittorio Lanternari, *The Religions of the Oppressed*.(New York: Mentor, 1965); Jacob Katz, *Exclusiveness and Tolerance*. (New York: Schocken, 1961); Wilfred Cantwell Smith, *The Meaning and End of Religion*. (New York: Mentor, 1964; Alfred Schutz, "Symbol, Reality and Society," in *Collected Papers*, Vol. 1 (The Hague: Martinus Nijhoff, 1967, pp. 287–356).

⁶Quoted from Darrow's *The Story of My Life* (New York: Scribner, 1932) by Althea J. Horner, "Genetic Aspects of Creativity," in *The Course of Human Life* eds. Charlotte Buhler and Fred Massarik, (New York: Springer, 1968, p. 135.)

⁷"The Eternal Now," in *The Meaning of Death* ed. Herman Feifel, (New York: McGraw-Hill, 1965, p. 32.)

⁸Quite common in literature, this theme of the fatal flaw is well exemplified in Leon Tolstoy's *The Death of Ivan Ilyitch* and in Arthur Koestler's *Darkness at Noon*. The personalization of mortality is, of course, a prominent theme among

Sartre. See Robert G. Olson, *An Introduction to Existentialism* (New York: Dover, 1962, pp. 192–212); Jacques Choron, *Death and Western Thought* (New York: Collier, 1963, pp. 222–61); Walter Kaufman, "Existentialism and Death," in Feifel, *op. cit.,* pp. 39–63.

[9]Donne's views are expressed in a diary of his own illness; Malraux's especially in *Man's Fate;* Mann's in *The Magic Mountain, Buddenbrooks,* and *Death in Venice.*

[10]Both Bergman and Boorman start from the premise that death is presently inevitable. But whereas Bergman's films have focused on personal responses to this inevitability, Boorman's *Zardoz* is, among other things, an elaborate *reductio ad absurdum* which attempts to show that death is in fact desirable, especially if science should eventually render it no longer inevitable.

[11]*On Death and Dying.* (New York: Macmillan, 1969.)

[12]Quoted from *Through the Looking Glass* in *The Life of Man* (Waukesha, Wis.: Country Beautiful, 1973, p. 182.)

[13]"Budapest 1956," in *From the Hungarian Revolution: A Collection of Poems* ed. David Ray, (Ithaca, N. Y.: Cornell University Press, 1966, pp. 107–8).

[14]Gerontological research is now discovering a cellular basis for this degenerative view of human life and, accordingly, might one day lead to means of overcoming it. See Rona Cherry and Laurence Cherry, "Slowing the Clock of Age," *The New York Times Magazine,* May 12, 1974, pp. 20ff.

[15]*The Life of Man, op. cit.,* p. 114.

[16]*Ibid.,* p. 162.

[17]Quoted by Arnold A. Hutschnecker, "Personality Factors in Dying Patients," in Feifel, *op. cit.,* p. 247.

[18]Maria H. Nagy, "The Child's View of Death," in Feifel, *op. cit.,* pp. 79–98.

[19]"The Idealogy of Death," in Feifel, *op. cit.,* p. 76. This lucid critique of the existentialists' emphasis on human finitude is on the whole complementary to views here being espoused.

[20]I say "generally speaking" because there are obvious qualifications which point to the need for a more careful statement than my documentation would allow. "Unwillingness to die," for example, cannot be taken to mean mere physical rebellion against dying; for, this might in fact do more harm than good, as in the case of one falling to the ground from a considerable height (here relaxation is probably the most salutary attitude to take). What an "unwillingness to die" does mean is well illustrated by the case of Louis Washkansky, the first recipient of a human heart transplant: Christian Barnard and Curtis Bill Pepper, *op. cit.,* pp. 337–53. See also Grosser/Wechsler/Greenblatt, eds., *The Threat of Impending Disaster.* (Cambridge, Mass.: MIT Press, 1964.)

[21]An appeal to the development of geriatrics as counter-evidence in this regard is muted most effectively just by noting the almost total neglect of the

aged, except as an economic problem, in most studies of the problems of society as a whole. For example, in all of the over 400 pages of his *Future Shock* (New York: Random House, 1970), Alvin Toffler barely manages to note in one passing line that ours is "a nation in which legions of elderly folk vegetate and die in loneliness" (p. 325). Yet even this brief observation is more than will be found in Philip Slater's *The Pursuit of Loneliness* (Boston: Beacon Press, 1970) or in Riesman/Glazer/Denny's *The Lonely Crowd* (New Haven: Yale University Press, 1950). Films such as NET's *Old Age—The Wasted Years* (1966) are correctives, as are such recent publications as Susan Jacoby, "Waiting for the End: On Nursing Homes," *The New York Times Magazine,* March 31, 1974, pp. 13ff.; and especially Mary Adelaide Mendelson, *Tender Loving Greed.* (New York: Knopf, 1974). Controversy over the latter work in particular seems to indicate the American conscience is not prepared to admit in the wake of such programs as Medicare that Michael Harrington's description of "The Golden Years" in his *The Other America* (Baltimore: Penguin, 1963, pp. 101–18) might still be essentially accurate.

[22]This standard model is even accepted by Charlotte Buhler and Fred Massaryk in their *The Course of Human Life* (*op. cit.*), which is subtitled "A Study of Goals in the Humanistic Perspective" and in which are acknowledged "late culmination" and "late-age peaks" (p. 62). See in this regard pp. 44 and 60.

[23]"The Soul and Death," in Feifel, *op. cit.,* p. 5.

[24]*Ibid.,* pp. 5–15.

[25]*From Death-Camp to Existentialism* (Boston: Beacon, 1959, pp. 64–84.)

[26]See, for example, John Beishon and Geoff Peters, eds., *Systems Behavior.* (New York: Harper & Row for Open University Press, 1972.)

[27]The need for wisdom in today's world has been stressed in various ways by such writers as Karl Jaspers, Pierre Teilhard de Chardin, Kenneth Boulding, Josiah Royce, and many others. A serious and knowledgeable attempt to articulate this need systematically is John David Garcia's *The Moral Society* (New York: Julian, 1971), which calls for "generalists" who have "total awareness."

[28]*Community and Society,* tr. C. P. Loomis, New York: Harper Torchbooks, 1963.

[29]*Culture and Commitment,* Garden City, N. Y.: Doubleday, 1970.

[30]Empirical support for this speculation has been reported by Alexander Leaf, "Getting Old," *Scientific American,* Vol. 229, n. 3 (September 1973) 44–52, especially p. 50: "It is characteristic of each of the areas I visited that the old people continue to be contributing members of their society . . . The old people, with their accumulated experience of life, are expected to be wise, and they respond accordingly."

[31]Carlos Castenada, *The Teachings of Don Juan* (New York: Ballantine, 1968, p. 83.) See also *A Separate Reality* (New York: Simon & Schuster, 1971, pp. 183–7.)

[32]Quoted by James L. Christian, *Philosophy: An Introduction to the Art of Wondering* (San Francisco: Rinehart, 1973, p. 476.)

[33]Quoted in *The Life of Man, op. cit.*, p. 173.

[34]This same model will also be found in Hermann Hesse's *Siddhartha*.

[35]See Maurice Friedman, *To Deny Our Nothingness*. (New York: Delta, 1967, pp. 62–79.)

SELECTED BIBLIOGRAPHY

One version of the philosophy of activism is typified in the "leisure ethic" of many retirement communities. For a critical evaluation of this form of the philosophy of activism see Jerry Jacobs, *Fun City*, (New York: Holt, Rinehart and Winston, 1974). Conceptual problems in defining "successful" aging are examined in Richard Williams and Martin Loeb, "The Adult's Social Life Space and Successful Aging: Some Suggestions for a Conceptual Framework," a paper presented to the annual meeting of the American Gerontological Society, Chicago, 1968; reprinted in Neugarten, MAA. Conceptual aspects of a philosophy of aging are also analyzed in Marjorie Fiske Lowenthal's essay "Psychosocial Variations Across the Adult Life Course: Frontiers for Research and Policy," *G,* 1975. Psychological phenomena related to the basic choices posed in philosophy of aging, including the increased "interiority" associated with arguments for a philosophy of disengagement, are described in Bernice Neugarten, "Adult Personality: Toward a Psychology of the Life Cycle," in Edgar Vinackex (ed.), *Readings in General Psychology* (New York:

American Book, 1968). Neugarten's influential contributions to the field of gerontology, mostly in the field of psychology, almost always have a humanistic and philosophical dimension. Other prominent gerontologists of whom the same could be said are Richard Kalish, David Guttman, Robert Butler, Charlotte Buhler, Robert Kastenbaum, Robert Kleemeier, Robert Havighurst and Marjorie Fiske Lowenthal. A popularized expression of the philosophy of activity is given in Gail Sheehy, *Passages: Predictable Crises of Adult Life* (New York: Dutton, 1976), Chapter 25. A general discussion of the losses and gains in old age and possible responses to them, which has a largely philosophical perspective, is Paul W. Pruyser's essay "Aging: Downward, Upward or Forward?" in Seward Hiltner (ed.), *Toward a Theology of Aging* (New York: Human Sciences Press, 1975). In the same book see Don S. Browning, "Preface to a Practical Theology of Aging" and Seward Hiltner, "Discussion and Comment." One of the most important texts in philosophy of old age, Simone de Beauvoir's *The Coming of Age*, is an overall recommendation of the philosophy of disengagement. An activist philosophy of aging, and discussion of a number of ethical questions related to old age, including agism and social justice, are found in Paul Klegman, *Senior Power: Growing Old Rebelliously* (San Francisco: Glide Publications, 1974). The activist philosophy is also advocated, from a perspective of normative ethics, in Doris Jonas and David Jones, *Young Till We Die* (New York: Coward, McCann and Geoghegan, 1973). An excellent general overview of the philosophy of aging, written from an activist perspective by Margaret E. Kuhn, founder of the Gray Panthers, is found in her essay "Learning by Living," *IJAHD*, 1978.

An interesting essay on learning activity in old age, written with an activist orientation, is "Cultural Therapy in the Old Person's Home," by Ignat Petrov and Lilia Vlahalizska, *G*, 1972. A similar view is expressed in "Continued Growth and Life Satisfaction" by John Kurtz and Stephen Wolk, *G*, 1975. A philosophy of education for retirement, including an analysis of ethical issues related to the "worthy" use of leisure time, is found in Hyman

Hirsch, "Higher Education in Retirement: The Institute for Retired Professionals," *IJAHD,* 1978. For more extensive discussion of the same theme, see W. Donahue et al. (eds), *The Way of A Liberal Education—Free Time—A Challenge To Later Maturity* (Ann Arbor: University of Michigan Press, 1958). An extensive bibliography of works related to education resources and opportunities for the elderly and retired person is found in "Education for Older Adults: Selected Bibliography," by Jeanne Bader, *IJAHD,* 1978.

The classic formulation of the philosophy of disengagement in modern gerontological literature is in Elaine Cumming and William Henry, *Growing Old: The Process of Disengagement* (New York: Basic Books, 1961), a portion of which is included in Section Four of this book. The disengagement philosophy is defended in D. B. Bromley, *The Psychology of Human Aging* (Baltimore: Pelican Books, 1966), especially in Chapters One and Three. Disengagement, successful aging, and related concepts are incisively analyzed by the psychologist Jack Botwinick in Chapter Five, "Turning Inward," of his book *Aging and Behavior* (New York: Atherton Press, 1965). Like Cumming and Henry's *Growing Old* this last book is an attempt to provide a theoretical interpretation of the data collected by the well-known longitudinal study, The Kansas City Study of Adult Life. Several essays analyzing key concepts of the disengagement philosophy and containing useful material on ethical and phenomenological aspects of aging are found in Volume 6, Number 3, (1975), of *IJAHD.* A work that supports the disengagement theory by arguing that in most people creative powers peak during the thirties is C. Lehman, *Age and Achievement* (Princeton: Princeton University Press, 1953). Counterarguments to Lehman, and a version of the philosophy of activism, are systematically developed in John A. B. McLeish, *The Ulyssean Adult* (New York: McGraw Hill Ryerson, 1976). How the concept of disengagement applies to religious belief and activity is analyzed by Charles Mendel and C. Edwin Vaughn in their essay "Multidimensional Approach to Religiosity and Disengagement," *JG,* 1978.

The traditional Hindu philosophy of old age is explained and related to Erik Erikson's "life-cycle" psychology in Sudhir Kakar, "The Human Life Cycle: The Traditional Hindu View and the Psychology of Erik Erikson," *Philosophy East and West,* 1968. Much of Erik Erikson's essay "Reflections on Doctor Borg's Life Cycle," *Daedelus,* 1968, an interpretive study of the aged hero of Ingmar Bergman's film *Wild Strawberries,* is of general philosophical interest. An interpretation of the philosophy of disengagement generally reflecting the Hindu view of stages of life is presented by Rabindranath Tagore in *The Religion of Man* (Boston: Beacon Press, 1961, Chap. 14.)

Evelyn Whitehead's essay "Religious Images of Aging: An Examination of Themes in Contemporary Christian Thought," in Stuart Spicker, Kathleen Woodward and David VanTassel, *AEHPG,* is richly suggestive of patterns of personal growth in old age, with a vaguely disengagement orientation.

Georgias Koumakis reviews Aristotle's view of the place of the elderly in society in "Aristotle's Opinions on Old Age From A Social Point of View," *Philosophia,* 1974. Various details of Plato's philosophy of old age are stated in *Laws,* Book I, 631C–634E; Book II, 664B–674C; Book XII, 964B–969D.

An area of gerontologic research with direct relevance to the philosophy of aging not represented in the selections included in the present text, centers around the concept of "life satisfaction," its measurement, and its relation to classical philosophical ideals of happiness. Gerontological literature on this subject is vast. For a summary of the key concepts, issues and theories, see Linda George, "The Happiness Syndrome: Methodological and Substantive Issues in the Study of Social Psychological Well-Being in Adulthood," *G,* 1979. Pioneering papers in this area of inquiry, themselves of substantial philosophical sophistication and interest, and all coauthored by Robert J. Havighurst, Bernice Neugarten and Sheldon S. Tobin, are: "The Measurement of Life Satisfaction," *JG,* 1961; "Personality and Aging," *G,* 1968 (reprinted in Neugarten, MAA), and "Personality and Patterns of Aging," Neugarten, MAA. A conceptual analysis of happiness in old age which follows these early papers in relativizing it to prior expectations of the aging individual is given in Erdman Palmore and Vira Kivett, "Changes in Life Satisfaction: A Longitudinal Study of Persons Aged 46–70," in *JG*, 1977. The same idea is criticized in Bill D. Bell, "Cognitive Dissonance and the Life Satisfaction of Older Adults," *JG*, 1974. Another perspective on the same topic that should be equally interesting to philosophers is found in Morris Medley, "Satisfaction with Life Among Persons Sixty-five and Older: A Causal Model," in *JG*, 1976, and in "A Causal Theory of Life Satisfaction Among the Elderly" by K. Markides and Harry Martin, *JG*, 1979. A useful overview and provocative discussion of "quality of life" in old age is found in Barry Lebowitz, "Age and Fearfulness: Personal and Situational Factors," *JG*, 1975. Conceptual problems relating to attempts to measure life satisfaction and happiness are raised in all of the following: M. Bloom, "Discontent With Contentment Scales," *G*, 1975: C. Nydeger, "Introduction," and M. P. Lawton, "Morale: What Are We Measuring?" both in C. Nydeger (ed.) *Measuring Morale* (Washington, D.C. Gerontological Society, 1977); and the essay by Linda George, "The Happiness Syndrome . . ." in *G*, 1979, just mentioned.

Ethical and conceptual problems in defining "successful" aging are analyzed in H. Thomae, "Patterns of 'Successful' Aging" and U. Lehr and R. Schmitz-Scherzer, "Survivors and Non-Survivors-Two Fundamental Patterns of Aging," both in H. Thomae (ed.), *Patterns of Aging* (Basel, Switzerland: S. Karger, 1976). What could be called a "formalist" theory of successful aging—the view that fulfillment in the course of personal development lies in the expression of a natural developmental order or pattern—is presented, with biographical support, in Part I of Daniel Levinson, *The Seasons of a Man's Life* (New York: Alfred A. Knopf, 1978). Numerous observations about successful aging, and a number of observations useful for developing a phenomenology of the experience of growing old, are made in "How does it Feel to Grow Old—Eleven Essayists Answer," by Jean Roberts and Larry Kimsly, *G*, 1972. A self-actualization ideal of happiness and fulfillment in old age, based on a philosophy of ethical individualism, is found in Chapters 6 and 7 of David L. Norton, *Personal Destinies* (Princeton: Princeton University Press, 1976).

Interpretations of successful aging from the perspective of existentialist philosophy have been developed in several works by James Crumbaugh and also by Gene Acuff. For examples of this work and further bibliography, see Gene Acuff and Donald Allen, "Hiatus in 'Meaning':Disengagement for Retired Professors," *JG,* 1970, and James Crumbaugh, "Aging and Adjustment: The Applicability of Logotherapy and the Purpose-In-Life Test," *G,* 1972. The experience of normlessness and alienation in old age are examined from a broad sociological and psychological perspective in Wilbert M. Leonard, "Social and Social Psychological Correlates of Anomia Among A Random Sample of Aged," *JG,* 1977. A partial review of recent literary descriptions of old age which have general overtones of the disengagement ethic is made by Celeste Loughman in "Novels of Senescence, A New Naturalism," *G,* 1977. A very useful bibliography of novels of aging is found in the same volume, in Mary Sohngren, "The Experience of Old Age as Depicted in Contemporary Novels." See also David A. Peterson and Elizabeth Karnes, "Older People in Adolescent Literature," *G,* 1976, and the following essays in Spicker, Woodward and VanTassel, AEHPG: Righard Freedman, "Sufficiently Decayed: Gerontophobia in English Literature"; Susan Tamke, "Human Values and Aging: The Perspective of the Victorian Nursery"; Kathleen Woodward, "Master Songs of Meditation: The Late Poems of Eliot, Pound, Stevens and Williams"; David Luke, "How Is It That You Live, and What Is It That You Do? The Question of Old Age in English Romantic Literature"; Walter Moss, "Why the Anxious Fear?: Aging and Death in the Works of Turgenev"; and David Bronsen, "Consuming Struggle vs. Killing Time: Preludes to Dying in the Dramas of Ibsen and Becket." A literary illustration of the disengagement philosophy is described by Sister Rachel M. Ricciardelli in "King Lear and the Theory of Disengagement," *G,* 1973. A summary and commentary on some Biblicial interpretations of Old Age are found in "The Bible and

Old Age," by J. J. Griffin, *JG*, 1946. Furturistic predictions of changes in political philosophy affecting old age, drawn from historical observation, are ventured in "Aging in America, Toward the Year 2000," by David Peterson, Chuck Powell and Lawrie Robertson, *G*, 1976.

Books which offer general discussion of old age from perspectives that are wholly or to a significant degree philosophical are: A. L. Vischer, *On Growing Old* (Boston: Houghton Mifflin Company, 1967 [translated from the German by Gerald Onn]); Paul Tournier, *Learn To Grow Old* (New York: Harper & Row, 1971 (translated from the French by Edwin Hudson)); and Ethel Sabin Smith, *The Dynamics of Aging* (New York: W. W. Norton, 1956). Robert N. Butler's *Why Survive? Being Old in America* (New York: Harper & Row, 1975) contains philosophical analysis and argumentation on almost every page, and can easily be read as a major work in the philosophy of old age with a generally activist orientation. Questions pertaining to the overall response to aging, including the continuing need to find meaning in life, are discussed in a general way by Jack Weinberg in "On Adding Insight to Injury," *G*, 1976. In the same volume, see Erdman Palmore and Dan Blazer, "Religion and Aging in a Longitudinal Panel." Several aspects of the philosophy of old age are examined from a sociological perspective in Majda Thurnher, "Goals, Values and Life Evaluations at the Preretirement Stage," *JG*, 1974.

A group of philosophically important essays on successful aging that are difficult to classify in terms of activity or disengagement perspectives are featured in the Fall 1977 issue of the journal *Humanitas*. These include: "Aging: Potentials for Personal Liberation," by Joseph Kuypers, which has certain affinities with the disengagement theory in stressing inwardness during old age; "Authentic Living-Graceful Aging," by Germaine Hustedde, in which moral authenticity and integrity is defended as a condition for happiness in old age; "Does Old Age Make Sense?" by Avery Weisman, in which a very useful distinction is made between the concepts of "growing older" and "decline," and "Fulfillment in the Later Years," by Adeline Hoffman.

The philosopher Albert Chandler contributed the following historical essays on philosophy of aging to *JG:* "Aristotle on Mental Aging" and "Cicero's Ideal Old Man," 1948; "The Chinese Attitude Toward Old Age," 1949. A historical survey of the concept of aging in philosophical thought, with a discussion of the theme that aging is "learning to die," is found in Horace M. Kallen, "Philosophy, Aging and the Aged," *JVI,* 1972.

Part II

ETHICAL ASPECTS OF AGING

INTRODUCTION

Recent public discussion has raised a number of important questions about the ethical values underlying contemporary treatment of the elderly. As a result, such ethical problems of old age as life extension, alienation of the aged, economic justice for retirees, filial obligation, euthanasia, and others have received increased attention from moral philosophers in recent years. The increasing political, demographic, and educational advantages of the aged population insure that debate about these and related problems will continue for the indefinite future. The present part is devoted to essays that illuminate some of the philosophical principles underlying that evolving discussion.

Lin Yutang's "On Growing Old Gracefully" is a rich source of observations basic for an ethics of old age. He reminds us of the tendency to regard old people as having diminished human worth. He suggests that old people have certain rights deriving from their former service to others, and that their claim to basic human dignity is enhanced by long experience of life. Finally, in an interesting critique of the Western cultural aesthetic, Lin suggests that there is something morally deficient in the eye of the beholder who sees ugliness rather than beauty in the aged human face and body.

Some of Lin's perspective on old age has its origin in the classic Confucian text *The Book of Filial Piety*. This text presents the central Confucian principle that respect and love for one's parents is the moral virtue presupposed by all other moral virtues. It should be noted that the duty of filial piety is not seen as being satisfied by providing for parents materially, nor by external conformity to their wishes. It is concerned with our inner disposition to value old people as well as with external behavior. It is important to see also that this virtue has a foundational role in Confucian ethics similar to the role of good will in the ethical theory of Immanuel Kant. In other words, all morally valuable feelings, attitudes, and actions are said to derive their moral worth from their origin in an inner disposition of filial piety, and ostensibly good acts in an unfilial person are seen as morally empty.

Of the many social problems that currently afflict old people, none is more damaging to quality of life than our failure to provide for their economic well-being. In the essay "The Ethics of Providing for the Economic Well-Being of the Aging," B. J. Diggs discusses the problem of achieving economic justice for the aged. According to Diggs, we must distinguish between economic support flowing from benevolence for the aged and support to which the aged are entitled as a matter of human rights. He explains his view that such rights are conventional, and therefore within our power to establish through appropriate social conventions and institutions. He also relates his view of the economic rights of the aged to recent philosophical discussion of justice between generations.

Old age is perhaps too closely associated with death in popular thinking. The image of the old as people who are near death and therefore "finished" is one of the more harmful negative stereotypes of old age. We need to be reminded that being old is not the same as waiting around to die.

Nevertheless, old age does bring us into confrontation with

death, both through the death of persons close to us, and because the likelihood of our own death becomes increasingly real as we grow into old age. Two ethical problems concerning death seem especially relevant to a philosophy of aging: life extension and euthanasia. The first of these is discussed in the essays by James Goddard and James Gustafson.

Goddard raises a number of important ethical questions related to extending the human life span. First, there is the problem of deciding whether current scientific understanding and ability warrant a significant commitment of resources to the goal of life extension. Goddard believes that such a commitment is warranted, as far as our scientific readiness for it is concerned. He suggests that adoption of an extended life span as a national goal be modeled on such earlier systematic commitments of national resources as the commitment to eradicate polio and the commitment to develop technology for going to the moon. A second kind of ethical problem relates specifically to pursuing more detailed knowledge of the aging process. Among these is the problem of establishing the place of life extension in the scale of national priorities, especially establishing its importance in relation to the more immediate problems of sustaining and enhancing life for the current generation. Another problem concerns limitations on research methods, especially the selection and use of human subjects. Finally, there is the problem of coping with the ethical dilemmas that would result from successful large-scale extension of the aging process. Increasing the life span for just a few years, Goddard argues, would have important predictable effects on the allocation of goods and services in society, on the pattern of the life cycle, and on interpersonal relationships. Many of these changes would involve disruption of established ethical norms.

In contrast to Goddard, James Gustafson believes that there is need for a much enlarged basis of factual knowledge before responsible decisions about life extension policies can be made. According to Gustafson, we do not in fact have knowledge about how to extend life, nor of what consequences would follow upon doing so. But even if we did, a moral basis for a public policy of life extension would have to go beyond that empirical knowledge to include ethical reasoning and justification. Gustafson examines three different kinds of ethical reasons that might be given for such a policy. He looks unfavorably on the idea that a policy of life extension could be morally justified either by the natural desire or wish to live as long as possible or by the tenuous social benefits that might accrue from such a policy. A much stronger ethical justification, he thinks, can be found in the basic human right of each individual to live as long as possible.

It should be noted that the life extension at issue here is not equivalent to increasing longevity. The former carries the connotation of intervening medically or biologically with the aging process itself, so as to slow down the specific process of growing older and stretch it out over a longer period of time. This is different from postponing death through the control of killing diseases. The latter process does not increase the length of the lifespan that is "natural" for the human species, but rather insures that we can live to its upper limit.

Chapter 7

ON GROWING OLD GRACEFULLY

Lin Yutang

The Chinese family system, as I conceive it, is largely an arrangement of particular provision for the young and the old, for since childhood and youth and old age occupy half of our life, it is important that the young and the old live a satisfactory life. It is true that the young are more helpless and can take less care of themselves, but on the other hand, they can get along better without material comforts than the old people. A child is often scarcely aware of material hardships, with the result that a poor child is often as happy as, if not happier than, a rich child. He may go barefooted, but that is a comfort, rather than a hardship to him, whereas going barefooted is often an intolerable hardship for old people. This comes from the child's greater vitality, the bounce of youth. He may have his temporary sorrows, but how easily he forgets them. He has no idea of money and no millionaire complex, as the old man has. At the worst, he collects only cigar

From Lin Yutang, *The Importance of Living* (London: Wm. Heinemann, Ltd. 1931). Reprinted by permission of the publisher.

coupons for buying a pop-gun, whereas the dowager collects Liberty Bonds. Between the fun of these two kinds of collection there is no comparison. The reason is the child is not yet intimidated by life as all grown-ups are. His personal habits are as yet unformed, and he is not a slave to a particular brand of coffee, and he takes whatever comes along. He has very little racial prejudice and absolutely no religious prejudice. His thoughts and ideas have not fallen into certain ruts. Therefore, strange as it may seem, old people are even more dependent than the young because their fears are more definite and their desires are more delimited.

Something of this tenderness toward old age existed already in the primeval consciousness of the Chinese people, a feeling that I can compare only to the Western chivalry and feeling of tenderness toward women. If the early Chinese people had any chivalry, it was manifested not toward women and children, but toward the old people. That feeling of chivalry found clear expression in Mencius in some such saying as, "The people with grey hair should not be seen carrying burdens on the street," which was expressed as the final goal of a good government. Mencius also described the four classes of the world's most helpless people as: "The widows, widowers, orphans, and old people without children." Of these four classes, the first two were to be taken care of by a political economy that should be so arranged that there would be no unmarried men and women. What was to be done about the orphans Mencius did not say, so far as we know, although orphanages have always existed throughout the ages, as well as pensions for old people. Every one realizes, however, that orphanages and old age pensions are poor substitutes for the home. The feeling is that the home alone can provide anything resembling a satisfactory arrangement for the old and the young. But for the young, it is to be taken for granted that not much need be said, since there is natural paternal affection. "Water flows downwards and not upwards," the Chinese always say, and therefore the affection for parents and grandparents is something that stands more in need of being taught by culture. A natural man loves his children, but a cultured man loves his parents. In the end, the teaching of love and respect for old people became a generally accepted principle, and if we are to believe some of the writers, the desire to have the privilege of serving their parents in their old age actually became a consuming passion. The greatest regret a Chinese gentleman could have was the eternally lost opportunity of serving his old parents with medicine and soup on their deathbed, or not to be present when they died. For a high official in his fifties or sixties not to be able to invite his parents to come from their native village and stay with his family at the capital, "seeing them to bed every night and greeting them every morning," was to commit a moral sin of which he should be ashamed and for which he had constantly to offer excuses and explanations to his friends and colleagues. This regret was expressed in two lines by a man who returned too late to his home, when his parents had already died:

> The tree desires repose, but the wind will not stop;
> The son desires to serve, but his parents are already gone.

It is to be assumed that if man were to live this life like a poem, he would be able to look upon the sunset of his life as his happiest period, and instead of trying to postpone the much feared old age, be able actually to look forward to it, and gradually build up to it as the best and happiest period of his existence. In my efforts to compare and contrast Eastern and Western life, I have found no differences that are absolute except in this matter of the attitude towards age, which is sharp and clearcut and permits of no intermediate positions. The differences in our attitude towards sex, toward women, and toward work, play, and achievement are all relative. The relationship between husband and wife in China is not essentially different from that in the West, nor even the relationship between parent and child. Not even the ideas of individual liberty and democracy and the relationship between the people and their ruler are, after all, so very different. But in the matter of our attitude toward age, the difference is absolute, and the East and the West take exactly opposite points of view. This is clearest in the matter of asking about a person's age or telling one's own. In China, the first question a person asks the other on an official call, after asking about his name and surname is, "What is your glorious age?" If the person replies apologetically that he is twenty-three or twenty-eight, the other party generally comforts him by saying that he has still a glorious future, and that one day he may become old. But if the person replies that he is thirty-five or thirty-eight, the other party immediately exclaims with deep respect, "Good luck!"; enthusiasm grows in proportion as the gentleman is able to report a higher and higher age, and if the person is anywhere over fifty, the inquirer immediately drops his voice in humility and respect. That is why all old people, if they can, should go and live in China, where even a beggar with a white beard is treated with extra kindness. People in middle age actually look forward to the time when they can celebrate their fifty-first birthday, and in the case of successful merchants or officials, they would celebrate even their forty-first birthday with great pomp and glory. But the fifty-first birthday, or the half-century mark, is an occasion of rejoicing for people of all classes. The sixty-first is a happier and grander occasion than the fifty-first and the seventy-first is still happier and grander, while a man able to celebrate his eighty-first birthday is actually looked upon as one specially favored by heaven. The wearing of a beard becomes the special prerogative of those who have become grandparents, and a man doing so without the necessary qualifications, either of being a grandfather or being on the other side of fifty, stands in danger of being sneered at behind his back. The result is that young men try to pass themselves off as older than they are by imitating the pose and dignity and point of view of the old people, and I have known young Chinese writers graduated from the middle schools, anywhere between twenty-one and twenty-five, writing articles in the magazines to advise what "the young men ought and ought not to read," and discussing the pitfalls of youth with a fatherly condescension.

This desire to grow old and in any case to appear old is understandable when one understands the premium generally placed upon old age in China. In the first place, it is a privilege of the old people to talk, while the young must listen and hold their tongue. "A young man is supposed to have ears and no mouth," as a Chinese saying goes. Men of twenty are supposed to listen when people of thirty are talking, and these in turn are supposed to listen when men of forty are talking. As the desire to talk and to be listened to is almost universal, it is evident that the further along one gets in years, the better chance he has to talk and to be listened to when he goes about in society. It is a game of life in which no one is favored, for everyone has a chance of becoming old in his time. Thus a father lecturing his son is obliged to stop suddenly and change his demeanor the moment the grandmother opens her mouth. Of course he wishes to be in the grandmother's place. And it is quite fair, for what right have the young to open their mouth when the old men can say, "I have crossed more bridges than you have crossed streets!" What right have the young got to talk?

In spite of my acquaintance with Western life and the Western attitude toward age, I am still continually shocked by certain expressions for which I am totally unprepared. Fresh illustrations of this attitude come up on every side. I have heard an old lady remarking that she has had several grandchildren, but, "It was the first one that hurt." With the full knowledge that American people hate to be thought of as old, one still doesn't quite expect to have it put that way. I have made allowance for people in middle age this side of fifty, who, I can understand, wish to leave the impression that they are still active and vigorous, but I am not quite prepared to meet an old lady with gray hair facetiously switching the topic of conversation to the weather, when the conversation without any fault of mine naturally drifted toward her age. One continually forgets it when allowing an old man to enter an elevator or a car first; the habitual expression "after age" comes to my lips, then I restrain myself and am at a loss for what to say in its place. One day, being forgetful, I blurted out the usual phrase in deference to an extremely dignified and charming old man, and the old man seated in the car turned to his wife and remarked jokingly to her, "This young man has the cheek to think that he is younger than myself!"

The whole thing is as senseless as can be. I just don't see the point. I can understand young and middle-aged unmarried women refusing to tell their age, because there the premium upon youth is entirely natural. Chinese girls, too, get a little scared when they reach twenty-two and are unmarried or not engaged. The years are slipping by mercilessly. There is a feeling of fear of being left out, what the Germans called a *Torschlusspanik*, the fear of being left in the park when the gates close at night. Hence it has been said that the longest year of a woman's life is when she is twenty-nine; she remains twenty-nine for three or four or five years. But apart from this, the fear of letting people know one's age is nonsensical. How can one be thought wise unless one is thought to be old? And what do the young really know about life, about marriage and about the true values? Again I can understand that the whole pattern of Western life places a premium on youth and therefore makes men and women shrink from telling people their age. A perfectly efficient and vigorous woman secretary of forty-five is, by a curious twist of reasoning, immediately thought of as worthless when her age becomes known. What wonder that she wants to hide her age in order to keep her job? But then the pattern of life itself and this premium placed upon youth are nonsensical. There is absolutely no meaning to it, so far as I can see. This sort of thing is undoubtedly brought about by business life, for I have no doubt there must be more respect for old age in the home than in the office. I see no way out of it until the American people begin somewhat to despise work and efficiency and achievement. I suspect when an American father looks upon the home and not the office as his ideal place in life, and can openly tell people, as Chinese parents do, with absolute equanimity that now he has a good son taking his place and is honored to be fed by him, he will be anxiously looking forward to that happy time, and will count the years impatiently before he reaches fifty.

It seems a linguistic misfortune that hale and hearty old men in America tell people that they are "young," or are told that they are "young" when really what is meant is that they are healthy. To enjoy health in old age, or to be "old and healthy," is the greatest of human luck, but to call it "healthy and young" is but to detract from that glamour and impute imperfection to what is really perfect. After all, there is nothing more beautiful in this world than a healthy wise old man, with "ruddy cheeks and white hair," talking in a soothing voice about life as one who knows it. The Chinese realize this, and have always pictured an old man with "ruddy cheeks and white hair" as the symbol of ultimate earthly happiness. Many Americans must have seen Chinese pictures of the God of Longevity, with his high forehead, his ruddy face, his white beard—and how he smiles! The picture is so vivid. He runs his fingers through the thin flowing beard coming down to the breast and gently strokes it in peace and contentment, dignified because he is surrounded with respect, self-assured because no one ever questions his wisdom, and kind because he has seen so much of human sorrow. To persons of great vitality, we also pay the compliment of saying that "the older they grow, the more vigorous they are," and a person like David Lloyd George would be referred to as "Old Ginger," because he gains in pungency with age.

On the whole, I find grand old men with white beards missing in the American picture. I know that they exist, but they are perhaps in a conspiracy to hide themselves from me. Only once, in New Jersey, did I meet an old man with anything like a respectable beard. Perhaps it is the safety razor that has done it, a process as deplorable and ignorant and stupid as the deforestation of the Chinese hills by ignorant farmers, who have deprived North China of its beautiful forests and left the hills as bald and ugly as the American old men's chins. There is yet a mine to be discovered in America, a mine of beauty and wisdom that is pleasing to the eye and thrilling to the soul, when the American has opened his eyes to it and starts a general program of reclamation and reforestation. Gone are the grand old men of America! Gone is Uncle Sam with his goatee, for he has taken a safety razor and shaved it off, to make himself look like a frivolous young fool with his chin sticking out instead of being drawn in gracefully, and a hard glint shining behind horn-rimmed spectacles. What a poor substitute that is for the grand old figure! My attitude on the Supreme Court question (although it is none of my business) is purely determined by my love for the face of Charles Evans Hughes. Is he the only grand old man left in America, or are there more of them? He should retire, of course, for that it only being kind to him, but any accusation of senility seems to me an intolerable insult. He has a face that we would call "a sculptor's dream."

I have no doubt that the fact that the old men of America still insist on being so busy and active can be directly traced to individualism carried to a foolish extent. It is their pride and their love of independence and their shame of being dependent upon their children. But among the many human rights the American people have provided for in the Constitution, they have strangely forgotten about the right to be fed by their children, for it is a right and an obligation growing out of service. How can any one deny that parents who have toiled for their children in their youth, have lost many a good night's sleep when they were ill, have washed their diapers long before they could talk and have spent about a quarter of a century bringing them up and fitting them for life, have the right to be fed by them and loved and respected when they are old? Can one not forget the individual and his pride of self in a general scheme of home life in which men are justly taken care of by their parents and, having in turn taken care of their children, are also justly taken care of by the latter? The Chinese have not got the sense of individual independence because the whole conception of life is based upon mutual help within the home; hence there is no shame attached to the circumstance of one's being served by his children in the sunset of one's life. Rather it is considered good luck to have children who can take care of one. One lives for nothing else in China.

In the West, the old people efface themselves and prefer to live alone in some hotel with a restaurant on the ground floor, out of consideration for their children and an entirely unselfish desire not to interfere in their home life. But the old people have the right to interfere, and if interference is unpleasant, it is nevertheless natural, for all life, particularly the domestic life, is a lesson in restraint. Parents interfere with their children anyway when they are young, and the logic of noninterference is already seen in the results of the Behaviorists, who think that all children should be taken away from their parents. If one cannot tolerate one's own parents when they are old and comparatively helpless, parents who have done so much for us, whom else can one tolerate in the home? One has to learn self-restraint anyway, or even marriage will go on the rocks. And how can the personal service and devotion and adoration of loving children ever be replaced by the best hotel waiters?

The Chinese idea supporting this personal service to old parents is expressly defended on the sole ground of gratitude. The debts to one's friends may be numbered, but the debts to one's parents are beyond number. Again and again, Chinese essays on filial piety mention the fact of washing diapers, which takes on significance when one becomes a parent himself. In return, therefore, is it not right that in their old age, the parents should be served with the best food and have their favorite dishes placed before them? The duties of a son serving his parents are pretty hard, but it is sacrilege to make a comparison between nursing one's own parents and nursing a stranger in a hospital. For instance, the following are some of the duties of the junior at home, as prescribed by T'u Hsishih and incorporated in a book of moral instruction very popular as a text in the old schools:

> In the summer months, one should, while attending to his parents, stand by their side and fan them, to drive away the heat and the flies and mosquitoes. In winter, he should see that the bed quilts are warm enough and the stove fire is hot enough, and see that it is just right by attending to it constantly. He should also see if there are holes or crevices in the doors and windows, that there may be no draft, to the end that his parents are comfortable and happy.

> A child above ten should get up before his parents in the morning, and after the toilet go to their bed and ask if they have had a good night. If his parents have already gotten up, he should first curtsy to them before inquiring after their health, and should retire with another curtsy after the question. Before going to bed at night,

he should prepare the bed, when the parents are going to sleep, and
stand by until he sees that they have fallen off to sleep and then pull
down the bed curtain and retire himself.

Who, therefore, wouldn't want to be an old man or an old father or
grandfather in China?

This sort of thing is being very much laughed at by the
proletarian writers of China as "feudalistic," but there is a charm to
it which makes any old gentleman inland cling to it and think that
modern China is going to the dogs. The important point is that
every man grows old in time, if he lives long enough, as he
certainly desires to. If one forgets this foolish individualism which
seems to assume that an individual can exist in the abstract and be
literally independent, one must admit that we must so plan our
pattern of life that the golden period lies ahead in old age and not
behind us in youth and innocence. For if we take the reverse
attitude, we are committed without our knowing to a race with the
merciless course of time, forever afraid of what lies ahead of us—a
race, it is hardly necessary to point out, which is quite hopeless and
in which we are eventually all defeated. No one can really stop
growing old; he can only cheat himself by not admitting that he is
growing old. And since there is no use fighting against nature, one
might just as well grow old gracefully. The symphony of life
should end with a grand finale of peace and serenity and material
comfort and spiritual contentment, and not with the crash of a
broken drum or cracked cymbals.

Chapter 8

THE BOOK OF FILIAL PIETY

Confucius

CHAPTER I: THE GENERAL THEME

Chung-ni* was at leisure, and Tseng Tzu attended him. The Master said: "The early kings possessed the supreme virtue and the basic Tao for the regulation of the world. On account of this, the people lived in peace and harmony; neither superiors nor inferiors had any complaints. Do you know this?"

Tseng Tzu rose from his seat and said: "How can Sheng,† dull of intelligence, know this?"

The Master said: "Filial piety is the basis of virtue and the source of culture. Sit down again, and I will explain it to you. The body and the limbs, the hair and the skin, are given to one by one's

From *The Humanist Way in Ancient China: Essential Works of Confucianism,* edited and translated by Ch'u Chai and Winberg Chai (New York: Bantam Books, 1965). Reprinted by permission of the publisher.
*Confucius' name.
†Tseng Tzu's name.

parents, and to them no injury should come; this is where filial piety begins. To establish oneself and practice the Tao is to immortalize one's name and thereby to glorify one's parents; this is where filial piety ends. Thus filial piety commences with service to parents; it proceeds with service to the sovereign; it is completed by the establishment of one's own personality.

"In the Shih it is said:

> May you think of your ancestors,
> And so cultivate their virtues!"

CHAPTER II: THE SON OF HEAVEN

The Master said: "One who loves one's parents does not dare to hate others. One who reveres one's parents does not dare to spurn others. When love and reverence are thus cherished in the service of one's parents, one's moral influence transforms the people, and one becomes a pattern to all within the four seas. This is the filial piety of the Son of Heaven.

"In the Fu Code, it is said:

> When the One Man has blessings,
> The millions of people rely on him."

CHAPTER III: THE FEUDAL PRINCES

When the prince is not proud and arrogant, he will be secure in his position, however high it may be. When the prince is frugal and prudent, he will keep his wealth, however abundant it may be. When he secures himself in his high position, he will remain unimpaired in his dignity; when he keeps his abundant wealth, he will remain rich. And thus, preserving his wealth and dignity, he will be able to protect his country and pacify his people. This is the filial piety of feudal princes.

In the Shih it is said:

In fear and trembling,
With caution and care,
As if standing by a deep abyss,
As if treading on thin ice.

CHAPTER IV: THE HIGH OFFICERS

They do not presume to be in costume not prescribed by the early kings; they do not presume to use words not sanctioned by the early kings; they do not presume to act contrary to the virtuous conduct of the early kings. Thus, none of their words are contrary to sanctions, and none of their actions are not in accordance with the Tao. Their words are not improper; nor are their actions indecent. Their words spread over the world, and yet no fault is found in them. Their actions spread over the world, and yet no complaint is caused by them. When these three things are properly observed, they will be able to preserve their ancestral temples. This is the filial piety of high officers.

In the Shih it is said:

Day and night, never slacken
In the service of the One Man.

CHAPTER V: THE SCHOLARS

One serves one's mother in the same manner in which one serves one's father, and the love toward them is the same. One serves one's prince in the same manner in which one serves one's father, and the reverence toward them is the same. Thus, to the mother one shows love and to the prince one shows reverence, but to the father one shows both love and reverence. Therefore, to serve the prince with filial piety is to show loyalty; to serve the senior with reverence is to show obedience. Not failing in loyalty and obedience in the service of one's superiors, one will be able to preserve one's emolument and position and to carry on one's family sacrifices. This is the filial piety of scholars.

In the Shih it is said:

> Rise early and go to sleep late,
> Never disgrace those who bore you.

Chapter VI: The Common People

In order to support their parents, they follow the Tao of Heaven; they utilize the earth in accordance with the quality of its soil, and they are prudent and frugal in their expenditure. This is the filial piety of the common people.

Therefore, from the Son of Heaven down to the common people, there has never been one on whom, if filial piety was not pursued from the beginning to end, disasters did not befall.

Chapter VII: The Trinity—Heaven, Earth, and Man

Tseng Tzu said: "How great is filial piety!" The Master said: "Filial piety is the basic principle of Heaven, the ultimate standard of earth, and the norm of conduct for the people. Men ought to abide by the guiding principle of Heaven and earth as the pattern of their lives, so that by the brightness of Heaven and the benefits of earth they would be able to keep all in the world in harmony and in unison. On this account, their teachings, though not stringent, are followed, and their government, though not rigorous, is well ordered. The early kings, knowing that their teachings could transform the people, made themselves an example of practicing all-embracing love; thereby the people did not neglect their parents. They expounded the virtuous and righteous conduct, and the people enthusiastically complied. They made of themselves an example of respectful and prudent behavior, and the people were not contentious. They guided themselves with li and music, and the people lived in concord. They verified the distinction between good and evil, and the people knew restraint.

"In the Shih it is said:

> Oh, majestic Master Yin,
> The people all look up to thee!"

CHAPTER VIII: GOVERNMENT BY FILIAL PIETY

The Master said: "Formerly the enlightened kings governed the world by filial piety. They did not dare to neglect the ministers of small states—to say nothing of the dukes, marquises, earls, viscounts, and barons! They thereby gained the good will of all the states to serve their early kings.

"Those who governed the states did not dare to ignore the widows and widowers—to say nothing of scholars and the people! They thereby gained the good will of all the subjects to serve their early kings.

"Those who regulated their families did not dare to mistreat their servants and concubines—to say nothing of their wives and children! They thereby gained the good will of others who served their parents.

"Accordingly, while living, the parents enjoyed comfort; after their death, sacrifices were offered to their spirits. In this way the world was kept in peace; disasters did not arise, nor did riots occur. Such was the way in which the early enlightened governed the world by filial piety.

"In the Shih it is said:

> Glorious was his virtuous conduct,
> And all states submitted themselves."

CHAPTER IX: GOVERNMENT BY THE SAGE

Tseng Tzu said: "I venture to ask whether in the virtue of the sage there is anything that surpasses filial piety."

The Master said: "It is the nature of Heaven and earth that man is the most honorable of all beings. Of all human conduct none is greater than filial piety. In filial piety nothing is greater than to revere one's father. In revering one's father, nothing is greater than making him a peer of Heaven. The Duke of Chou did this. Formerly the Duke of Chou sacrificed to Hou Chi in the suburbs as the peer of Heaven. He sacrificed to King Wen [his father] at the Ming T'ang [Bright Temple] as the peer of Shang Ti [Supreme Being]. Therefore, all the feudal princes within the four seas came, each with his tribute, to join in the sacrifices. How can there be anything in the virtue of the sage that surpasses filial piety?

"Affection is fostered by parents during childhood, and from there springs the child's reverence, which grows daily, while sustaining his parents. The sage was to follow this innate development by teaching reverence and to follow this innate feeling of affection by teaching love. Thus, the teachings of the sage, though not stringent, were followed, and his government, though not rigorous, was well ordered. All this was brought about because of this innate disposition.

"The Tao of father and son is rooted in the Heaven-endowed nature, and develops into the equity between sovereign and ministers. Parents give one life; no bond is stronger. They bring up and care for their child; no kindness is greater. Therefore, one who does not love one's parents, but others, acts to the detriment of virtue. One who does not revere one's parents, but others, acts to the detriment of li. Should the rules of conduct be modeled on such perversity the people would have no true norm by which to abide. Therein is found no goodness but only evil. Although such a person may gain a high position, the chün-tzu will not esteem him.

"The chün-tzu is not like this. His speech is consistent with the Tao, his action with what is good. His virtuous equity is respected; his administration is commendable; his demeanor is pleasing; his movements are proper. In this way he governs the people, and therefore they look upon him with awe and love— make him their model and follow him. Thus he is able to realize his virtuous teachings and to carry out his edicts and orders.

"In the Shih it is said:

> The chün-tzu our princely lord—
> His fine demeanor is without fault."

CHAPTER X: THE PRACTICE OF FILIAL PIETY

The Master said: "In serving his parents, a filial son reveres them in daily life; he makes them happy while he nourishes them; he takes anxious care of them in sickness; he shows great sorrow over their death; and he sacrifices to them with solemnity. When he has performed these five duties, he has truly served his parents.

"He who really serves his parents will not be proud in a high position; he will not be rebellious in an inferior position; among the multitude he will not be contentious. To be proud in a high position is to be ruined; to be rebellious in an inferior position is to insure punishment; to be contentious among the multitude is to bring about violence. As long as these three evils are not discarded, a son cannot be called filial, even though he treats his parents daily with the three kinds of meat."

CHAPTER XI: THE FIVE PUNISHMENTS

The Master said: "There are five punishments for three thousand offenses, and of these offenses there is no greater crime than lack of filial piety. To intimidate the sovereign is to defy a superior; to denounce the sage is to disregard the law; to decry filial piety is to not acknowledge parents. This is the way to great chaos."

CHAPTER XII: ILLUSTRATION OF THE BASIC TAO

The Master said: "There is nothing better than filial piety to teach the people love for one another. There is nothing better than brotherly deference to teach the people propriety and prudence. There is nothing better than music to transform their manners and to change customs. There is nothing better than li to safeguard the sovereign and to govern the people.

"Li is but reverence. When the parents are revered, the son is pleased; when the elder brother is revered, the younger brother is pleased; when the sovereign is revered, the ministers are pleased; when the One Man is revered, the millions of men are pleased. Thus, those who are revered are few, but those who are pleased are many. This is said to be the 'basic Tao.'"

CHAPTER XIII: ILLUSTRATION OF THE SUPREME VIRTUE

The Master said: "The chün-tzu in teaching filial piety need not go daily to visit the families. He need only teach filial piety and he will show reverence due to all the fathers of the world. He need only teach brotherly deference and thereby show reverence due to all the elder brothers of the world. He need only teach the duties of ministers and thereby show reverence due to all the sovereigns of the world.

"In the Shih it is said:

> The princely man, cheerful and pleasant,
> Is the father and mother of the people!

"Without possessing the supreme virtue how can he keep the people in such harmony?"

CHAPTER XIV: ILLUSTRATION OF PERPETUATING THE NAME

The Master said: "The chün-tzu serves his parents with filial piety; thus his loyalty can be transferred to his sovereign. He serves his elder brother with brotherly deference; thus his respect can be transferred to his superiors. He orders his family well; thus his good order can be transferred to his public administration.

"Therefore, when one cultivates one's conduct within oneself, one's name will be perpetuated for future generations."

CHAPTER XV: THE DUTY OF ADMONITION

Tseng Tzu said: "I have heard about parental love, loving respect, cherishing care for parents, and making their name known. I venture to ask whether a son, by obeying every command of his father, can be called filial?"

The Master said: "What are you talking about? What are you talking about? In the old days, the Son of Heaven, who had seven ministers to admonish him, would not have lost his world, even if he were devoid of virtue. A state prince, who had five officers to admonish him, would not have lost his state, even if he were devoid of virtue. A minister, who had three assistants to admonish him, would not have lost his family, even if he were devoid of virtue.

"Thus, if a scholar has a friend to admonish him, he will not deviate from his good name. If a father has a son to admonish him, he will not commit gross wrong. In case of gross wrong, the son should never fail to admonish his father against it; nor should the minister fail to admonish his sovereign. Hence when there is gross wrong, there should be admonition. How can a son, by obeying the command of his father, be called filial?"

CHAPTER XVI: INFLUENCE AND EFFECT

The Master said: "Formerly the enlightened kings were filial in the service of their fathers and thereby became enlightened in the service of Heaven. They were filial in the service of their mothers and thereby became discreet in the service of earth. When the young deferred to the elders, superiors governed inferiors well. When they were enlightened and discreet in the service of Heaven and earth, the blessings of spirits were manifest.

"Hence, even the Son of Heaven has someone to honor—his father. He has someone to respect—his elder brothers. He sacrifices at the ancestral temple, lest he forget his parents. He cultivates his person and acts with prudence, lest he disgrace his elders. He pays reverence, at the ancestral temples, to the spirits and ghosts, so as to enjoy their blessings. When his filial piety and brotherly deference reach perfection, he is endowed with divine enlightenment. His virtuous influence illuminates the four seas and penetrates far and wide.

"In the Shih it is said:

> From the west to the east.
> From the south to the north,
> None thought of not submitting."

CHAPTER XVII: SERVING THE SOVEREIGN

The Master said: "In serving his sovereign, the chün-tzu endeavors to be utterly loyal when he is in office; he contemplates, in retirement, to remedy his shortcomings. Then he tries to conform to what is good in the sovereign, and to rectify what is wrong in him. In this way a mutual affection will be fostered between superiors and inferiors.

"In the Shih it is said:

> In my heart I love him,
> Why should I not tell it?
> I keep him in my heart,
> When shall I forget him?

CHAPTER XVIII: MOURNING FOR PARENTS

The Master said: "In mourning for his parents, a filial son weeps without wailing, he observes funeral rites without heeding his personal appearance, he speaks without regard for eloquence, he finds no comfort in fine clothing, he feels no joy on hearing music, he has no appetite for good food; all this is the innate expression of grief and sorrow. After three days, he breaks his fast, so as to teach the people that the dead should not hurt the living and that disfigurement should not destroy life; this is the rules of the sages. Mourning only extends to the period of three years, so as to show the people that sorrow comes to an end.

"The body, dressed in fine robes, is placed in the encased coffin. The sacrificial vessels are set out with grief and sorrow. Beating the breasts and stamping the feet, weeping and wailing, the mourners escort the coffin to the resting-place selected by divination. A shrine is built, and there offerings are made to the spirits. Spring and autumn sacrificial rites are performed, for the purpose of thinking about them at the proper season.

"When parents are alive, they are served with love and reverence; when they are dead, they are mourned with grief and sorrow. This is the performance of man's supreme duty, fulfillment of the mutual affection between the living and the dead, and the accomplishment of the filial son's service to his parents."

Chapter 9

THE ETHICS OF PROVIDING FOR THE ECONOMIC WELL-BEING OF THE AGING

B. J. Diggs

Providing for the well-being of older people confronts one with a tangle of ethical or moral issues. Because older people first of all, are people, all the basic traditional issues of ethics are involved. Then there are further issues arising from the question whether older people, because of factors related to their age, are entitled to special treatment, or have, or ought to have, special rights. Furthermore, if we examine the variety of institutional systems that assist the aged, we find that these systems involve mixed motives and complex procedures, many with ethical implications. Social Security, Supplemental Security Income, private pensions, family help, personal savings, and insurance are a very mixed bag. In what follows, I shall try to disentangle the most important considerations and to sort out the issues.

From B. J. Diggs, "The Ethics of Providing for the Economic Well-Being of the Aging," in *Social Policy, Social Ethics and the Aging Society*, ed. Bernice Neugarten and Robert Havighurst (Washington, D.C.: National Science Foundation, 1976). Reprinted by permission of the author.

To begin with some of the fundamental characteristics of morality. We might think of moral requirements as having two different sources. One is our benevolence. Some philosophers of the past have looked at benevolence as the source of all moral requirements. Because we are benevolent, or have "a feeling for others" as well as for ourselves, we endorse acts that promote the good and relieve the distress of persons taken individually and collectively. We praise unselfishness, beneficence, and (when we are not fighting) we help one another, at times to a remarkable degree. We might think of the members of a moral community, those who have the same general moral views, as enjoying a certain "moral friendship" with one another, whether or not they are citizens of the same country or speak the same language. Of course, people do not always display this friendship or generosity, but they are not always moral.

The second source of moral requirements is harder to locate. We assume here that it is different from the first because the requirements that stem from it are so very different, as different as "fidelity" and "justice" are from "charity." Besides being asked to be benevolent or charitable, we are taught to tell the truth, to keep our promises, not to steal, not to cheat, to be a good parent, a faithful child, a good citizen, and more generally to be honest, trustworthy, and just in our dealings with others.

Requirements of this latter sort depend on commonly accepted institutions, or social practices, or forms of social life. One could not keep or even make a promise unless there was a common understanding among people concerning the meaning or "force" that certain linguistic expressions possess. Nor could one steal without a commonly accepted system of property, nor cheat without commonly accepted rules of games or ways of doing business, nor be a good parent without an accepted family structure, and so on. The common understanding or common acceptance of these practices and institutions creates social roles and the rights and obligations associated with these roles. One who makes a promise, or does business, or becomes a parent assumes a role to which duties, obligations, and rights attach. Promisors, players,

businessmen, and parents have obligations or duties; and promises, other players, businessmen, and children have corresponding
rights. The question whether older people have (or ought to have)
special *rights* thus depends on whether we have (or ought to have)
certain institutions or social practices that give them rights.

The social forms to which I have referred—promises, property, rules of games and business, the family structure—are basical-
ly nonmoral. How then does it happen that morality endorses the
obligations and rights associated with these institutions and practices, telling us to discharge the obligations and respect the rights?
One way in which we can make sense of morality is by looking at
these social forms as devices of cooperation. Although subject to
improvement, the social forms allow persons to pursue highly
individual goals, with the general consequence that everyone is
better off. But the complex system of cooperation will work only if
persons voluntarily accept the restraints involved in discharging
their obligations; only then will they have any effective rights.
This is where morality comes in: it tells people to restrict the
pursuit of their self-interests within the bounds of a just system of
restraints—in simplest terms, assuming that many of the social
forms are not unjust, it tells persons that when they assume social
roles, they should "do their part." This basic moral principle is
essential to the well-being of every person. In this sense, it is a
principle to which all persons can freely and reasonably subscribe.
Everyone is so dependent on it that, by and large, people teach it to
their children and they themselves accept the principle, openly
advocating it even when secretly violating it, and forcing compliance on others when necessary.

Principles of this sort, and the moral rules to which they give
rise, constitute a social morality, a system of moral articles (principles and rules) governing persons' acts toward one another, that is
voluntarily accepted by those whose acts are governed by it. In this
sense, a social morality is a descriptive concept; and anthropologists can examine the morality of a society. But when we want to
consider moral issues—for example, how old people ought morally to be treated—we need to distinguish the "morality" that persons
do live under from the kind of morality that persons *ought* to live

under. We might characterize morality in the latter sense as the system of articles or requirements to which all persons *together* can *reasonably* and *without coercion* subscribe. Morality in this latter sense is an ideal, our moral ideal, and, distinguished from morality in the descriptive sense, is most simply conceived as the most reasonable way for persons to live together. If pressed to do so, this is how the ordinary person with a moral conscience is apt to describe it.

That the central features of this ideal, reasonableness and freedom, are basic characteristics of our morality is evident in our moral teaching. We try to show children that moral articles, although they do impose restraints, impose reasonable restraints. And we regard our moral teaching as successful only if children voluntarily accept the restraints.

Although our morality is an ideal, it is not hopelessly abstract. It makes a difference in how we act. In effect, if a person is to act morally, he must act in ways that are as reasonable from other persons' points of view as from his own. And to determine what these moral ways are, he must develop the habit of putting himself in another's place, and, after having done so, of dispassionately judging what is reasonable. Moreover, he cannot impose a solution on others, even a reasonable solution. If he imposes his will, then he is living only half morally with others; in order to achieve the other half, coercion must give way to a free and voluntary acceptance of restraints. (If this seems a hopeless goal, one should recall our success in attaining religious toleration.)

These formal requirements, implicit in our ideal of a moral community, illuminate the traditional notion of moral respect of persons. In order to treat another as a person, and not as a thing, one must weigh his point of view and his good equally with one's own; one must treat the other as a rational being and not simply impose one's will on him. Moreover, because it is impossible to have a moral community unless persons treat one another in this way, each person has the basic moral duty to respect every other person, and each person has a corresponding moral right to be treated with respect.

Because people often have mistaken ideas about what is

good, even for themselves, it is often difficult to reconcile the two requirements involved in respect for persons. People do not always voluntarily agree to an act that is for their good. However, we have the best chance of avoiding general coercion if we develop social forms, practices, and institutions that do reasonably serve the good of all, and that in this sense are reasonably acceptable to all. Democratic societies have, in this sense, a number of social forms that may be regarded as devices for promoting respect. Among them are rights to freedom of one's person, freedom of speech, freedom of conscience, and the like (which protect one from encroachments), and also rights to vote, hold office, and the like (which enable one to exercise some control over social legislation). But there is also a need for more substantive and less procedural social forms if people are not to suffer coercion. These latter constitute one of the greatest needs of the aged, if the aged are to be treated as persons and if they are not to be treated as things outworn, to be shoved into spare rooms or stacked in nursing homes. Social security, of course, is a social or institutional form of promoting respect.

At least this much moral theory is necessary to begin to think clearly about how, morally, we ought to treat the aged.

Is Age a Morally Relevant Characteristic?

In considering ethical issues in providing for older people, the first and most important point is that age, *as such,* is not a morally relevant characteristic. Older people are members of our moral community. Moral respect is owed them not because they are old, but simply because they are persons and fellow members of the community. One who shows them this kind of respect will be concerned about their views and their good, as much as and no more than the views and the good of any other group. He will not yield to the temptation to impose his will on those among the old who are weak, even if they have become accustomed to being told what to do. Only if the old are treated in this general way can we expect them to preserve their moral dignity, or moral respect for themselves. If some old people make a special appeal to our sympathy, others among them even more insistently arouse our admiration. Many of those who arouse our sympathy do so because they have not been treated as moral equals.

Once the moral irrelevancy of age has been emphasized, it should be acknowledged, on the other side, that age is typically correlated with a number of characteristics that *are* morally relevant. The old are not all alike. Some are too feeble to conduct their own affairs. There is no use pretending that these people command the same *kind* of respect as the others; and we unhesitatingly make decisions for them. It is not that such persons are without all rights; many institutions and practices, morally endorsed, impose obligations and give them rights. But what rights they have must be protected by a trustee. How should such persons be treated? Surely their rights should be respected, and surely some homes and nursing homes are incomparably better than others. Somehow we must find a way of caring for these people and making them as comfortable as possible. Beyond this, what can one say other than the obvious, namely, that from the moral point of view such persons make a special call on our benevolence, and that a moral people will heed the call.

It is important to notice that even in the case of these infirm aged the appeal for benevolence and morality is not based on age, but on infirmity.

Another characteristic often associated with old age that justifies special treatment is poverty. A society as wealthy as ours will surely undertake, in the name of justice, to eliminate poverty. There are strong arguments for establishing a social minimum or poverty level. We need not resort to the fuzzy claim that all persons have a "natural right" to the necessities of life. This claim, as it is sometimes literally and grandly made, would imply that nature, in the form of a drought, can deprive persons of their natural rights. It would also imply that one person is under an obligation to feed another able-bodied person who does nothing to feed himself. But in view of the difficulty of establishing a public system of employment in which there is a decent "willingness to work" test, and in view of the fact that a governmental agency (like the Federal Reserve System) can adopt a policy whereby thousands lose their jobs, justice requires that we adopt measures to protect everyone at least from abject misery and helplessness. It is hard to see how a moral society could settle for less. And this has nothing to do with old age as such.

Other characteristics that call for special treatment are also not peculiar to old age, such as being out of work, or being in need of medical attention. Persons often have these characteristics through no fault of their own. Justice surely requires that we develop some set of social institutions that will allow them to be insured against such contingencies, regardless of their age.

Where then does age come in?

It is not clear that there are any really significant moral requirements owed to older people simply because they are old. Old age has been taken to be grounds for special treatment because it has in fact been correlated with such positive attributes as the "wisdom of experience," and with such deficiencies as physical infirmity, poverty, unemployment, and need of medical help. The question is whether these negative correlations are not reflections of our social system rather than part of the nature of things. Perhaps old age and these negative characteristics are related because of the way in which persons live in our society and the way they are treated by our institutions before they get old, as well as the way they are treated once they are old.

There is certainly a point to Simone de Beauvoir's comment at the end of her book on old age, "It is the whole system that is at issue . . . "[1] If persons were not treated so much as things, if labor were not regarded so often as only a commodity, we could reasonably expect old age to be very different from what it is today. It might be much more interesting, less passive, and perhaps the old would suffer fewer ailments. We might even be able to cut our medical costs. It may be true to say, as my mother-in-law used to say, "There is no friend in your old age like money." But she was able to enjoy her later years because she was not only above the poverty level in wealth, but also much above it in ideas and interests.

If we want to do right by old people, we must begin before they get old. And we must conceive the problem of satisfying people's wants in terms that are not wholly materialistic. As we all know, the best way of satisfying old people's desires for patent medicines is by education—that alone would save them millions of dollars. The same is true of many other of their needs, and of our own needs as well. The difficulty is that one wonders whom one is addressing when one says something of this kind. The large-scale changes that are needed for people to be treated as rational beings, persons rather than things, ends rather than means—these are everyone's business, and thus tend to be no one's business. We need not accept Marxist idyllic or collectivist solutions (although we might profit from taking the Marxian critique seriously). There is a large reservoir of intelligence and good will that needs to be tapped in revitalizing our good institutions and inventing some new ones. We certainly should not fool ourselves into thinking that we can do right by old people until we do better by ourselves.

In this spirit, without waiting for the millenium and without despairing because the millenium will never come, we might address ourselves to one large problem or one characteristic typically associated with the aged that might yield to institutional experimentation, namely, unemployment of older people. This is a particularly important problem both from the moral and from the economic point of view.

There appears to be an inevitable correlation between being old and not having the powers one formerly had. There is a consequent correlation between age and becoming marginally unproductive on the job. In view of the difficult institutional and personal problems in trying to use "marginal unproductivity" as a criterion of retirement, it is natural (at least in large institutions) to substitute age as the criterion. This is a terrible compromise—on the order of using SAT scores in determining university admissions—and we probably fall for such schemes too readily.

Having persons retire when they are able and willing to work is a serious enough problem just from the standpoint of the Social Security System. But it is even more serious if one considers the importance of work for the productivity of society, and its ethical importance in the lives of individuals. Taking the latter point first: From the moral point of view, in the sense indicated earlier, society is a cooperative system. When an able and willing person is excluded from the ranks of the contributors, he feels alienated and to some degree humiliated, whether or not he *should* feel this way. The point has often been made with respect to those who are on welfare and the same point applies to many who are forced to retire, even when they have rights to things they have earned such as retirement or pension benefits. A person who is excluded against his will, simply because of his age, "put on the shelf" as we say, is apt to suffer unless he has developed substantial personal resources and interests. The point especially applies when workers are forced into early retirement and cannot get another job. Any such person has natural cause to wonder whether he is not being manipulated by the rules of the system. If persons are to be treated justly and with respect, we must find ways of meeting the demand of the first part of the old socialist slogan of justice, "from each according to his talents . . . ."

This is not simply a matter of some persons being oversensitive, and feeling alienated and humiliated too readily. Perhaps because so many jobs in an industrial society involve drudgery, and afford very little opportunity to use or develop talents, we tend to regard it as the goal to stop work and relax. Such a view, if understandable in the circumstances, is both peculiar on the face of it and contrary to our best ethical tradition. The single most important ethical lesson the Greeks had to teach us is that our well-being and happiness lie in activity, or the exercise of our talents and virtues. If the kinds of jobs we offer people drive this lesson out of our minds, we had better do something about the jobs.

Not all jobs from which able people are forcibly retired, however, are drudgery. When able and willing persons are forced to retire from jobs that *do* allow them to exercise their talents, then a forced retirement system also deprives them of a large part of their lives. Not surprisingly some of them feel they may as well be dead. Inactivity, in the Greek sense, is so psychologically debilitating that some workers feel this way even after leaving jobs that are dull. Where nothing much can be done to make these dull jobs more interesting, we try to provide significant "outside work" or "outside interests," ways of being active that are personally rewarding.

Improvement in our general retirement system could be reasonably expected to increase significantly the productivity of our society. Our attitudes toward retirement are formed by a system that makes 65 (or less) a magic number. This confronts us, even in times of relative full employment, with the social spectacle of large numbers of persons with enormous leisure time needing many things they do not have, and with many younger people who are downright impoverished. This is one place where social experimentation and research might do some good for all concerned.

Notwithstanding the desirability of keeping persons on the job—if the job is interesting and useful—it is probably inevitable that we shall use one age or another as a criterion of retirement, for lack of better alternatives. The advantages of using age as a criterion might possibly be combined with the advantages of keeping persons productively and interestedly active. It is not necessarily true that the best solution to all our problems, for all workers, is to keep people on the *same* jobs forever. Retired persons have considerable talents, and we ought to find ways of putting them to good use. Many retirees have been very inventive on their own. There have been a few recent experiments in having the old teach the young. If we could find some sensible institutional way for retired persons to teach the technical skills they have to the impoverished unskilled young, the benefits might be large, not only for the parties involved, but for society as a whole. This would be a kind of social service in reverse, it might produce great advantages for many individuals, and much less national waste. It might even heal some wounds.

If as much thought were given to this matter as has been given to retirement villages, there is no telling what benefits might accrue. Surely we need to change the social climate for the old. Persons who are denied the opportunity to do anything for others become preoccupied with themselves, and have diminished their chances of happiness.

Thus the main point is that we ought to regard old people primarily as people, and not as old. The secondary point is that if we are to provide for the well-being of the old, we must think about far more than money.

Providing for Economic Well-Being

Notwithstanding the importance of these points, it is wholly unrealistic to think of keeping the old at work until they drop; and money is of course important. Thus we shall continue to need ways of providing for retirees. There are two general alternative ways, both of which are morally endorsed: The first is for retirees to be supported by private benevolence; the second is for them to be supported by means of social institutional arrangements that, in the general way indicated earlier, give them *rights* to that support by imposing correlative obligations on others.

The alternatives are not mutually exclusive. As mentioned earlier, there is surely a place for benevolence in providing for the aged. Some older persons have serious needs that social institutions cannot easily satisfy. And many older persons have had a considerable share of suffering and misfortune. If they cannot properly be granted a host of special privileges in the name of justice, it seems only fitting to allot them a share of our sympathetic understanding and benevolence. I see no reason why they should not be granted some public favors, if not a lower rate on their taxes. Moreover, most older persons may be assumed to have had a wider and deeper experience of life, and this experience itself is worthy of esteem. It appears salutary to breed a special respect for one's elders among the young, who need to learn to appreciate the value of experience and the practical wisdom that depends on it. Such a respect, which should not be confused with the moral respect for persons outlined above, may also stimulate a more general sympathy and benevolence.

As a way of providing for the aged, however, private benevolence and respect for one's elders have serious limitations. Although happily received, they are apt to be haphazard and unpredictable—certainly no firmer than the lives of the donors. They consequently do not offer the kind of support on which retirees will reasonably want to depend, and on this account such dependence is incompatible with a genuine moral respect for retirees. The only apparent way of escaping the limitations of private benevolence as a means of support is by establishing social forms and institutions that provide for retirees as a matter of right.

Within our society we can distinguish at least four different kinds of institutional or social arrangements: (1) systems of insurance or savings, which allow a person to accumulate rights to future consumption and thereby provide for himself as much protection as he can afford and wants; (2) the family institution, in which an older person normally is regarded as having rights by virtue of what he has done for other members of the family; (3) the business firm, which sometimes allots retirees rights to certain benefits in return for their having served the firm; (4) political institutions, which grant citizens certain rights and benefits as a consequence of the State's exercising its function of promoting the common good. There are other institutions—for example, private associations like the union or lodge. There is no hope of carefully examining here all the different social forms under which retirees gain rights to support. Instead, I shall concentrate on a general moral question that has attracted recent attention, the question, as it is usually put, of justice between generations. How much should workers be asked to put up for the benefit of the aged? Is the amount they presently contribute a fair amount? Let us consider these questions as they relate to the first three institutional systems mentioned above.

It may be helpful, first, to remove a confusion. As a result of the influence of Rawls' recent work,[2] there has been a growing interest in something called "the problem of justice between generations." The problem that Rawls discusses is *not* the problem that concerns those who worry about the cost to workers of retirement benefits, although it is indirectly related to it. Rawls' question is not the question of how much workers should be asked to contribute to retirees, but the question of how much each generation should save for the benefit of succeeding generations. If a generation consumes more than it produces, other things equal, the generation would be thought to have been unjust to later generations. Moreover, it seems reasonable to ask a generation to save for future generations in view of the capital it has received from antecedent generations. From this point of view, what one can reasonably ask of one's child, in return for what was given him, is equal concern by the child for *his* child. To be sure, the child, in return for what was given him, also owes something to the parent. But the obligation in the latter case is a different obligation from the former, and the two should not be confused. Quite different institutions might be needed to secure justice in the two respects; different rights and obligations are involved. It is worth bearing in mind, however, in the present context, that if there is to be any progress a generation cannot expect to receive as much as it gives or to consume as much as it produces. What it is owed should be limited by a just savings principle of some kind, which allots a fair share of capital to succeeding generations. After all, if there had been no saving in the past, we would be in a wretched state today.

A SYSTEM OF SAVINGS

Now let us briefly consider the first of the four systems that our society makes available in providing for retirees, namely, a system of insurance or savings that allows a person to provide for himself. What is the "just" amount of savings or insurance a person should accumulate, bearing in mind that this saving for the future creates a claim on what future workers will produce? This last consideration is a signal that we have an economic problem on our hands, as well as an ethical one. In creating this claim on future production, one assumes that future workers will produce enough more than they themselves consume—otherwise, there will be trouble. In view of the requirement of justice that a generation save something not for itself but for future generations, and as something of a guarantee that enough surplus will be produced in the future to cover savers' claims, it would seem highly desirable for savings to be used to increase productive capacity. I am not expert in economics, but I shall assume, for the purposes of this paper, that some invisible hand, or one not so invisible, will see to it that, at least in this kind of case, the saver's or insurer's claim will be honored.

If we assume that the economic problem will somehow take care of itself, and ask "what is the just amount of savings or insurance a person should accumulate?", the question sounds odd. We can give it a meaning, however, if we regard a person as owing something to his future self. We might think of a person asking himself how much he should save now, so that he can say both now and later "This is the right amount." We may even think of him as seeking a reasonable agreement between his present and his future self, or a solution that reasonably attends to the needs and desires of the two and shows respect for the rights of both. This is an ethical problem, all right, of a kind with which all of us are acquainted, and it may even be described as a problem of justice between generations. But it is peculiar when put in these terms, and hardly need worry us in the present context.

(We should notice, in passing, that a person cannot be just to himself by saving properly unless he is paid a just amount for his services, and unless there are honest and fair ways of saving and insuring one's future. Doing justice to oneself depends in many ways on a just society.)

THE FAMILY

The second institutional way we have of providing for retirees is constituted by our family structure. Children have traditionally felt an obligation to take care of their dependent parents—it seems only right because their parents took care of them. The rights and obligations are commonly felt to vary with the amount of care that was given; certainly, being a biological parent is not enough to constitute a right, as we discover in the phrase "he was no father to me." Does one have a right to be cared for in proportion to the care one has given?

What proportion of a person's income and wealth should he spend on his parents, his children, himself? Views vary: some have regarded it as especially important to provide kinds of opportunities for children that they and their parents never dreamt of having for themselves. Is this the "just savings principle" carried in some cases to an absurd extreme? Was this an unjust system? It is by no means clear that it was, since many parents and grandparents regarded the system as just and fair, or, rather, a proper way of providing a fair opportunity to grandchildren. If there were unfairness in some cases, and surely there was, it lay partly in the social structure itself, which required so heavy a burden to be put on working parents and grandparents. I mention this case because it shows (1) how hard it is to generalize about "how much" should be provided *any* member of a family, and (2) the importance of institutions other than the family in determining "how much." Pretty clearly, "how much" is not the same when there is a Social Security system and Supplemental Security Income, or when there is neither.

In general, a family union is such that no person is deemed to have a right to benefits if it means that other family members are not provided for. The idea is that each person shall get what he needs and wants within the limit of a family's resources. And if this principle is violated—for example, if the working members neglect their dependent parents or children, or favor one over another—injustice is thought to be done. But when there is a background of social institutions devoted to providing for dependents—for example, Social Security, or public schools—the requirements imposed on the workers is to see to it that the dependents are cared for, but not necessarily to put up all the cash.

Our family structure is confusing from a moral point of view because it is such a curious mixture of rights and obligations on the one hand, and benevolence and friendship, on the other. The two often get in the way of the other: when a family member stands on his rights, benevolence tends to dry up, and *vice versa;* and extensive benevolence may be regarded as "more than one deserves." With the family, we seem to come as close as possible to institutionalized benevolence, if that is not a contradiction in terms. Because the family, in discharging its obligations, typically gives benevolence such a central place, it provides many retirees with the best "home" they could possibly have. Government, in providing financial help and health care for the aged, should be mindful of the family's role and be careful not to encourage other institutions, such as nursing homes, to be put in its place.

With respect to the problem of allocating family resources to its members, it is hard to see any clearer principles than have been given. In the case of the family, there does not appear to be any large-scale problems of justice between generations of the kind that has recently caused concern. We have no clear indications that the presumed smaller number of children providing for the welfare of a proportionally larger number of parents will cause future strain in the family—although this might become a problem. If retirement benefits from other sources can be improved, family relations may be better, not worse.

THE BUSINESS FIRM

We now turn to the role of the business firm or business organization in providing for the welfare of retirees. There are many complexities, such as the problem of determining whether it is possible realistically to have a firm contribute to the retirement of workers without its indirectly deducting the contribution from workers' wages. I shall have to bypass such complexities here.

From the moral point of view, the basic obligation of a business firm is to give the worker a fair share of the income of the firm in return for the worker's service. (There does not appear to be any simple way of determining a fair share. In principle, we might think of a fair share, in terms of what Rawls calls "pure procedural justice," as the outcome of fair bargaining procedures conducted within a just economic system.) Whether the fair share is given wholly in the form of wages, or partly in the form of benefits, including contributions to public or private pension systems, does not seem to matter from the standpoint of justice to the worker—although practically it appears to be greatly to the worker's advantage to have an institutional way of providing for his life after retirement. Some moralists have thought that it is important for persons freely to provide for themselves, that otherwise persons will not develop the virtue of caring for themselves. But it is highly questionable that a retirement system, whether wholly voluntary or not, detracts from a person's concern for his future. A good case can be made that even a compulsory retirement system encourages such concern, by giving a person a monetary stake in the future that he might not otherwise have. Actually, private pension plans appear to result most often from collective bargaining; in this case an individual's rights and powers are restricted by those of other union members. Such a system should not be conceived as imposed on the worker insofar as the union process is itself democratic.

Moreover, how well a person can provide for himself depends directly on efficient retirement systems being available. This availability in turn depends on large numbers of workers being committed to a system. As in any kind of cooperative arrangement, such a commitment restricts a person's freedom. But the loss of freedom in any good pension system would appear to be more than offset by the benefits. All things considered, it does not seem reasonable to complain that every kind of private "compulsory" retirement system that a firm establishes, or contributes to, is an unwholesome infringement on individual freedom.

There appears to be one possible significant byproduct of a firm's contributing to the retirement income of workers. As we all know, such a contributory system does not by any means guarantee it, but it may help a firm to regard its workers as persons, rather than as simply a commodity. The growth in private pension systems seems to be an expression of a greater consciousness by management of their responsibility to their workers, and it may stimulate further growth of this consciousness. From a moral point of view, such a development would be most welcome.

How much of a claim on (the products of) future labor constitutes a just claim? How much can present workers accumulate? How much can they justly save? Such questions signal again the economic problems that were mentioned earlier. Assuming that the economy will take care of itself, the only sensible answers to such questions parallel the answer given in the case of individual savings and insurance: namely, a firm's laborers should save as much in the form of future retirement benefits as they are willing to sacrifice in the form of wages or rights to present consumption. The problem of justice between generations again seems to reduce itself to the problem of being fair to present and future selves, although the decision in this case is a group decision, probably involving both labor and management, rather than an individual decision.

Thus, it appears that in the case of all three of these institutional forms for supporting the aged, individual savings, the family, and the firm, there is no special cause for the recent worry about workers having to do too much for retirees—no problem of justice between generations in this sense. If the economy does not function properly, however, there may well be a problem of justice or injustice in the opposite direction for those retirees who depend on personal savings or on private pensions. If future production is not sufficient to honor their claims to a certain level of real income in the future, then these people, and not the future workers, will get the short end of the stick. We are well acquainted with this kind of injustice, having seen the real income of many retirees steadily decline. The essential palliative is to adjust retirement benefits for inflation, as we have done with Social Security. The only real long-term solution seems to be a healthy and just economy. A sound economy and a just economy are not the same thing, but they seem to be closely interwoven.

THE GOVERNMENT

In our society, the most prominent institutional means of providing for the aged is the fourth one mentioned earlier, the public and political. In exercising its function of promoting the common good, government distributes benefits and assigns rights to the aged. It may appear that government differs from the other institutional forms that support older people in a very important respect. Because government's function is to promote the common good, it may be thought that a person is entitled to rights and benefits without having to earn them. He is entitled to them simply by being a citizen. In each of the three previous institutional forms, by contrast, a person acquires a right to something only by earning it, whether it be by saving for the future, by caring for his children, or by serving a firm.

There is a certain element of truth in this claim, at least with respect to government's support of the aged. In providing for the needy old (as is the case with the disabled) government requires no service, only proof of need. But this method of providing for some of its citizens is a desperation move; it is a move suitable only for the desperate. Government's aim is to prevent people falling into this class, so far as possible. With this latter goal in mind, it is fitting for government to establish an institutional system that will enable people to help themselves and keep them from becoming wards of the State. Within this system, people acquire rights, not as a gift, but by earning them. Social Security, at least in part, is such a system. To prevent misunderstanding, this part of Social Security should be carefully distinguished from Supplemental Security Income and all other institutional ways of providing for the needy.

One may reasonably ask for justification of a governmental system which compulsorily assigns obligations and rights in an area served by other institutional forms. This is a taller order than I can supply, but the main outline seems to be as follows: the justification of a state system derives from its important advantages over other institutional forms. It is more advantageous than the first form we discussed, private savings or insurance, because it covers almost all workers, and because it is impossible to offer comparable private protection at the same cost. It is thus said to be the most efficient way of protecting everyone and keeping the number of persons on welfare to a minimum—it may even stimulate individuals to have greater care for their future. It is more advantageous than the second form, the family, because family support varies and is unpredictable. It is more advantageous than the third form, the business organization, because businesses are much more vulnerable to economic forces than governmental insurance system and because labor is mobile between firms.

In view of all these advantages, a State system is generally thought to be needed. At the same time, there should be a clear understanding that our Social Security system is misleadingly described as a governmental system of retirement protection. It is actually a combination of the first and third institutional forms, the individual and the business organization (and it is a welfare or transfer system as well), with government serving as coordinator and administrator. In sum, government in this case serves the common good not by passing out benefits, but by establishing and operating a more extensive and more efficient system than private individuals and private firms can do.

The Social Security system contains so many diverse elements, however, that the proper economic analysis of the system is open to disagreement. It has been said that we should regard it as (1) a system that guarantees a level of income for those older people who wish or are forced to retire—in contrast to one that provides annuities, strictly speaking, and (2) a system that enables people to help themselves—in contrast to a welfare or transfer system. Points of this sort have many moral implications. For example, we may agree with the first, but at the same time acknowledge that it is morally very important not to adopt policies that encourage retirement. And on the second point: Social Security is often regarded as a welfare or transfer system, partly because of its origins, and partly because of some persons' aversion to the state's assuming welfare functions. To the degree to which the system is not clearly understood—and the misunderstanding appears to be considerable—legislators not only make proposals that are foreign to its spirit and intent, but people accept or object to the system for the wrong reasons. The misunderstanding thus not only endangers the system, from a pragmatic point of view, but interferes with the free and rational consideration of the system on its merit. As suggested in the first section of this paper, this latter kind of defect is morally serious.

It thus seems of utmost importance to distinguish the insurance elements in Social Security from the welfare elements. If welfare elements in the system are expanded, a governmental contribution to the system from general taxation would seem to be in order. I am not competent either to analyze the Social Security system or to make recommendations. But structuring the system in such a way that it *can* be understood, and then promoting this understanding—are not only technically and pragmatically but also morally important.

In the case of Social Security, how much should workers contribute to the system? How much of a claim on future workers should they be allowed to build up? As a result of the way Social Security is financed, questions of this sort have an entirely different significance from those asked about the other institutional forms of providing for retirees. The worry that some have expressed about whether workers will be asked to bear too large a burden in providing for the aged, the question of "justice between generations" in this sense, seems really to be a question about proper Social Security financing. One will become excited about the problem of "justice between generations," to the extent to which he regards Social Security financing as posing a problem.

The problem arises because, in Social Security financing, reserves are not held to each workers' account sufficiently to pay off future claims. As Robert Ball put it in an earlier paper,[3] Social Security is financed on a "current-cost basis"—the funds to pay for current beneficiaries are advanced by current workers. In view of the breadth of the system, and its compulsory feature, there may be nothing improper in this method of financing. But, by way of conclusion to this paper, I want to raise two large questions about it, one economic, and the other ethical.

The economic question is whether this is the best mode of financing, in view of the great need of capital for expansion and modernization of plant and equipment, about which we hear more and more. I referred indirectly to this need in connection with the problem of justice between generations. I am poorly equipped to estimate how serious this economic need is, or how Social Security financing might be modified in order to help meet the need. I presume that large-scale changes would have to be made, and they may not be at all feasible. It nevertheless seems important to keep the economic problem before us because the welfare of older people in the future will so greatly depend on how well the problem is solved. It probably deserves much more serious consideration than it is likely to get.

The ethical question concerns what is a just and fair contribution for each generation of workers, in view of the way Social Security is financed. Consider the financing problem that is expected to arise about the year 2010 because of the declining proportion of workers to retirees. There are ominous predictions that, unless some changes are made, the contributions of workers and employees will have to be increased substantially. Perhaps, the changes will be made. Or perhaps workers will not retire so early, productivity will increase, and the fertility rate will go up, so that the predictions will not come true. If the changes are not made and the predictions do come true, however, then workers beginning in about 2010 will have good reason to feel unjustly treated. In that case, the increased number of retirees would not have contributed over the years, as a group, in proportion to the benefits they would receive. With current cost financing, they would have supported a smaller number of beneficiaries than they would be asking workers in 2010 to support. This injustice would probably be apparent to all. It would be even more apparent to those workers in 2010, if when *they* retired, because of their smaller number, the contributions of the workers who follow them were *decreased* again.

It appears to me that justice between generations, in the sense indicated, does require that changes be made. The factors that will shape the financing problem beginning in 2010, as Mr. Ball has pointed out, are predictable. If the ominous financing problem begins to develop, it appears to me that in the name of justice, politics notwithstanding, those who will begin to retire in 2010 ought to be asked well ahead of that date to increase their contributions.

NOTES

[1] Simone de Beauvoir, *The Coming of Age*, trans. of *La Viellesse*. (New York: Putnam, 1972, p. 543.)

[2] John Rawls, *A Theory of Justice*. (Cambridge, Mass.: Belknap Press of Harvard University Press, 1971.)

[3] Robert M. Ball, "Critical Choices in the Federal Social Security Program," paper prepared for the Commission on Critical Choices for Americans.

Chapter 10

EXTENSION OF THE LIFE SPAN: A NATIONAL GOAL?

James L. Goddard

In the United States today there are several thousand individuals who are over 100 years of age. The probability of any of us joining that select group is very slight in spite of the astonishing advances made in the medical sciences in recent decades. Most of us will, in fact, have to be content with the traditional three score and ten as evidenced by today's average age of death for men at 69 ½ years, and for women, 75 ⅔ years. There are those, however, who believe that these averages can be substantially increased in the not too distant future through the development of methods to slow the rate of aging. If so, becoming a centenarian could become the norm rather than the exception. What lies behind this belief? What would be involved in accomplishing such a change? What ethical and social issues would confront society if such a development were to occur?

From James L. Goddard, "Extension of the Life Span: A National Goal?" in *Extending the Human Life Span: Social Policy and Social Ethics*, ed. Bernice L. Neugarten and Robert J. Havighurst (Washington, D.C.: National Science Foundation, 1977). Reprinted by permission of the author.

The belief that it might be possible for man to extend his life span seems to be age-old. Its roots are in the myths and religions of early societies and in the early era of modern man, when it was observed that some individuals lived many decades beyond their contemporaries. Such observations led alchemists during mediéval times to seek a magical formula, led explorers such as Ponce de Leon to search for the "fountain of youth," and in the late nineteenth and early twentieth centuries enticed scientists to undertake investigation of the phenomena associated with aging in the hopes of discovering a method to prolong life. Metchnikov, of the Pasteur Institute in Paris, published in 1903 a treatise called "The Nature of Man" in which he set forth the hypothesis that autointoxication caused by bacterial pathogens in the digestive tract was the major factor in the mechanism of aging.[1] He was wrong, but his work was an early landmark in the study of the processes involved in aging (more commonly called gerontology, as opposed to geriatrics which is a study of the diseases of the aged). Since then the scientific community and the public at large have periodically been exposed to new "discoveries" which held forth the hope that man's cherished dream of postponement of death was indeed at hand. In turn, we have witnessed the rise and fall of the yogurt diet fad, the era of glandular transplants, cytotoxic serum, and the current rages of cell therapy and Gerovital.[2] Over this same period of time, less spectacular but more important developments have occurred that must be appreciated in order to understand why many scientists feel we are in a position to tackle the job of extending man's lifespan.

NEW RESEARCH DIRECTIONS

First of all, scientists have been conducting laboratory experiments on a variety of nonhuman species throughout most of this century in an attempt to understand the aging process and how to alter it. These experiments have resulted in a substantial body of knowledge that suggests that life processes can be extended beyond their normal range. Some of the more significant experiments and their implications are these:

1. Cooling experiments, reported as early as 1917, indicate that lowering the internal temperature of an organism will result in longer life. One such study showed that a common pond organism, the rotifer, if kept in water 10°C below its normal environment will almost double its life span. Currently there is considerable interest in determining if alteration of the temperature-regulating mechanisms of subhuman primates to achieve a lower internal temperature will produce increased longevity. Results to date indicate that the internal temperature of monkeys can be lowered by 7°F.

The potential of this approach is that scientists estimate that a 3°F decrease in internal body temperature of humans could extend life by as much as 30 years. How long the lower temperature can be maintained in monkeys is yet to be determined, and whether the change will indeed enhance their longevity.

2. Changing the ability of animals to resist infections has been tested through manipulation of their immune systems in order to prolong life. Old mice when injected with virulent bacteria die off very quickly; but when protected by the injection of selected cells from young mice, the same dosage levels of virulent organisms are not lethal and the mice live on for several more months with this "acquired immunity." Similarly in experiments in which the thymus gland of a young mouse is transplanted to an older mouse, along with bone marrow cells and the spleen, the recipient's ability to combat infections and live longer is enhanced. A comparable effect has been produced by extracting a hormone, Thymosin, from the thymus glands of young mice and injecting it into older mice. The importance of this hormone in man is as yet unknown, but it has been reported that the level of Thymosin decreases significantly during the middle years of life and thus may set the stage for the initiation of the aging process.

3. Experiments with rats and mice have demonstrated that sharply reducing their caloric intake throughout their early life will enable them to live as much as 30 to 50 percent longer. The

implications of such findings for humans is uncertain. It has been noted that persons surviving to very old age are usually lean and have generally been moderate throughout life in their dietary intake, but extrapolation from such meager data is not sound.

4. Dietary experiments have also been carried out involving the use of additives of varying types. The addition of antioxidants in order to combat "free radicals" within the body cells is a method that has been used by a number of researchers. The "free radicals" are fragments of molecules which are thought to combine in deleterious ways with other intracellular elements and thus cause cell aging. The addition of an antioxidant such as vitamin E has been tried in an experiment involving mice, but it had no effect on life span. Other antioxidants have been tested in a similar fashion and several have resulted in extending life. One of these tested, dimethylaminoethanol, prolonged life by as much as 40 percent when fed to young mice. None of the chemicals tested in this fashion have as yet been used for trials in humans, although it is not unlikely that such a trial could be carried out in the near future.

5. Scientists have developed new techniques to study aging that permit greater insight into the processes involved. The most significant of the new techniques involved that of studying cell behavior in the laboratory. With the ability to grow generation after generation of cells derived from human or animal tissues, scientists can undertake a wide variety of experiments which had previously been impractical or impossible. Without presenting a comprehensive review of the field of molecular biology, it is difficult to appreciate the substantial accomplishments that have followed. Two brief statements will hopefully provide some insight into this area:

5a. The discovery by Dr. Leonard Hayflick in 1961 was a milestone; namely, that normal cells grown in laboratory culture systems have a finite capacity for reproduction before they deteriorate, show changes characteristic of aging, and die.[3] Prior to his now classic experiments it was assumed that cell lines could be maintained indefinitely in the laboratory, provided the proper nutrients were supplied and provided that the environment was carefully controlled. Dr. Hayflick not only demonstrated the fallibility of this assumption, but also showed, along with other experimenters, that the capacity for cell division varies with the species involved and is related to the longevity of the species. Thus, the longer the species life span, the greater the number of cell divisions before death occurs.

The underlying implications of Hayflick's findings are indeed substantial. We may well possess within our body cells a "biological clock," genetically preset, which determines maximum age. If so, it may be possible, using normal human cells systems, to discover ways to safely alter the rate of aging within the cell without having to understand the basic cause(s) of the changes that occur with aging. This could greatly facilitate the discovery of an antiaging agent or technique.

5b. The technology has been developed to study in exquisite detail the inner workings of the cell, including its genetic material. Just how complex the processes are can be appreciated by contemplating Dr. Samuel Goldstein's description of the role of genetic factors within the cell. "Every cellular component, whether it is the surface of cytoplasmic receptor for a drug, hormone, or nutrient, an enzyme, or a structural component, is coded for by genes. The same applies to other gene factors exported from cells, including hormones and interstitial factors such as collagen and related ground substances that heretofore had been regarded as informationally inert."[4] These new techniques involving normal cell culture lines, microanalysis, electron microscopy, and genetic manipulation have fostered the development of a new area of gerontological research which Dr. Hayflick has termed *cytogerontology*, meaning the study of the aging processes in cultured cells. The cell is, according to Hayflick, " . . . where the gerontological action lies."

THEORIES OF AGING

From the expanded research permitted by the development of these approaches over the past several decades, a host of clues to aging have emerged that have led to the development of several theories as to cause(s). The major theories now being tested include Hayflick's concept that lifespan is limited by a "biological clock" within the cell that permits a finite number of cell divisions before deterioration sets in and cell death occurs; a genetic program within the cells which "runs out" and ceases to provide information to the cellular components, thus causing disorganization and malfunction; and an "error" theory which says that mistakes occur at a low rate throughout the life of a cell and their accumulation reaches a lethal threshold.

Which theory will prove to be correct is, at this stage, relatively unimportant. What is of significance is that the field of gerontology has advanced to a stage where a theoretical framework has been formulated for its future research efforts. With a theoretical framework, based on a substantial body of experimental data, and with a highly sophisticated technology, we seem to be in a position to move rapidly towards fulfilling man's age-old dream of extending life.

THE LOW PRIORITY OF AGING RESEARCH

When one examines the resources being alloted to the field today, it is quickly apparent that aging research is a relatively low priority at the national level.[5] We will have spent, depending on how one defines the field, betwen $15 and $25 million during fiscal year 1975 on gerontological research. It has been estimated that we spend 2 dollars in cancer research for every 3 cents spent in research on aging. This disparity is due in part to the relative newness of gerontology as a special field of interest. It is due also to the absence of major public support groups, such as the National Cancer Society or the American Heart Association, who, along with leaders from the professional organizations within these fields, lobby effectively for the limited funds available from both public and private sources.

Another factor is that aging characteristically has been viewed as an inevitable consequence of living and not subject to attack in the same fashion that enabled us to eliminate polio and other communicable diseases. Only within the past 5 years have we begun to hear experts voice the opinion that aging, although a normal physiological process, can someday in the not too distant future be deferred or even perhaps eliminated. Some of these statements are noteworthy because they constitute unique appraisals of the field of aging, or they express expert views of what our goals should be, how successful we may be in our endeavors, and when a significant breakthrough may occur.

For example, Dr. Nathan Shock, Director of the Gerontology Research Center of the National Institute on Aging, recently stated, "We are not interested in our laboratory in increasing the life span. I don't buy that as a legitimate goal. I'd rather make the years that we have into good years."[6]

Dr. Leonard Hayflick has said, "The goal that appears to be not only more desirable, but indeed more attainable, is not the extension of longevity per se, but the extension of our most vigorous and productive years."[7]

Dr. Alexander Comfort, former director of the Research Group in Aging of University College of London, has commented, "The aging process can be slowed down,"[8] seeming to suggest that not only would the middle vigorous years of life be extended but also that the lifespan would be increased in the process.

Dr. Ivan Asimov suggests that by understanding the biochemical and biophysical process, we may by the year 2000 ". . . face a future society in which men and women will routinely live to be over 100, perhaps far beyond 100."[9] Others in this field are even more optimistic as to what can be accomplished.

Pierre Auer of France has said, "Death may be a manipulable genetic characteristic."[10]

Dr. Bernard Strehler of the University of Southern California has been quoted as saying "Someday we may live indefinitely."[11] It is obvious that Dr. Strehler does not hold the view expressed by one skeptic, Dr. Sobel, who said "Man will, if present research trends continue, be able to live for 300 years, 50 years of virility and 250 years of senility"[12] for Strehler says ". . . there is no way to appreciably increase the life span except by improving the body's physical state."

As to the probability of success, there is substantial agreement among the experts. Dr. Hayflick has said "The notion that the biology of sensecence is too vastly complex to yield to experimentation is, I believe, a myth."[13]

Dr. Alexander Comfort has predicted the probability of a breakthrough as being ". . . one hundred percent, given the time and resources," and " . . . we shall probably get the method of altering the rate of aging before we get the theory." On the timing of the breakthrough, he said that by 1990 " . . . we will know of an experimental way of slowing down age changes in man that offers an increase of 20% in life span."[14]

Given these perspectives, it seems that at this juncture we should seriously consider altering our national priorities to provide the funding necessary to ensure a reasonable chance of fulfilling man's age-old dream. How can this best be done? Should we, as has been suggested, establish the extension of the life span as a national goal for the year 2000?

ADOPTING A NATIONAL GOAL

The process of establishing a national goal is much more complex than generally recognized. It usually requires a coalition of outstanding leadership, strong political support, the presence of strong vested interests, a constellation of pressures which combine to cause substantial public support, the economic wherewithal, and in those few instances which have involved science, the existence of a capability that can reasonably be expected to lead to a successful outcome. Thus in the instance of the space program we had the leadership of President Kennedy, the public appreciation which had been heightened by desire to outdo the Russians, the political support stimulated by the vested interest groups, and the underlying scientific capability.

Obviously not every element is required before a goal can be adopted, as witnessed by the Manhattan Project initiated just prior to the outbreak of World War II. National Health Insurance is an example of a seemingly desirable national goal that we have failed consistently to adopt, in spite of substantial public support, economic wherewithal, and technical capability. The lack of outstanding leadership, the lack of strong political support, and the presence of powerful vested interest opposition have been more than enough to preclude its adoption.

What then would be involved in adopting the extension of the life span as a goal for the year 2000? A prime requisite would be the presence of outstanding national leadership. Without it sufficient public support will be lacking. The leadership may come from an individual, such as a national political figure, or from an organization. (The National Polio Foundation comes to mind as an example of organizational leadership, although the conquest of polio had the added advantage of President Roosevelt's personal interest and support.) A more remote possibility is that the "leadership" would come from industry.

A second prerequisite would be creation of substantial public support. How easy this would be to obtain is difficult to assess. My own experience in discussing this issue with groups of scientists and academicians during the past 3 years leads me to believe that widespread public acceptance can be obtained. There are, however, ethical and social issues to be considered.

ETHICAL ISSUES

One of the ethical issues certain to be raised is whether it is right for man to alter life processes in such a profound fashion. It can be anticipated that philosophers will present a range of opinions on this issue. Yet it would seem for the most part that our society, and Western societies in general, have accepted medical intervention for the improvement of health and the preservation of life as a part of their ethos. Paradoxically, this view is so widely accepted that we are now, because of technical innovations, confronted with the ethical issue in dealing with terminally ill patients of their "right to die." An extension of that ethical issue would no doubt arise in the future if the life-extending process were to involve an irreversible change such as a surgical procedure in early adulthood, or an alteration of the genetic coding instructions within the cells. Would euthanasia be available in later life, if desired? To whom, and under what circumstances? This issue would not arise if the life-extending process were to be not only voluntary but controllable by the individual, such as would be the case if one were to take pills each day.

A somewhat different ethical issue would present itself initially. Are we justified in adopting extension of the life span as a national goal in view of our current domestic and international problems? It seems certain that arguments will be advanced that adoption of such a goal would be unethical—because of the potential impact on world population; because of the need to enhance the quality of life for today's elderly before reaching for a new goal involving aging; because of the serious disruption to health care services in the future; and so on. The reasoning would be that a society must solve its existing ills before taking an action that could produce new problems.

But societies, as we know, do not operate in this fashion, and it would be no more unethical to adopt life extension as a national goal than one calling for a permanent Earth colony to be located on the Moon. More appropriate would be such concerns as, How much of our resources should we commit? What changes would these resource commitments generate? What types of changes would be expected in the future with respect to the individual, the family, and society?

CHANGES IN BIOMEDICAL RESEARCH PROGRAMS

If life extension were to be adopted as a national goal, the most immediate changes would involve our current biomedical programs with respect to research and training programs. We have in recent years substantially increased the funding for research and training related to the first three causes of death—diseases of the heart, malignant neoplasms, and cerebrovascular accidents. Our funding in these three areas accounts for almost 50 percent of our current total health research investment, but in terms of what is spent on health care *services* (an estimated $94 billion in 1973), it is a fairly modest amount. To have a reasonable chance of reaching the goal by the year 2000, it may be necessary to expend as much as $25 billion in total, or slightly less than the amount spent by the space agency in its program to put man on the Moon.

Could we expend funds at this level and not adversely affect the efforts to discover causes of heart disease, cancer, and stroke? It seems doubtful that both efforts could be sustained at such high levels, especially during the early years—not from the point of view of impact on the national budget, but because we are limited largely by the availability of qualified persons to conduct the necessary research. Many of the persons now involved in cancer and cardiovascular research would be the very ones most needed in the new effort. It would therefore be essential in the early phases to underwrite a very substantial training program, beginning at the college level and extending through pre- and postdoctoral levels. Only through substantial investment, perhaps as much as $5 billion over the next 10 to 20 years, could enough personnel become available to implement the research program at an optimal level.

To minimize the disruption in both research and training, an assessment of our resource allocation would be required that would permit a redefinition of priorities in light of the new goal; the identification of current programs and projects that fit within the new scheme of priorities; the exposition of areas requiring research effort; the definition of short- and long-range manpower requirements; the matching up of capabilities and interests of organizations and individuals with the tasks to be performed; and the institution of a management system that would couple an appropriate degree of monitoring sensitivity with the capability for periodic reassessment and redefinition of tasks.

HUMAN TRIALS AND ETHICAL PROBLEMS

One special aspect of the experimental phase is worthy of note. It seems almost certain, as the research programs expand and the efforts to determine cause(s) of aging intensify, that one or more developments will occur which will suggest the feasibility of human trials even though the basic cause(s) of aging has not been determined. As a result of cell culture studies, and of trials in one or more short-lived species of animals, an agent or technique (relatively nontoxic) will be demonstrated to prolong life. Are there any ethical issues to be resolved before undertaking long-term clinical trials in a selected population of humans?

No matter how many tissue cell lines are used, no matter how many mice, rats, guinea pigs, dogs, and chimpanzees will have been used in testing efficacy and safety, we will be confronted with not knowing how safe or how effective the approach will be when applied to humans. The same, of course, is true today with regard to all new drugs, but here we are generally dealing with pathological conditions, and usually ones that will *not* require long-term administration, or we are dealing with conditions where the drug used will not produce an effect that may last for the remainder of the person's life. But in extending the life span, we will be attempting to alter a normal physiological process, either by a one-time irreversible process or by administration of an agent over a prolonged period of time, perhaps the remainder of the person's life.

How will we select persons to be included in the initial trials? Much will depend on the nature of the data derived from tissue studies and animal trials. If the data show that the method extends life even when first used late in the life span, we would be able to minimize the risk in human studies. We would first test the method in persons age 75 or more, and as experience warranted, we would gradually reduce the age of entry into the test group in a stepwise fashion. Each new age group would then be followed carefully to determine that the only significant change was a decrease in the rate of aging. All other physiological process, including those involved in reproduction, should remain normal and there should be no unusual incidence of tumors or other pathological processes.

If, however, animal data suggested that benefits could only be obtained if treatment were instituted in early adulthood, a different approach would need to be used. Then indeed there would be some thorny issues. Could we ethically recruit volunteers when the risks would be so poorly defined and the benefits so long deferred? This would be quite unlike the trial, say, of oral contraceptives, where long-term risk was undefined, but where the short-term benefits were highly desirable to their participants.

Even if we could recruit sufficient volunteers, we might be faced with the difficult problem of maintaining their interest in participation over the long period required. Especially difficult would be to ensure compliance if daily medication were to be involved. Could we ethically in this instance offer any additional incentives without beclouding the risk issues? Would we be justified in encouraging the use of special groups such as prisoners, to overcome some of the methodological problems? Would we be forced to again start testing with the 75-year-old persons and gradually work down to the age groups most apt to benefit, in order that safety could be assured? If so, how could we justify exposure of participants to unknown risks when there would be no reasonable expectation of benefits for the individual?

In the event a surgical procedure were involved, such as the implantation of crystals into the temperature regulating center of the body, no social controls exist today comparable to the controls developed in the field of drugs. No institutional review programs exist in hospitals, medical schools, or large clinics to review in advance whether the new procedure to be tested is appropriate, or whether adequate safeguards for protecting the rights of the individual have been provided for. This is also an issue that would have to be resolved.

If the agent proposed for trial were a chemical, then the approval of the U.S. Food and Drug Administration (FDA) would be required before any clinical trials could take place. FDA requirements call for proof of safety and efficacy through animal experimentation. Once these minimal requirements are met, an exemption from the new drug regulation is issued (Investigational New Drug Approval, or IND) that permits the trial to be started on humans. In the normal course of events, with successful completion of the trial, an approval from FDA could be obtained by a private firm, without awareness of this fact on the part of the scientific community or the general public. A handful of overburdened medical officers, pharmacologists, and chemists in FDA could make a decision that would have inestimable effects upon future societies.

Is this FDA process any longer adequate? Must we not be concerned with more than safety and efficacy? Should we not at an early point involve a broader spectrum of the scientific community? If an effective method is perceived as being probable, should there not be provision for consideration by social scientists, politicians, ethicists, and theologians? It has been my concern for almost a decade that our present system is inadequate to appropriately assess the highly sophisticated drugs and devices being developed by the scientific community. The existence today of a valid Investigational New Drug Exemption to permit assessment of an agent with potential for life extension adds considerably to my concern for the adequacy of the system. Should this not be the occasion for a reappraisal of the FDA's role?

One final note of caution concerning the human trials needed to demonstrate safety—the numbers of participants needed would be very substantial. This is related to the need to detect changes in the rate of occurrence of rare events, such as malignant tumors or diabetes, in order to properly assess safety. It would be even more important that all foreseeable precautions were taken at the outset, and that the utmost efforts were made to ensure proper followup throughout the trial. Finally, we would need to accept at the outset the possibility that some of the participants would be adversely affected. Should we not be prepared to provide appropriate compensatory benefits? How this could be done without unduly influencing the judgments of potential volunteers is another unresearched issue.

THE AFTERMATH

Successful conclusion of the research phase, and validation of a method to defer aging, will create a new problem and many important social issues will arise. If one assumes usage by those age 40 and over, and if one assumes that optimum benefits, in terms of number of years by which life will be expanded, would decline according to the age at which use is initiated, then it is apparent there will be a lag period between introduction of an agent or technique and the time of maximum impact as measured by survivors in the population. The precise period of time will be a function of the rate change generated by the agent and extent to which it is utilized. It would not be unreasonable to assume, however, that the minimum time available for adjustment would be roughly 40 years. At first blush, this would seem to be more than adequate for even significant social change to occur, but when one begins to assess the nature and magnitude of changes that an age-retarding agent would induce, 40 years may indeed be grossly inadequate. What types of changes could reasonably be expected to occur, and what social issues would they generate?

The most obvious change would be the impact on the population group over 65 years of age. The change in life span by 20 to 25 percent (or 15 years on the average) would markedly increase the proportion of persons over 75 years of age, and it would noticeably affect the numbers in the 65 to 74 age group. (Even without any such antiaging treatment, the over-65 age group in this country is expected to constitute approximately 15 percent of the population by the year 2040—this assumes no improvements in death rates due to better health habits or improved health services, and it assumes a birth rate equal to that of 1972.)

With the increase in the over-65 age group, there would be an increased demand for health and social services. The magnitudes of these increases cannot be specified with great precision, but they would be substantial. When we realize that today, in spite of our current emphasis on acute rather than chronic health care, some 27 percent of all health expenditures are made for care of the elderly (now 10 percent of our population), we can easily visualize what would be involved if there were to be any significant lengthening of the life span. If we are successful in the intervening years in developing means of coping with chronic illnesses, in providing adequate home health and social services, and in developing a modicum of preventive services, it is not unreasonable to assume that the health care industry would become the major industry in our society if life were to be extended by 20 to 25 percent. (This, despite the desideratum advanced which stipulates that any method of extending life is not worth developing unless it extends the useful vigorous years, and not merely the years of senility.)

The increased life span would require substantial adjustments in retirement income programs of all types, if adequate income levels are to be maintained. An increased demand for housing of all types would occur as the population expands; and if present trends towards separate housing for the elderly continue, there would be a substantial requirement for new construction after the year 2040.

Less obvious are changes that might occur with respect to family structure, life styles, especially with respect to leisure time, educational patterns, work patterns, and political processes. One could speculate that with greater longevity assured, divorce might increase and new partnerships might be formed after the end of the child-rearing years. Multigenerational families of five generations would become more common. This would pose new problems: What kinds of relationships would exist between generations so greatly separated, not only by years, but by life experiences? Life styles would be expected to change markedly in response to changes in work patterns and education patterns. If, as postulated, work weeks would be truncated, and two or perhaps three careers would become the norm, then education and leisure activities would assume greater importance throughout life than they do today. With a greater proportion of the population over 55 years of age, one could reasonably expect that political processes would be biased toward the elderly. Beyond these potential changes lie many others that would be even more taxing upon our society.

The social issues which such changes would create are even less predictable. What type of income distribution system would be necessary to accommodate the varying needs and demands of the expanded society? Could enough employment opportunities be generated to permit the labor market to operate in essentially the same fashion as it does today, or would we be forced to some new system of job allocation with built-in requirements for periods of community service and reeducation, in order to preserve some semblance of equity? What could be done on an international basis to prevent excessive population growth as usage of the antiagent grows? What could be done to foster a reallocation of resources to minimize the possibility of nuclear blackmail by the have-not nations? How could we alter the "Protestant work ethic" to stimulate the intelligent use of the increased amounts of leisure time available? Would we adopt a permissive attitude towards euthanasia for those who find the quality of life during the extended years not worthwhile? Would use of the life-extending technique be restricted, or available to all? If restricted, how would we select those to benefit? Would we consider it a privilege, as we do voting rights, and deny it to any who commit felonies?

Others, more perceptive than I am with respect to the social sciences, can enlarge upon the partial listing of changes that might occur and the issues which could arise. It is apparent even with this incomplete listing that the disruptions to our society would be serious unless appropriate measures were to be initiated at the earliest signs of success derived from the limited human trials.

How concerned should we be that the scientific endeavor now underway will be successful? When are we likely to have our first trial of an agent or method on humans, and when would we be likely to have the method available for all? In my opinion, there is a high probability of success. The indications are now that one chemical currently under study could be tested within the next 2 to 3 years if funds become available. Others will certainly follow.

The early efforts may fail, but if we expand our research base and adopt the extension of useful life as a national goal, it seems likely that by the year 2000 we will have completed the initial trials in humans and be on the threshold of accomplishing man's cherished dream. As for today, perhaps it is appropriate to remember the advice given by Carlyle, who said, "Our main business is not to see what lies dimly at a distance, but to do what lies clearly at hand."

NOTES

[1] E. Metchnikov, *The Nature of Man* (New York: Putnam, 1903).

[2] R. Cherry and L. Cherry, "Slowing the Clock of Age," *New York Times,* May 12, 1974, p. 20.

[3] L. Hayflick and P. D. Moorhead, "The Serial Cultivation of Human Diploid Cell Strains." *Experimental Cell Research,* vol. 25, 1961, pp. 585–621.

[4] S. Goldstein, "Biological Aging: An Essentially Normal Process," *Journal of the American Medical Association,* vol. 230, no. 12, 1974, p. 1651.

[5] L. Hayflick, "The Strategy of Senescence," *Gerontologist,* Vol. 14, No. 1, 1974, p. 39.

[6] Reported in a column by Victor Cohn, *Washington Post,* March 16, 1975, p. C-2.

[7] Hayflick, 1974, *op. cit.*

[8] A. Comfort, "We Know the Aging Process Can Be Slowed Down," *The Center Eclectics,* No. 11, 1974. Center for the Study of Democratic Institutions, Santa Barbara, California.

[9] V. Cohn, 1975, *op. cit.*

[10] V. Cohn, 1975, *op. cit.*

[11] V. Cohn, 1975, *op. cit.*

[12] H. Sobel, in E. Palmore and F. Jeffers (eds.), *Predictions of Life Span: Recent Findings.* (Lexington, Mass.: D. C. Heath, 1971, p. 275.)

[13] Hayflick, 1974, *op. cit.*

[14] Comfort, 1974, *op. cit.*

Chapter 11

EXTENSION OF THE ACTIVE LIFE: ETHICAL ISSUES

James M. Gustafson

In order to write a fully satisfactory assessment of the issues of ethics and human values that emerge from the prospects for the extension of active life, some conditions are necessary that cannot be met at this time. First, insofar as a critical assessment is to be made of the benefits and the deleterious consequences of the extension of active life, certain data needed for evaluation are not readily available. One would need to know what would be the actual consequences for individuals, for particular societies, and for the human species. If such information could be developed, there would be a better factual basis on which to raise the more particular ethical questions of what consequences are to be judged to be of value, or of value to whom and for what. My limited study of the literature available, and the hypothetical character of much

From James M. Gustafson, "Extension of the Active Life: Ethical Issues," in *Extending the Human Life Span: Social Policy and Social Ethics,* ed. Bernice L. Neugarten and Robert J. Havighurst (Washington, D.C.: National Science Foundation, 1977). Reprinted by permission of the author.

of that literature both militate against accurate and precise analysis.

Second, while there is literature that makes evaluative judgments about the consequences of life extension and raises consciousness about the need for evaluative studies of the consequences, neither moral philosophers nor moral theologians have given much attention to this arena. If one compares the amount of literature on clinical medical problems as moral issues, for example, with literature on social policy with references to aging, it is clear that both in its amount and in its degree of sophistication the medical field is far ahead. Thus, there is little literature in relation to which these exploratory efforts can be developed or assessed.

These limitations dictate that the present effort be more formal and procedural than is desirable. Its basic content is a clarification of questions and a development of hypothetical arguments in favor of or against proposals that are in themselves somewhat hypothetical. Some illustrative material will indicate how the more formal issues could be developed with reference to the extension of active life. Hopefully, the reader will find sufficient clarity to be able to engage in his or her own revisions of the questions, criticisms of the arguments proposed, and extension of the procedures to other matters in the field of social gerontology.

Ethical analysis is primarily concerned to explore what reasons are given for choices, and particularly the reasons that are moral in tone and character. It is concerned to explore why someone might say, for example, that to deter the rate of biological aging in humans is the "right" thing to do, or is a "good" thing to do. What would count as warrants for supporting the rightness or the goodness of such activity? In a discussion of the extension of *active* life, it is quite apparent that a valuation is already implied in the stipulation of the topic, namely that "active" connotes something that is worthy, whereas "inactive" suggests something that is not of value. Thus, the qualifier "active" seems to imply that there would be reasons for not considering the prolongation simply of human biological life itself as a worthy purpose. "Active" suggests certain human capacities that are either of value in themselves, or are the conditions (and thus of instrumental value) for realizing or achieving other values. Thus the principal question of this paper can be stated as follows: What reasons can be given to justify the extension of life in conditions that make possible human "activity"? That "active" and "activity" are susceptible to more refined analysis in terms of their value-laden but ambiguous weight I hope I have suggested. We will simply presume that there is sufficient clarity about the connotations to proceed to develop three different types of reasons that might be given in favor of life extension.

The three types of reasons are as follows:

1. Individual persons desire to live as long as it is possible for them to be active.
2. Society would benefit from having a larger number of individuals live longer active lives.
3. Individuals have a moral right to live as long as possible in conditions that insure activity.

In the course of the elaboration of these reasons I shall note difficulties involved in each, and also the sorts of arguments that might counter them.

A delineation of limits or perimeters to the expectancy of life that is assumed in the following parts of the paper is necessary. For purposes of this paper we will assume what are reasonable expectations with reference to the coming decades, and not speculate upon more imaginative prospects. The assumption is that persons will be able to live actively for 3 to 5 years more than has been the case in the immediate past, and with the same extent and severity of disabilities in the last few years of life that now occur. Stated differently, we are working on the assumption that persons at the ages of 78 or 80 will have the same level of vigor and function of capacities as is normal for persons at the age of 75 at the present time. As noted, this assumption seems to be a reasonable one with reference to the next decades on the basis of projections by demographers.

LIFE EXTENSION IS DESIRABLE TO INDIVIDUALS

This reason for extending active life, like the other two reasons that will be analyzed, has imbedded in it certain ethical and practical difficulties when it is spelled out in terms of a social policy. We begin with what will be presumed to be a generally valid empirical statement: Individual persons desire to live as long as it is possible for them to be active. This empirical statement becomes one premise for a social policy. Because individuals desire to live longer, research, social policy, and relevant resources ought to be developed to extend the period of active life. Briefly, what is involved can be seen in the following form:

1. Individuals desire to extend their active lives.
2. The desires of individuals are the basis for what is good or valuable.
3. Therefore it is good or valuable to have active life extended.
4. Therefore research, policies, and resources *ought* to be developed to extend active life.

One important assumption to be noted is that the basis for determining both what is "good" to do, and what ought to be done, is the desires of individuals. What is desirable for individuals is good or valuable. Here we confront two complications worthy of note. First, persons in the history of Western ethics who have thought in these terms have had to find ways to distinguish between an "apparent" good for an individual, and a "real" good. For example, an aging person might desire to eat all the rich foods that he or she can, or might desire to engage in as much strenuous exercise as possible. To do so, however, might be only apparently good, for each of these activities might create grave threats to health. Health would be judged to be a "real" good; at least it would have a more fundamental position in an ordering of values than the pleasure of rich food or strenuous exercise. The general point to be noted is that to ground values in desires requires a

process of determining which desires are more worthy of fulfillment than others, or even which are "essential" to active life, and
which are optional.

The second complication is readily noted when account is
taken of the social and even natural context in which desires are to
be fulfilled. The words "good" or "valuable" invite the questions,
"Good for whom?" and "Good for what?" Good, or value, it can be
argued, is always in relation to some person, or some community,
or even in relation to the natural world. What is good (fulfills the
desires) of one individual might be in conflict with what is good for
another individual. Prolongation of active life of a person might
not be beneficial to members of that person's family, or to a
community in which there are limited resources available for the
fulfillment of the desires of all individuals. Indeed, prolongation
might not be good for the human species as a biological class. To
introduce this complication is to force recognition of the necessity
of a *distributive* principle in reasoning about policy. When the
desires of all cannot be fulfilled, some principles and procedures
need to be introduced that help to determine how the resources
available can be distributed justly or fairly among all whose desires
make claims upon them.

From these two complications we see the need for more
generalized principles to sort out, if not to resolve, the ambiguities
that are confronted. With reference to the need to order desires, or
goods, or values, some might argue that the crucial factor is
power, or capacity to purchase or in other ways secure what fulfills
desires. Thus, for example, an individual who desires health and
has the economic means to secure health care is the person who
properly has access to it, while the person without those means has
no right to it. While this offends the moral sensibilities of many
persons, desire plus power has usually been crucial in determining
whose desires are fulfilled.

Others might argue that social custom determines not only
whose desires are to be fulfilled, but what desires have priority.
For example, if one lives in a society that is generally "youth
oriented," advanced age itself becomes a disqualifying factor in

determining whose desires shall be met. Or, if one lives in a society that has determined that high-quality health care for all citizens takes priority over the desire of some to enjoy winter vacations in Spain, ramifications for public policy follow. Others might argue that the ordering of desires, or of values, must be grounded in the ontological structure of the human. Thus, on the basis of philosophical reflection about what constitutes the "truly" human, the "really" human, one can come to some ordering of values to be realized for persons. One would, in effect, determine what "goods" are really good and therefore necessary; what "goods" are not necessary, but nonetheless worthy of pursuit if resources are available; and what desires are only "apparently" good.

With reference to the need for a distributive principle (and the two complications overlap, as has already become apparent), various delineations of the concept of distributive justice would be invoked. Some would argue that justice requires that each individual has a right to fulfill his or her desires until the fulfillment infringes upon the right of others to fulfill their desires. Because, in social experience, this comes quickly, the practical task of justice is to determine the proper limits to free pursuit of individual desires. Others would argue that equals shall be treated equally, and that those who are equal to each other are those who have the same needs. "The same needs" requires further specification in the reality of social experience; some would then argue that a judgment has to be made about which human needs are more basic. Those that are basic ought to be fulfilled for all individuals. Thus, for example, what constitutes proper health care ought to be provided to all aging persons, but what constitutes desirable recreational opportunities might be secondary, or at least might be optional with reference to the desires for recreation that different individuals have. Further permutations on distributive justice can be left to the reflections of the reader.

A further difficulty in working out this first reason is seen in the multivalent or multidimensional character of certain crucial terms that are used to simplify the basic thrust. Aristotle, for example, judged that what all persons desire as an end in itself, and not as a means to any other end, is happiness. Others have used the notion of fulfillment. The extension of *active* life, as I have indicated, already suggests that extension of biological life is not an end in itself; it provides a necessary condition for the realization of other desires or values. Presumably happiness would be one of these. Both happiness and fulfillment are multivalent or multi-dimensional concepts when they are carefully formulated. In order to provide more specific justification for extending life in order to pursue happiness, these complications need to be taken into account. Clearly, the conditions that make one individual happy are not necessarily the same as those that make another person happy. I take it that social policy is directed to providing those conditions. If the final end of a policy is to prolong the pursuit or the realization of a state of happiness, the proximate ends must be plural. Some persons will be happy if they can live their aging years in the company of the younger generations of their families; others desire greater solitude and greater distance from families. Some persons will be fulfilled if they can continue in their vocations or professions as long as they have the capacities to do so; others find happiness in the opportunity to engage in activities deferred by their preoccupation with work during their earlier lives. For some persons the extension of physical pleasures is a major element in their happiness; for others a richness of cultural life is more important.

Proposals for social policy necessarily are based upon generalizations about what significant numbers of persons desire. The limitations of resources dictate that variations in provision of conditions deemed necessary for happiness be limited. It is not unreasonable to note that a principle of utility frequently is invoked at this juncture. The social policies that ought to be pursued are those that will provide the conditions for the greatest amount of happiness for the greatest number of persons. The difficulties frequently pointed to with reference to utilitarian ethics pertain here quite aptly. The major one is that a quantification of an elusive quality—happiness—is required to provide more acceptable reasons for particular choices.

It is not my intention to make an overall judgment about the adequacy or inadequacy of the first reason for the prolongation of active life. In our culture, which has cherished as central the value of individuals, and has organized both law and social life along the principle that persons ought to have the maximum possibilities to pursue their individual desires, this reason for life extension comes almost "naturally" to mind. The complications I have suggested are in no sense novel, but the delineation of them might be of practical significance to persons who choose to develop policy primarily on the basis of this reason.

SOCIETY WOULD BENEFIT

The second reason noted for the extension of life is as follows: Society would benefit from having a larger number of individuals live longer, active lives. Note the predictive aspect of this: society *would* benefit. The empirical generalization involved in the first reason is no doubt more valid than is the predictive generalization involved in this second, for its validity is more susceptible to empirical verification. This second reason is based upon prediction of social consequences, and therefore has greater uncertainty. Both reasons involve judgments about the value of certain consequences. One could at least turn the first reason into a statement that the prolongation of active life is likely to lead to greater, for example, happiness. The consequences of happiness function to support the proposal to prolong life. In the second reason, judgments of the consequences are made with reference to what is good, or of value, for society. The first had its grounding in the *desires of* individuals; the second is grounded in what is *"desirable" for* society.

Briefly, what is involved can be seen in the following form:

1. Society would benefit from having a larger number of individuals live longer, active lives.
2. The benefits to society are the basis for what ought to be done with reference to individuals.

3. Therefore, it is good to have active life of individuals extended.
4. Therefore research, policies, and resources *ought* to be developed to extend active life.

One important assumption to be noted is that the utility or instrumental value of individuals to society determines what ought to be done with reference to them. The "collective" good, or the "common" good, or the good of society is of prior value to the good of individuals. Taken in its starkest form, this reason runs counter to the maxim that persons are to be treated as ends in themselves, and not as means to other ends. To deprive the society or community of potential benefits to itself by not extending active life would be wrong.

Two complications of this second reason have been briefly noted, and now require more development. The first is that the prediction has not been established by sufficient evidence to permit it to carry the weight that it must. Consensus could be established that the extension of the active lives of certain individuals might benefit society—the care of a vigorous genius whose research or ideas contribute to the cause of health or justice in a society in some immediate or direct way would raise no question. One could with greater ease than in the case of a person of less social significance make a rough "cost/benefit" calculation that would come out on the affirmative side of the equation. The quality and quantity of benefits could be roughly adduced, because relative to the ordinary person they would be palpably greater. It is not so clear that the same sort of argument could be made for the majority of aging persons.

Another aspect of the prediction problem pertains to what society or what community a policy has in mind when it judges benefits. If one were to suggest that the most universal human group, the species homo sapiens, is the proper object of concern, one would have to justify the policy in terms of contributions to the survival of the species, as well as the biologically qualitative characteristics of the species that survives. To establish this would

require a considerable amount of biological research, extrapolat-
ing from the known to the predictable, and then turning back from
the predictable to its implications for policy.

If one were to suggest that a particular nation/state is the
proper object of concern, a large number of consequences would
have to be brought into consideration. The good of a nation is
multidimensional or multivalent. Consequences for economic
growth and stability would have to be calculated; consequences for
allocation of resources, and particularly allocation between distinguishable age groups would have to be predicted. Some judgments about the social dislocations and the political effects would
have to be made. (Further suggestions are unnecessary to indicate
what would be involved for a nation/state.) *Pari passu,* the same
process pertains to judgments about ethnic groups, families,
neighborhoods, professions, friends, and so forth. The best possible factual evidences for potential consequences would have to be
adduced in order to make the strongest possible case.

The second difficulty can be stated in the form of a question.
What constitutes benefits for society? A historic and knotty issue
comes to mind immediately. Does one think of benefits for society
in terms of a concept of the common good that in effect claims that
the common good is the sum of the beneficial effects of individuals
pursuing their own goods and desires? Or does one think of the
common good as the good of the community as a whole, in such a
way that the common good requires an ordered distribution of the
goods of individuals, and in some instances the elimination of
certain individuals for the sake of the common good? It makes a
difference whether an affirmative answer is given to the first or the
second of these questions about the meaning of the common good.
If one affirms that the common good is the sum of individual
contributions, then whatever the extension of active life that would
permit the continuation of benefits by individuals would contribute
to the good of society. If, however, one affirms that the common
good is the good of the whole and that it must be determined
whether that common good is being enhanced by the extension of

active life, it is likely that the extension of the active life of all members of the society would not be justified.

There is a further difficulty in judging what constitutes benefits to society. In contemporary technological societies, it is easy to slip into the assumption that benefits are to be judged in terms of contributions to productivity and other aspects of the economy. Persons contribute to society by their capacities to produce. Little reflection is required, however, to grasp the limitations of this notion of social benefits. Society benefits from the capacities of persons to render social services that might not make significant contributions to economic growth or economic stability. Society benefits from contributions to its cultural life, to the quality of interpersonal relationships that exist, to the richness of its symbolic and "spiritual" life. Specification of the kinds of activities that would be beneficial to society would be required if a strong argument were to be sustained. Because the benefits are not likely to be easily comparable or commensurable, the calculations and the assessments of their significance will be rather loose and more inconclusive than is desirable.

In comparing the first and second reasons for life extension, the decisive significance of a basic moral choice becomes clear. The choice is between the domination of the valuation of individuals, their desires, and their freedom, on the one hand, and the domination of the valuation of societies or communities, their "common good" and their requisite restraints upon individual desires and freedom, on the other hand. An illustration of this will make the point clearer. Physicians engaged in the treatment of aging persons have what Paul Ramsey calls a "covenant relationship" with individual patients. Their discerned obligation is to enable the patient to survive in the best possible health for the longest possible time. Medical care locates the dominant value in individuals. One would be surprised to find a physician refusing to treat an aging person because his or her continuation of life would be detrimental to the survival of the species. Population geneticists and other biologists, in contrast, think of benefits in terms of survival of the species. They are more prone to consider the survival of individuals in the context of the consequences for the species as a whole. While it is possible in theory to overcome the tensions between these two primacies of valuation, in practical policy formation the tensions are not resolvable.

Practical policy proposals in the area of aging as in other areas are frequently buttressed by mixed arguments; persons will argue that both extreme positions can be properly defended and that each carries some "grain of truth." In effect, then, as the argument for a policy is developed one finds tolerable compromises, or "trade-offs" which take into account both poles. (Absence of conscious-ness of the use of mixed arguments, however, sometimes leads to "rationalizations" in the worst sense for impulsive or intuitive moral responses. Persons, to justify their policy preferences, occa-sionally argue from whichever starting point seems to give them the greatest support in particular circumstances.)

As in the discussion of the first reason, I have introduced no novel ethical considerations, but have attempted to indicate the soft points in this second reason for extending the active life.

INDIVIDUALS HAVE A RIGHT TO LIVE AS LONG AS POSSIBLE

The third reason for life extension invokes a very different language and a different basic concept. Individuals have a moral right to live as long as possible in conditions that insure activity. The ground reason is not the desires of individuals, nor the benefits for society. It is stated as a *right*. While there was an "empirical" premise in the argument that developed from the first reason, and a predictive empirical premise in the second, the statement of a right is not subject to the same tests of validity; it is not verifiable in the same way. The reason for life extension is not conditioned by consequences either to individuals or to society. Indeed, it is awkward on the face of it to introduce the language of instrumental values. Individuals are, in this reason, inherently valuable; simply because they are human beings they ought be treated as ends rather than as means to other ends. The major premise is clear and forthright:

1. Inherent in being a member of the human species is the right to life, which includes the right to live as long as possible.
2. Aging persons are members of the human species.
3. Therefore, the conditions which permit them to extend their lives ought to be developed.

Similar arguments are made with reference to clinical decisions in medical care. For example, there are those who argue that a terminally ill patient ought to receive whatever therapy medical science and technology can provide, even if it requires "heroic" procedures, on the grounds that humans have a right to have their lives preserved. (It should be noted that no significant moral philosophers or moral theologians argue in this way; even the most conservative Roman Catholic theologians distinguish between ordinary and extraordinary means for the prolongation of life. Some physicians, however, act as if there was an inherent right to prolongation regardless of the consequences for the "quality" of life of the patient.) There are those who argue that radically defective newborns have a right to every possible medical intervention to preserve their lives, regardless of the incapacities with which they are destined to live, simply because they are human in biological parentage.

Clearly, if the grounds for the assertion of a right can be defended, this argument is the strongest possible argument for extending the active life. The grounds for the assertion might be secular: ("There are natural rights"); or they might be religious ("Rights are God-given"). They might also be prudential: if one did not assert that individuals have a right to the extension of life, one would have grounded the value of life in the quagmire of desires or social consequences or social utility. Apart from the assertion of rights, the values of individuals or of classes of individuals like the aging, are instrumental or conditional. If they are instrumental or conditional, one is on an exceptionally slippery slope. Rights are then conferred by others who determine the value of persons or age groups, and it is more difficult to avoid great moral harm because of the vagaries of those who have power to determine who has rights.

To argue for the extension of active life from a doctrine of rights, of course, does not avoid the problem of conflicting rights, or of conflicts in the allocation of resources when persons with equal rights compete for scarce resources. Classic "triage" situations occur, for example, in which persons with equal basic human rights to life are competing for seriously limited resources for survival. To use an expression found frequently in Jewish literature on these situations, "one man's blood is not redder than another's." In the sight of God each is of equal value. It is not important to rehearse classic resolutions of such extreme situations, and the reasons for alternative ones. The most frequent resolution is that in extreme situations it is morally licit to deny resources to some in order to save others, and the others chosen to be saved are usually those who would have greatest prospects for survival or greatest utility value to the community, or both.

To extend life from 3 to 5 years does not place the human race at the present time in a "lifeboat ethic" situation, or in a triage situation. If, however, one sets the claims of various groups within the context of limited resources, and if age classifications are used to group persons, the distributive question again emerges. Those who have special interest in the rights of the aging would need to make clear their grounds for either equal treatment with other age groups, or for special preference to the aging. If all age groups in society have equal rights to resources for health and other benefits, is there a good reason why the rights of the aging should take any priority over the rights of other age groups? Those who would argue this third reason, and whose arguments would lead to preferential treatment for the aging, would have to provide persuasive answers to the question just posed.

EPILOGUE

Clearly my intention has not been to state and defend a position with reference to the extension of active life. I have attempted to make a relatively simple and modest clarification of the issues that must be faced in defending policies in favor of life extension. I hope this paper is quickly superseded by work that is both more learned in the literature about social gerontology and by more sophisticated ethical analysis and arguments.

SELECTED BIBLIOGRAPHY

A number of ethical problems related to old age are systematically analyzed, from a variety of perspectives, in Nancy Datan and Leon H. Ginsberg (eds.), *Life Span Developmental Psychology: Normative Life Crises* (New York: Academic Press, 1975). A compelling indictment of abuses and inequities suffered by the old in America is Sharon Curtin's *Nobody Ever Died of Old Age* (Boston: Little, Brown, 1972), a book which also has moments of inspired appreciation of aesthetic beauty in the aged face and body. A sociologic analysis of the major life problems old people see themselves as having is found in Louis Harris, *The Myth and Reality of Aging,* (Washington, D.C.: National Council on Aging, 1975), a study that undermines a large number of familiar assumptions about the everyday experiences of living in old age. Conceptual problems in defining economic deprivation are examined in *The Concept of Poverty* (Washington: United States Chamber of Commerce, 1965). In his essay "How to Grow Old and Poor in An Affluent Society," *IJAHD,* 1973, Robert Butler discusses the ethics of distributive justice in relation to the elderly poor. An important conceptual muddle of the "Catch-22" type often found in programs of economic support for the elderly poor is explained in Stanley Brody, "Comprehensive Health Care of the Elderly: An Analysis," *G*, 1973. Brody also discusses some basis questions in the general philosophy of medical care for the aged. Mary Adelaide Mendelson's *Tender Loving Greed* contains analyses of issues of economic justice relating to nursing home residents. Economic and other human rights issues in the nursing home industry are also examined in Claire Townsend's *Old Age: The Last Segregation* (New York: Bantam Books, 1971). An indictment of contemporary treatment of the elderly in America, and a pessimistic assessment of the future state of the elderly, is found in David Stannard, "Growing Up and Growing Old: Dilemmas of Aging in Bureaucratic America," in Stuart Spicker, Kathleen Woodward and David VanTassel, *AEHPG*.

A comprehensive proposal for more nearly approaching economic justice for the aged is outlined by Robert Butler in "Old Age Dividends For Lifetime Investments in America," *IJAHD*, 1970. Ethical conclusions relevant for economic policy are drawn from the study of happiness in old age by Walter Chatfield in "Economic and Sociological Factors Influencing Life Satisfaction of the Aged," *JG*, 1977, and in Francis Glasmer, "Determinants of a Positive Attitude Toward Retirement," *JG*, 1976. See also Douglas J. Brown, *An American Philosophy of Social Security: Evaluation and Issues* (Princeton: Princeton University Press, 1972) and Ben S. Seligman, "The Poverty of Aging" in *Permanent Poverty: An American Syndrome* (Chicago: Quadrangle Books, 1968). The philosophical basis for economic policies affecting the elderly is described in Ollie Randal, "Aging In America Today—New Aspects," *G*, 1977. Issues of social justice for the aged in relation to political organization are discussed by Robert Binstock in "Interest Group Liberalism and the Politics of Aging," *G*, 1972. An anthropologic examination of social justice and the aged in relation to the practice of information control and suppression is found in "Information and Esteem: Cultural Considerations in Treatment of the Aged," by Robert Maxwell and Philip Silverman, *IJAHD*,

1970. Normative and conceptual problems of economic justice for the elderly are examined in Richard Wendel, "The Economic Status of the Aged," and in Juanita Kreps, "Economic Policy and the Nation's Aged," both in *G*, 1978. See also Kreps' essay "Human Values, Economic Values and the Elderly," in David VanTassel (ed.), *Aging, Death and the Completion of Being* (Philadelphia: University of Pennsylvania Press, 1979). Ethical issues in economic justice related to the elderly are analyzed in Harold J. Wershow, "The Outer Limits of the Welfare State: Discrimination, Racism and Their Effect on Human Services," *IJAHD*, 1979 and in Chapter Three of Mirna Field's book *Aging With Honor and Dignity* (Springfield, Ill.: Charles C Thomas, 1968). An extended examination of human dignity and its relation to justice (though not specifically in relation to the elderly) is found in Michael S. Pritchard, "Human Dignity and Justice," *Ethics*, 1972. The relation between poverty and ethical values in the life style of one group of poor elderly is analyzed and criticized by Joyce Stephans in "Society of the Alone: Freedom, Privacy and Utilitarianism as Dominant Norms in the SRO," *JG*, 1975. The same topics are explored at greater length in Stephans' book, *Loners, Losers, and Lovers* (Seattle: University of Washington Press, 1976). The important distinction between absolute and relative economic deprivation is used as a basis for a conceptual analysis of economic status in old age in "Relative Deprivation and Perception of Financial Adequacy Among Aged," by Jersey Liang and Thomas Fairchild, *JG*, 1979. An analysis of rationality in allocation of resources to the aging is given by Donald Dwight in his "State and Local Resources, Allocation and the Elderly," *JG*, 1968. Dwight identifies factors influencing allocation that, he argues, reduce its status as rational action, and some which he argues enhance its rationality.

Erdman Palmore describes ethical issues in social discrimination against the aged in his essay "Agism Compared to Racism and Sexism," *JG*, 1973 and "Attitudes Toward Aging as Shown by Humor," *G*, 1971. A history of the concept of old age and the perceived obsolesence of old people during the period of emerging

Darwinian social theory is given in W. Andrew Achenbaum, "The Obsolesence of Old Age in America," 1865–1974, *Journal of Social History*, 1974. In "The Double Standard of Aging," *Saturday Review*, 1972, Susan Sontag argues that many ageist biases are also sexist, imposing one standard of successful aging for men, a more difficult one for women. Inge Bell Powell's essay "The Double Standard: Age," *Trans-Action*, 1970, also discusses aspects of double standard morality imposed on the aged, as does Tish Sommer's "The Compounding Impact of Age on Sex, Another Dimension of the Double Standard," *Civil Rights Digest*, 1974. Social Justice in relation to aged women is examined in Myrna Lewis and Robert Butler, "Why is Women's Lib Ignoring Old Women?" *IJAHD*, 1972, and in "Neglected by Women's Lib: Why Elderly Females Need Help Against Discrimination," *The National Observer*, July 20, 1972. Some of the discriminatory practices against older women are described in Vivian Wood's "The Plight of the Older Woman," Newsletter, Institute for the Study of Women in Transition, 1976.

In "The Etiquette of Filial Behavior," *IJAHD*, 1970, Elaine Brody argues that understanding of ethical practices and institutions of support for the elderly has eroded, with the effect that current supportive thought, programs and behavior toward the elderly rests on the comparatively thin reed of etiquette. A detailed discussion of a related theme is "Ethics and the Elderly: Some Problems" by Donald Marquis in Spicker, Woodward and Van Tassel, *AEHPG*. Marquis argues that we lack a genuine understanding of our duties to the aged because there never has been, and still isn't, an ethical theory sufficiently comprehensive to explain moral obligations to the elderly. The current status of the ethical principal of filial piety among poor Chinese is discussed in Charlotte Ikels, "Old Age in Hong Kong," *G*, 1975. See also Alvin L. Schorr, *Filial Responsibilities in the Modern American Family*, (Washington, D.C.: U.S. Department of Health, Education and Welfare, 1960). Ethical aspects of filial responsibilities and the rights of aged parents are discussed in Sidney Margolis, "Aged Parents and Dependent Kids: The Middle Aged Dilemma," *Family*

Circle, 1975, and in Jane English, "What Do Grown Children Owe Their Parents?" in Onora O'Neil and William Riddick, (eds.) *Having Children: Philosophical and Legal Reflections on Parenthood* (New York: Oxford University Press, 1978). Ethical values presupposed in the avoidance of dependency on grown children are examined in A. I. Goldfarb, "Responsibilities to Our Aged," *American Journal of Nursing,* Vol. 64 (1964), and in Richard Kalish, "Of Children and Grandfathers: A Speculative Essay on Dependency," *G,* 1967. An essay useful to philosophers interested in ethical relations between generations is "Generational Differences and the Developmental Stake," by Vern Bengtson and Joseph Kuypers in *IJAHD,* 1971, which contains an analysis of the concept of "generation gap" and identifies the role of philosophical beliefs in creating and ameliorating alienation between members of different generations. The same philosophers will find much of interest in James A. Christenson's "Generational Value Differences," *G,* 1977. Erdman Palmore describes and analyzes the practice of filial responsibility and the status of the elderly in contemporary Japan in *The Honorable Elders* (Durham, N.C.: Duke University Press, 1975).

A conceptual analysis of prejudice, as it is directed toward the elderly, is given by Ewald Busse in "Prejudice and Gerontology," *G,* 1967. Busse argues that prejudice consists in beliefs supported by unresolved conceptual and emotional conflicts, including beliefs that the old are sick, weak, confused, etc. supported by unresolved conflicts about such values as independence, physical competence and health. Ageist biases implicit in language are analyzed in Marvin R. Koller, *Social Gerontology* (New York: Random House, 1968), pp. 145–146, and in Carlos I. Reed, "Suggestions for Revision of Nomenclature on Aging," *G,* 1966. Age-related stereotyping unfavorable to the aged in television is analyzed in J. Scott Francher, "'Its the Pepsi Generation . . .' Accelerated Aging and the Television Commercial," *IJAHD,* 1973, and in Herbert C. Northcott, "Too Young, Too Old—Age in the World of Television," *G,* 1975. Social Scientists' treatment of "Age Grading" and "Age Classification" often contain philosophically interesting analyses of value assumptions and judgments; excellent examples are reported in M. Riley and A. Foner, *Aging and Society, Volume Three: A Sociology of Age Stratification;* Bernice Neugarten and Joan W. Moore, "The Changing Age Status System," in Neugarten, *MAA*; Bernice Neugarten, Joan W. Moore and John C. Lowe, "Age Norms, Age Constraints and Adult Socialization, *The American Journal of Sociology,* 1965; Arnold M. Rose, "The Subculture of the Aging," *G,* 1962; Gordon F. Streib, "Are the Aging a Minority Group?" in Alvin W. Gouldner and S. M. Miller, *Applied Sociology* (Glencoe: Free Press 1965). These last three essays are reprinted in Neugarten, *MAA*. Interdisciplinary perspectives on ageist discrimination, including humanistic perspectives, are given in Gordon Moss and Walter Moss (eds) *Growing Old* (New York: Pocket Books, 1975). See also U.S. Department of Labor, *The Law Against Age Discrimination in Employment* (Washington, D.C.: U.S. Government Printing Office, 1971). An incisive statistical analysis of age discrimination in employment, as well as an analysis of some of its subtler ethical implications, are given in Harold L. Sheppard, "On Age Discrimination" in *Toward An Industrial Gerontology,* 1970. A subtle ageist bias in certain empirically based assessments of intellectual capacities is analyzed in Ilene Wittels, "Age and Stimulus Meaningfulness in Paired-Associate Learning," *JG,* 1972. Aspects of the concepts of "deviance" and "stigma" in relation to old age are analyzed in "The Impact of Subjective Age and Stigma on Older Persons," by Russell Ward, *JG,* 1977. One particularly incisive analysis of the subtlety of ageist bias is found in Richard Kalish, "The New Ageism and the Failure Models: A Polemic," *G,* 1979. A historical commentary on the nature of negative stereotypes of the aged is given in Clark Tibbets, "Can We Invalidate Negative Stereotypes of the Aging?" *G,* 1979. Negative stereotypes of the aged are portrayed as mechanisms of social control and manipulation in J. A. Kuypers' and V. L. Bengtson's essay "Social Breakdown and Competence: A Model of Normal Aging," *HD,* 1973. Stereotypes of the elderly in children's literature are examined in Mildred Seltzer and Robert Atchley, "The

Concept of Old: Changing Attitudes and Stereotypes," *G*, 1971. See also "A Portrayal of Elders in Magazine Cartoons," by M. Dwayne Smith, *G*, 1979. An analysis of the concept of human dignity as it applies to the elderly is given by Bruce Senn and Joseph Steiner, in "Don't Tread on Me: Ethological Perspectives on Institutionalization," *IJAHD*, 1978, and by Drew Christianson in "Dignity in Aging," *Hastings Center Report*, Fall 1974.

There are several important ethical problems related to old age not represented in the selections of the present book, including retirement and uses of leisure, sexual morality, paternalism and interventionist behavior, and euthanasia. The injustices and discrimination implicit in mandatory retirement practices are analyzed by the philosopher Paul Weiss (himself a victim of mandatory retirement) in "Age is Not a Number," *New York Times*, Jan. 1, 1971. See also "Growing Up and Growing Old: The Politics of Age Exclusion," G. Johnson and J. Kanara, *IJAHD*, 1977. For a legal perspective, see Terry S. Kaplan, "Too Old to Work: The Constitutionality of Mandatory Retirement Plans," *Southern California Law Review* Vol. 44, 1971.

Ethical aspects of voluntary *versus* involuntary retirement, as well as of the relationship of retirement to the ethical values implicit in the philosophies of disengagement and activism, are examined in Robert Atchley, "Adjustment to Loss of Job at Retirement," *IJAHD*, 1975. Ethical questions arising from increased leisure time in retirement are examined in Robert J. Havighurst, "The Nature and Value of Meaningful Free-Time Activity" and Charlotte Buhler, "Meaningful Living in the Mature Years," both in Robert G. Kleemeier, *Aging and Leisure* (New York: Oxford University Press, 1961). In his essay "The Social Dilemma of the Aging Leisure Participant," in Arnold M. Rose and Warren A. Peterson, *Older People and Their Social World: The SubCulture of the Aging* (Philadelphia: F. A. Davis, 1965), Stephen J. Miller gives an account of the ethical values surrounding the use of leisure time in retirement. Similar issues are usefully, though less directly examined in Robert J. Havighurst and Kenneth Feigenbaum, "Leisure and Life Style" *American Journal of Sociology*, 1959. Several definitions of leisure, and some of the conceptual problems of defining leisure, are reviewed, and a general perspective on its ethical dimension that favors socially engaged leisure activities, is developed by Larry Peppers in "Patterns of Leisure and Adjustment to Retirement," *G*, 1976. See also Alexander Martin, "Urgent Need for a Philosophy of Leisure in an Aging Population," in *Journal of the American Geriatrics Society*, 1962. A major philosophical essay on the nature of leisure and its relation to loss of work role and personal fulfillment is Sebastian de Grazia's *Of Time, Work and Leisure* (Garden City, N.Y.: Anchor Books, 1964). De Grazia presents his major ideas specifically in relation to the elderly in "The Uses of Time," in Kleemeier's *Aging and Leisure*, just cited.

Ethical aspects of sexual behavior in old age, especially the perception of sexuality in old age as deviant, are discussed in James Peterson, "Marital and Family Therapy Involving the Aged," and K. Warner Schaie, "Reflections on papers by Looft, Petterson, and Sparks: Intervention Toward an Ageless Society?" both in *G*, 1973. A variety of innovations in sexual behavior in recent decades, including nonmarital cohabitation, acceptance of homosexuality, group marriage, communes, and others are discussed in relation to old people in "Speculation and Innovations to Conventional Marriage in Old Age," by Ruth Shoule Cavan, in *G*, 1973. Ethical aspects of sexuality of special relevance to the aged are examined in several works by Eric Pfeiffer, including "Sexual Behavior in Old Age," in Ewald Busse and Eric Pfeiffer (eds.), *Behavior and Adaptation in Late Life*, 2nd edition, (Boston: Little, Brown, 1977), and *Successful Aging* (Durham, N.C.: Duke University Center for the Study of Aging and Human Development, 1974). Other useful material on the same topic can be found in I. Rubin, *Sexual Life After Sixty* (New York: Basic Books, 1965), Alex Comfort, *A Good Age* (New York: Crown Publishers, 1976), p. 128, pp. 192ff, and Robert Butler and Myrna Lewis, *Sex After Sixty: A Guide for Men and Women in the Later Years* (New York: Harper & Row, 1976). A philosophical discussion of sexual values that addresses questions of sexual restraint likely to be of interest to many older persons is found in Chapter 5 of C. H. and W. N. Whiteley, *Sex and Morals* (New York: Basic Books, 1967), reprinted in Raxie L. Abelson and Marie Louise Friquegnon, *Ethics for Modern Life* (New York, St. Martin's Press, 1975). A recent classic in the philosophy of sexuality that will be valuable to those interested in combating the stereotype of sexuality among the aged as morally inappropriate behavior is Thomas Nagel's "Sexual Perversion," *JP*, 1969. Other recent philosophical works on the same and related topics are: Sara Ruddick, "Better Sex," D. P. Verence "Sexual Love and Moral Experience" and Bernard H. Baumrin, "Sexual Immorality Delineated," all in Robert Baker and Frederick Elliston, *Philosophy and Sex* (Buffalo, N.Y.: Prometheus Books, 1975), where Nagel's essay is also reprinted.

Philosophical analyses of conceptual and ethical aspects of interventionist and paternalist behavior are found in the following: G. Dworkin, "Paternalism" in R. Wasserstrom, *Morality and the Law* (Belmont, Ca.: Wadsworth Publishing Co., 1971), reprinted in J. Feinberg and H. Gross (eds.), *Philosophy of Law* (Encino, Ca.: Dickerson Publishing Co., 1975); J. Feinberg, "Legal Paternalism," *Canadian Journal of Philosophy*, 1971; H. L. A. Hart, *Law, Liberty and Morality* (Stanford: Stanford University Press, 1963), pp. 31ff; Martin Golding, *Philosophy of Law* (Englewood Cliffs, N.J.: Prentice-Hall, 1975), Chapter 3; John Rawls, *A Theory of Justice* (Cambridge, Mass.: Harvard University Press, 1971), pp. 248ff; Bernard Gert and Charles M. Culver, "Paternalistic Behavior," *Philosophy and Public Affairs*, 1976; N. Fotion, "Paternalism," *Ethics*, 1979, and Bernard Gert and Charles Culver, "The Justification of Paternalism," *Ethics*, 1979. A moderate defense of paternalism is found in Thomas Holper, "Paternalism and the Elderly," in Stuart Spicker, Kathleen Woodward and David VanTassel, *AEHPG*. A purely empirical essay which will nevertheless be of interest to those concerned with the ethical problem of paternalism is "The Moral Career of the Elderly Mental Patient," *G*, 1969, by Sally Hacker and Charles Gartz, which describes effects of psychiatric hospitalization on the normative outlook of elderly patients.

A classic defense of euthanasia is found in Glanville Williams, *The Sanctity of Life and the Criminal Law* (New York: Knopf, 1957). Williams' view is criticized by Yale Kasimar in "Some Non-Religious Views Against Proposed Mercy Killing Legislation," *Minnesota Law Review,* 1958. Williams in turn responds to Kasimar's arguments, in the same volume, in "Mercy Killing Legislation—A Rejoinder." Both essays have been reprinted in Raxiel Abelson and Marie Louise Friquegnon, *Ethics for Modern Life* (New York, St. Martin's Press, 1975) and in A. B. Downing, *Euthanasia and the Right to Die* (Los Angeles: Nash Publishing Co., 1970). The latter volume contains a number of other important essays on the philosophical problems surrounding euthanasia, including "The Principle of Euthanasia" by Anthony Flew. Conceptual and moral grounds for apprehension about "positive" euthanasia are analyzed in Richard L. Trammell, "The Presumption Against Taking Life," *JMP,* 1978. Euthanasia is defended, in the same volume, by Ellen Kappy Suckiel, in "Death and Benefit in the Permanently Unconscious Patient: A Justification of Euthanasia." Ethical principles, beliefs and assumptions about who should have control over life, and why, are analyzed in Glen Vernon, "Death Control," *O,* 1972. Conceptual relations between the ideas of death and human dignity are examined in Mary Louise Nash, "Dignity of Person in the Final Phase of Life," *O,* 1977. Basic value judgements bearing on the morality of euthanasia are examined in "When is Life Without Value? A Study of Life-Death Decisions in a Hemodialysis Unit," *O,* 1979. Ethical beliefs of old persons regarding euthanasia are reported in "Old People Talk About—The Right to Die," by Shura Saul and Sidney Saul, *O,* 1977. For extended examination of the subject, see Ruth Russell, *Freedom to Die: Moral and Legal Aspects of Euthanasia* (New York: Human Sciences Press, 1975) and Marvin Kohl, *Beneficient Euthanasia* (Buffalo, N.Y.: Prometheus Books, 1975). Both books offer wide ranging, in depth discussion of the ethical issues in the euthanasia controversy. Both support euthanasia on the basis of its potential for improving the quality of life and the dignity of the dying person. Logical features of the distinction between active and passive euthanasia are examined in Douglas Walton, "Active and Passive Euthanasia," *Ethics,* 1976.

A historical survey of thought about the morality of euthanasia and an extensive bibliography are found in Gerald Gruman, "An Historical Introduction to Ideas About Voluntary Euthanasia: With Bibliographic Survey and Guide for Interdisciplinary Studies," *O*, 1973. An essay that examines ethical beliefs about killing undesirable persons for reasons of social utility, with possible implications for a philosophy of euthanasia, is Helge Hilding Mansson, "Justifying the Final Solution," *O*, 1972.

In a major essay on the relation of ethical theory to elderly persons, Donald Marquis argues that our duties to the elderly cannot be adequately explained by any of the major theories of morality. See "Ethics and the Elderly: Some Problems" in Spicker, Woodward and VanTassel, *AEHPG*.

A bill of ten human rights of the elderly is formulated in an early but still cogent essay, " A Bill of Rights for Old Age," by George Lawton, *JG*, 1947. A system of geriatric ethics involving four fundamental ethical principles is formulated in Drew Christianson, "Dignity in Aging," *Hastings Center Report*, Fall, 1974. A discussion of human rights in relation to nursing home care is found in "Nursing Home Patient's Rights: Are they Enforceable?" by Sally Hart Wilson, *G*, 1978.

Part III

EPISTEMOLOGICAL ASPECTS OF AGING

INTRODUCTION

We turn in this part to epistemological ideas in the philosophy of aging. According to many philosophers, there are a variety of stages of epistemological progress or development in the course of a human life. Some of these philosphers, including Schopenhauer, Plato, and Manu, attribute the highest stages of epistemological development to old age. We have already seen two examples of this in Part I in Plato's contention that an understanding of things in terms of their relations to the Form of the Good should not be expected until well after the age of fifty, and in the Manu text (see sections 74 and 75), where it is said that the aged ascetic achieves a "true insight into the nature of the world." Another variation of this important theme is developed in Schopenhauer's essay presented in this part.

There are differences in the epistemologic advances these philosophers attribute to old age. Plato's ideal aged person achieves excellence in understanding the relation of worldly things to the Form of the Good, and in discriminating between right and wrong action in personal life and public policy. Schopenhauer's ideal aged person acquires the ability to see through worldly illusions and to understand the "emptiness and vanity" of human life. Manu's ideal aged person achieves understanding of the true nature and meaning of things. But there is a shared general view of the epistemology of old age underlying these differences. The main idea in this view is that old age brings with it increases in understanding of certain fundamental issues, including an increased ability to view one's own life and experience as deriving their meaning partly from their place in a wider whole.

The view that old age does or can bring increases in certain significant forms of understanding is supported by recent research in the psychology of adult cognitive development. Robert N. Butler's essay "The Life Review: An Interpretation of Reminiscence in the Aged" suggests that in old age a person can achieve cognitions that place earlier events in life within the framework of one's whole life, and achieve a new understanding of those events and their meaning in the light of that wider perspective.

It is evident from Butler's essay that the process he calls "life review" has long been of interest to narrative artists. A philosophically interesting aspect of life review, which literary descriptions often bring to light, is that it can lead to reversal of earlier opinion about important events, persons, and relationships in our past lives. A striking example of this appears in the life of the character Velchaninov in Dostoyevsky's *The Eternal Husband*.

> Some of the facts he remembered had been so completely forgotten that it seemed to him a miracle that they could be recalled . . . But the point was that all that was recalled came back now with a quite fresh, surprising and, till then, inconceivable point of view, and seemed as though someone were leading up to it on purpose. Why did some things he remembered strike him now as positive crimes? And it was not a question of the judgment of his mind only: . . . it reached the point of curses and almost of tears, inward tears.

Velchaninov's memory of an incident in which he had insulted a "harmless, bare-headed and absurd old clerk" involves just such a reversal of perspective:

> And now when Velchaninov remembered how the poor old man had sobbed and hidden his face in his hands like a child, it suddenly seemed to him as though he had never forgotten it. And, strange to say, it had all seemed to him very amusing at the time, especially some of the details, such as the way he had covered his face with his hands; but now it was quite the opposite.

There is an important philosophical dilemma implicit in the retrospective reversal of judgment that occurs in Velchaninov's life review. Which of his judgments is more nearly true to the remembered event as it actually was at the time it occurred: the judgment of the immediate situation or the retrospective judgment of life review? Was the remark to the clerk humorous, as it seemed at the time? Or cruel and self-aggrandizing, as it now seems in retrospect? Both judgments are subject to possible distortion—the contemporaneous judgment by the intensity and bias of immediate involvement, the life review judgment by the distortions of memory and distance. Each judgment has a special claim to credibility: the contemporaneous judgment has the benefit of immediate access to what is being judged; the retrospective judgment has the benefit of a broader perspective. These strengths seem to counterbalance each other, and so do not give a basis for accepting the testimony of one in favor of the other. Dostoyevsky seems to favor the life review judgment, at least in Velchaninov's case. In a similar vein, Schopenhauer contends that such reversals of earlier opinion are found in all accurate value judgments made from the perspective of old age. Schopenhauer believed that the retrospective perspective of old age is epistemologically superior to any other. Even if that view is rejected as overly simple, the reverse judgments at issue here do pose an important epistemological question; namely, by what criteria can we decide between conflicting earlier and later judgments in such cases? What final, settled judgment about the nature of the remembered thing would be rationally defensible, in light of the different but apparently equally defensible judgments about it? There is a strong suggestion in this inevitable line of questioning that an adequate and rational concept of the way a thing "really was" requires a complex, miltidimensional description, involving both the description of that thing from the perspective of life review and the description that would have been given or was given from the perspective of the moment. Finally, the philosophical question raised by life review does not depend upon its containing a reversal of judgment. Even if Velchaninov had judged his earlier remark to be innocent and harmless, just as it had seemed at the time, he would still be evaluating it from a new and different perspective, seeing it in a different way from before. It would still be important to the epistemologist to identify the contribution each perspective makes to our settled, final understanding of the remembered event, and that is a problem for philosophical analysis.

Like Manu, Plato, Schopenhauer, and Butler, the developmental psychologist K. Warner Schaie believes that a cognitive shift underlies some observed differences between the old and other age groups. In his essay "Toward a Stage Theory of Adult Cognitive Development" he outlines in general terms a developmental theory for understanding such differences. His contention that the cognitive skills of old age include elaboration of "cosmic interest of selected individuals who exemplify what folk myth describes as 'the wisdom of old age'" reiterates the idea that enhanced powers of metaphysical insight is an important feature of old age.

Schaie does not offer any very specific suggestions about what kinds of judgments he envisages as belonging to an "integrative" cognitive stage. To arrive at meaningful initial conjectures about what particular integrative forms of judgment might emerge or increase in strength during old age is a substantial challenge to the philosophy of old age. A large number of suggestions have been made in the recent literature of gerontology. These include Butler's suggestion that the life review of old age brings an increased ability to comprehend human lives as integrated wholes; the suggestion of a heightened sense of the relevance of past experience to present problems;[1] an ability to perceive as reconcilable, meaningful counterpoints such opposites as individual rights and social welfare, which others tend to perceive as mutually exclusive;[2] achievement of a less egocentric perspective in reasoning about values;[3] and achievement of insight into human life meanings from a rational metaphysical perspective.[4]

Several philosophically interesting aspects of old age are illustrated in the conversation between Socrates and Cephalus found at the beginning of Plato's *The Republic*. What is of special interest to us in this part is the insight into Cephalus's special mental habits and powers that Socrates elicits in the course of their exchange. Not that there is anything special about Cephalus as an intellectual or philosopher—his mind is ordinary in comparison to later participants in the dialogue, and he is soon perfunctorily exited from its main action. Still, Socrates approaches him with interest and respect—as a reliable source of important information about "the path ahead." Even the old person of ordinary mind, the suggestion is, may have valuable knowledge that younger people do not.

Three features of Cephalus's mental life that emerge in the ensuing discussion seem especially important for a philosophy of aging. First, the kind of knowledge Cephalus has of the path ahead is particular, not general. It is not a knowledge of generalization about trends and averages in the behavior of old people. Instead, it is an interpretive grasp of the meaning of his own life, expressed not in the language of statistical averages and graphs, but in the language of ethics, poetry, and religious theory. Cephalus does not attempt to illuminate the path ahead by suggesting any behavioral or developmental laws of aging. Instead the stress is on the particular circumstances of individual lives—old people are as different to Cephalus as they are alike. This is illustrated by the difference of character and behavior he sees between himself and many of his friends.

Second, his mental powers are primarily integrative rather than analytic. He resists the reductionist urge to explain his own successful adjustment to old age in terms of a single favored perspective. This integrative power is seen in the explanation that Cephalus and Socrates, working together, arrive at in order to understand Cephalus's achievement of happiness in old age.

ephalus exhibits a momentary impulse to explain this in terms of his own good moral character, but readily expands on this explanation to include environmental factors as well. Finally, a third characteristic of Cephalus's mental life lies in its general direction of interest, which is ethical and religious, directed at the questions of the meaning of man's life and its place in the larger universe.

In his essay "Aging, Catastrophe and Moral Reasoning," John Orr views moral reasoning in old age from the perspective of philosophy and developmental psychology. Drawing on the work of Jean Piaget, Lawrence Kohlberg, and other developmental psychologists, he suggests that achieving wisdom in old age cannot occur in a cultural vacuum, but requires the support of convincing models of cognitive achievement in old age. Regression in moral reasoning apparently found in some old people, Orr argues, may derive from the absence of convincing models of intellectual growth in old age. Orr calls upon philosophers to suggest such metaphors and images of epistemological growth in old age.

Some philosophers have viewed mental life in old age in primarily negative terms. This is the suggestion in Aristotle's remarks about mental life in old age, and in Simone de Beauvoir's book *The Coming of Age*. de Beauvoir's picture of old age is one of general cognitive decline that is not offset by any parallel intellectual growth. She seems to feel that the attempt to identify elements of positive cognitive growth in old age, or to suggest that old age can be a time of enriched understanding and wisdom, is an evasion or denial of the hard realities of life. In this connection, it is interesting to contrast her rather negative interpretation of the role of memory in old age with the more constructive one in Butler's essay.

The reasoning behind the widespread belief that mental changes in old age constitute an overall decline should be scrutinized very carefully. Researchers who adopt this view often cite evidence showing the existence of specific cognitive decrement in old age (such as relative loss in short-term verbal recall), and then treat this as suggesting that mental powers in old age are generally in decline. It is important to understand that any such general assessment of the epistemological status of old people is a normative, not factual, belief. It reflects a decision about whether to confer overriding importance on documented and possible losses, or upon documented and possible gains. This decision cannot be justified by empirically confirmed minor changes in specific mental abilities. Justice to the old in this matter requires an honest recognition of its normative aspect. It also requires a resolute and circumspect investigation of possible cognitive gains in old age, including those metamorphic alterations of perspective that philosophers and other thoughtful observers have alleged to occur in old age.

NOTES

[1] Bernice L. Neugarten, "The Awareness of Middle Age" in *Middle Age and Aging.* ed. Bernice L. Neugarten (Chicago: Chicago University Press, 1968).

[2] Erik Erikson and Joan Erikson, Introduction to Stuart Spicker, Kathleen Woodward, and David van Tassle, *Aging and the Elderly.* (Atlantic Highlands: Humanities Press, 1978).

[3] Robert C. Peck, "Psychological Developments in the Second Half of Life" in *Psychological Aspects of Aging.* Proceedings of a Conference on Planning Research, Bethesda, Maryland, April 24–27, 1955, edited by John E. Anderson (Washington, D.C.: American Psychological Association, 1956). Reprinted in Neugarten, *Middle Age and Aging.*

[4] Lawrence Kohlberg, "Continuities in Childhood and Adult Moral Development Revisited" in Paul B. Baltes and K. Warner Schaie, eds., *Life Span Developmental Psychology: Personality and Socialization.* (New York: Academic Press, 1973).

Chapter 12

SOCRATES AND CEPHALUS

Plato

I went down yesterday to the Piraeus with Glaucon, the son of Ariston, to pay my devotions to the goddess, and also because I wished to see how they would conduct the festival, since this was its inauguration.

I thought the procession of the citizens very fine, but it was no better than the show made by the marching of the Thracian contingent.

After we had said our prayers and seen the spectacle we were starting for town when Polemarchus, the son of Cephalus, caught sight of us from a distance as we were hastening homeward and ordered his boy run and bid us to wait for him, and the boy caught hold of my hem from behind and said, Polemarchus wants you to wait.

And I turned around and asked where his master was.

From Plato, *Republic:* I, trans. Paul Shorey, (Cambridge, Mass.: Harvard University Press, 1935). Reprinted by permission of the publishers and the Loeb Classical Library.

"There he is," he said, "behind you, coming this way. Wait for him."

"So we will," said Glaucon. And shortly after Polemarchus came up and Adimantus, the brother of Glaucon, and Nicias, and a few others apparently from the procession.

Whereupon Polemarchus said, "Socrates, you appear to have turned your faces townward and to be going to leave us."

"Not a bad guess," said I.

"But you see how many we are?" he said.

"Surely."

"You must either then prove yourselves the better men or stay here."

"Why, is there not left," said I, "the alternative of our persuading you that you ought to let us go?"

"But could you persuade us," said he, "if we refused to listen?"

"Nohow," said Glaucon.

"Well, we won't listen, and you might as well make up your minds to it."

"Do you mean to say," interposed Adimantus, "that you haven't heard that there is to be a torchlight race this evening on horseback in honor of the goddess?"

"On horseback?" said I. "That is a new idea. Will they carry torches and pass them along to one another as they race with the horses, or how do you mean?"

"That's the way of it," said Polemarchus, "and, besides, there is to be a night festival which will be worth seeing. For after dinner we will get up and go out and see the sights and meet a lot of the lads there and have good talk. So stay and do as we ask."

"It looks as if we should have to stay," said Glaucon.

"Well," said I, "if it so be, so be it."

So we went with them to Polemarchus' house, and there we found Lysias and Euthydemus, the brothers of Polemarchus, yes, and Thrasymachus, too, of Chalcedon, and Charmantides of the deme of Paeania, and Clitophon, the son of Aristonymus. And the father of Polemarchus, Cephalus, was also at home.

And I thought him much aged, for it was a long time since I had seen him. He was sitting on a sort of chair with cushions and he had a chaplet on his head, for he had just finished sacrificing in the court. So we went and sat down beside him, for there were seats there disposed in a circle.

As soon as he saw me Cephalus greeted me and said, "You are not a very frequent visitor, Socrates. You don't often come down to the Piraeus to see us. That is not right. For if I were still able to make the journey up to town easily there would be no need of your resorting hither, but we would go to visit you. But as it is you should not space so widely your visits here. For I would have you know that, for my part, as the satisfactions of the body decay, in the same measure my desire for the pleasures of good talk and my delight in them increase. Don't refuse then, but be yourself a companion to these lads and make our house your resort and regard us as your very good friends and intimates."

"Why, yes, Cephalus," said I, "and I enjoy talking with the very aged. For to my thinking we have to learn of them as it were from wayfarers who have preceded us on a road on which we too, it may be, must sometime fare—what it is like. Is it rough and hard-going or easy and pleasant to travel? And so now I would fain learn of you what you think of this thing, now that your time has come to it, the thing that the poets call 'the threshold of old age.' Is it a hard part of life to bear or what report have you to make of it?"

"Yes, indeed, Socrates," he said, "I will tell you my own feeling about it. For it often happens that some of us elders of about the same age come together and verify the old saw of like to like. At these reunions most of us make lament, longing for the lost joys of youth and recalling to mind the pleasures of wine, women, and feasts, and other things thereto appertaining, and they repine in the belief that the greatest things have been taken from them and that then they lived well and now it is no life at all. And some of them complain of the indignities that friends and kinsmen put upon old age and thereto recite a doleful litany of all the miseries for which they blame old age. But in my opinion, Socrates, they do not put the blame on the real cause. For if it were the cause I too should have had the same experience so far as old age is concerned, and so

would all others who have come to this time of life. But in fact I
have ere now met with others who do not feel in this way, and in
particular I remember hearing Sophocles the poet greeted by a
fellow who asked, How about your service of Aphrodite, Sophocles—is your natural force still unabated? And he replied, Hush,
man, most gladly have I escaped this thing you talk of, as if I had
run away from a raging and savage beast of a master. I thought it a
good answer then and now I think so still more. For in very truth
there comes to old age a great tranquillity in such matters and a
blessed release. When the fierce tensions of the passions and
desires relax, then is the word of Sophocles approved, and we are
rid of many and mad masters. But indeed, in respect of these
complaints and in the matter of our relations with kinsmen and
friends there is just one cause, Socrates—not old age, but the
character of the man. For if men are temperate and cheerful even
old age is only moderately burdensome. But if the reverse, old age,
Socrates, and youth are hard for such dispositions."

And I was filled with admiration for the man by these words,
and desirous of hearing more, I tried to draw him out and said, "I
fancy, Cephalus, that most people, when they hear you talk in this
way, are not convinced but think that you bear old age lightly not
because of your character but because of your wealth, for the rich,
they say, have many consolations."

"You are right," he said. "They don't accept my view and
there is something in their objection, though not so much as they
suppose. But the retort of Themistocles comes in pat here, who,
when a man from the little island of Seriphus grew abusive and told
him that he owed his fame not to himself but to the city from which
he came, replied that neither would he himself ever have made a
name if he had been born in Seriphus nor the other if he had been an
Athenian. And the same principle applies excellently to those who
not being rich take old age hard, for neither would the reasonable
man find it altogether easy to endure old age conjoined with
poverty, nor would the unreasonable man by the attainment of
riches ever attain to self-contentment and a cheerful temper."

"May I ask, Cephalus," said I, "whether you inherited most
of your possessions or acquired them yourself?"

"Acquired?" he said. "As a money maker, I hold a place somewhere halfway between my grandfather and my father. For my grandfather and namesake inherited about as much property as I now possess and multiplied it many times, my father Lysanias reduced it below the present amount, and I am content if I shall leave the estate to these boys not less but by some slight measure more than my inheritance."

"The reason I asked," I said, "is that you appear to me not to be overfond of money. And that is generally the case with those who have not earned it themselves. But those who have themselves acquired it have a double reason in comparison with other men for loving it. For just as poets feel complacency about their own poems and fathers about their own sons, so men who have made money take this money seriously as their own creation, and they also value it for its uses as other people do. So they are hard to talk to since they are unwilling to commend anything except wealth."

"You are right," he replied.

"I assuredly am," said I. "But tell me further this. What do you regard as the greatest benefit you have enjoyed from the possession of property?"

"Something," he said, "which I might not easily bring many to believe if I told them. For let me tell you, Socrates, he said, that when a man begins to realize that he is going to die, he is filled with apprehensions and concern about matters that before did not occur to him. The tales that are told of the world below and how the men who have done wrong here must pay the penalty there, though he may have laughed them down hitherto, they begin to torture his soul with the doubt that there may be some truth in them. And apart from that the man himself either from the weakness of old age or possibly as being now nearer to the things beyond has a somewhat clearer view of them. Be that as it may, he is filled with doubt, surmises, and alarms and begins to reckon up and consider whether he has ever wronged anyone. Now he to whom the ledger of his life shows an account of many evil deeds starts up even from his dreams like a child again and again in affright and his days are haunted by anticipations of worse to come. But on him who is conscious of no wrong that he has done a sweet hope ever attends and a goodly, to be nurse of his old age, as Pindar too says. For a beautiful saying it is, Socrates, of the poet, that when a man lives out his days in justice and piety, 'sweet companion with him, to cheer his heart and nurse his old age, accompanieth hope, who chiefly ruleth the changeful mind of mortals.' That is a fine saying and an admirable one. It is for this, then, that I affirm that the possession of wealth is of most value, not to every man but to the good man. Not to cheat any man even unintentionally or play him false, not remaining in debt to a god for some sacrifice or to a man for money, so to depart in fear to that other world—to this result the possession of property contributes not a little. It has also many other uses. But, setting one thing against another, I would lay it down, Socrates, that for a man of sense this is the chief service of wealth."

"An admirable sentiment, Cephalus," said I. "But speaking of this very thing, justice, are we to affirm thus without qualification that it is truthtelling and paying back what one has received from anyone, or may these very actions sometimes be just and sometimes unjust? I mean, for example, as everyone I presume would admit, if one took over weapons from a friend who was in his right mind and then the lender should go mad and demand them back, that we ought not to return them in that case and that he who did so return them would not be acting justly—nor yet would he who chose to speak nothing but the truth to one who was in that state."

"You are right," he replied.

"Then this is not the definition of justice—to tell the truth and return what one has received."

"Nay, but it is, Socrates," said Polemarchus breaking in, "if indeed we are to put any faith in Simonides."

"Very well," said Cephalus, "indeed I make over the whole argument to you. For it is time for me to attend the sacrifices."

"Well," said I, "is not Polemarchus the heir of everything that is yours?"

"Certainly." said he with a laugh, "and at the same time went out to the sacred rites."

Chapter 13

THE AGES OF LIFE

Arthur Schopenhauer

There is a very fine saying of Voltaire's to the effect that every age of life has its own peculiar mental character, and that a man will feel completely unhappy if his mind is not in accordance with his years

> Qui n'a pas l'esprit de son âge,
> De son âge atout le malheur.

It will, therefore, be a fitting close to our speculations upon the nature of happiness, if we glance at the changes which the various periods of life produce in us.

Our whole life long it is the present, and the present alone, that we actually possess: the only difference is that at the beginning of life we look forward to a long future, and that towards the end we look back upon a long past; also that our temperament, but not our character, undergoes certain well-known changes, which make the present wear a different color at each period of life.

From Arthur Schopenhauer, *Counsels and Maxims,* trans. T. Bailey Saunders (London: Swon Sonnenschein & Co, 1890).

I have elsewhere stated that in childhood we are more given to using our intellect than our will; and I have explained why this is so. It is just for this reason that the first quarter of life is so happy: as we look back upon it in after years, it seems a sort of lost paradise. In childhood our relations with others are limited, our wants are few—in a word, there is little stimulus for the will; and so our chief concern is the extension of our knowledge. The intellect—like the brain, which attains its full size in the seventh year, is developed early, though it takes time to mature; and it explores the whole world of its surroundings in its constant search for nutriment: it is then that existence is in itself an ever fresh delight, and all things sparkle with the charm of novelty.

This is why the years of childhood are like a long poem. For the function of poetry, as of all art, is to grasp the Idea—in the Platonic sense; in other words, to apprehend a particular object in such a way as to perceive its essential nature, the characteristics it has in common with all other objects of the same kind; so that a single object appears as the representative of a class, and the results of one experience hold good for a thousand.

It may be thought that my remarks are opposed to fact, and that the child is never occupied with anything beyond the individual objects or events that are presented to it from time to time, and then only in so far as they interest and excite its will for the moment; but this is not really the case. In those early years, life—in the full meaning of the word, is something so new and fresh, and its sensations are so keen and unblunted by repetition, that, in the midst of all its pursuits and without any clear consciousness of what it is doing, the child is always silently occupied in grasping the nature of life itself—in arriving at its fundamental character and general outline by means of separate scenes and experiences; or, to use Spinoza's phraseology, the child is learning to see the things and persons about it *sub specia aeternitatis*—as particular manifestations of universal law.

The younger we are, then, the more does every individual object represent for us the whole class to which it belongs; but as the years increase, this becomes less and less the case. That is the reason why youthful impressions are so different from those of old age. And that is also why the slight knowledge and experience gained in childhood and youth afterwards come to stand as the permanent rubric, or heading, for all the knowledge acquired in later life—those early forms of knowledge passing into categories, as it were, under which the results of subsequent experience are classified; though a clear consciousness of what is being done does not always attend upon the process.

In this way the earliest years of a man's life lay the foundation of his view of the world, whether it be shallow or deep; and although this view may be extended and perfected later on, it is not materially altered. It is an effect of this purely objective and therefore poetical view of the world—essential to the period of childhood and promoted by the as yet undeveloped state of the volitional energy—that, as children, we are concerned much more with the acquisition of pure knowledge than with exercising the power of will. Hence that grave, fixed look observable in so many children, of which Raphael makes such a happy use in his depiction of cherubs, especially in the picture of the *Sistine Madonna*. The years of childhood are thus rendered so full of bliss that the memory of them is always coupled with longing and regret.

While we thus eagerly apply ourselves to learning the outward aspect of things, as the primitive method of understanding the objects about us, education aims at instilling into us ideas. But ideas furnish no information as to the real and essential nature of objects, which, as the foundation and true content of all knowledge, can be reached only by the process called intuition. This is a kind of knowledge which can in no wise be instilled into us from without; we must arrive at it by and for ourselves.

Hence a man's intellectual as well as his moral qualities proceed from the depths of his own nature, and are not the result of external influences; and no educational scheme—of Pestalozzi, or of anyone else—can turn a born simpleton into a man of sense. The thing is impossible! He was born a simpleton, and a simpleton he will die.

It is the depth and intensity of this early intuitive knowledge

of the external world that explain why the experiences of childhood take such a firm hold on the memory. When we were young,
we were completely absorbed in our immediate surroundings;
there was nothing to distract our attention from them; we looked
upon the objects about us as though they were the only ones of their
kind, as though, indeed, nothing else existed at all. Later on, when
we come to find out how many things there are in the world, this
primitive state of mind vanishes, and with it our patience.

I have said elsewhere that the world, considered as object—in
other words, as it is presented to us objectively—wears in general a
pleasing aspect; but that in the world, considered as subject—that
is, in regard to its inner nature, which is will—pain and trouble
predominate. I may be allowed to express the matter, briefly, thus:
the world is glorious to look at, but dreadful in reality.

Accordingly, we find that, in the years of childhood, the
world is much better known to us on its outer or objective side,
namely, as the presentation of will, than on the side of its inner
nature, namely, as the will itself. Since the objective side wears a
pleasing aspect, and the inner or subjective side, with its tale of
horror, remains as yet unknown, the youth, as his intelligence
develops, takes all the forms of beauty that he sees, in nature and in
art, for so many objects of blissful existence; they are so beautiful
to the outward eye that, on their inner side, they must, he thinks,
be much more beautiful still. So the world lies before him like
another Eden; and this is the Arcadia in which we are all born.

A little later, this state of mind gives birth to a thirst for real
life—the impulse to do and suffer—which drives a man forth into
the hurly-burly of the world. There he learns the other side of
existence—the inner side, the will, which is thwarted at every
step. Then comes the great period of disillusion, a period of very
gradual growth; but once it has fairly begun, a man will tell you
that he has got over all his false notions—*l'âge des illusions est
passé;* and yet the process is only beginning, and it goes on
extending its sway and applying more and more to the whole of
life.

So it may be said that in childhood, life looks like the scenery in a theater, as you view it from a distance; and that in old age it is like the same scenery when you come up quite close to it.

And, last, there is another circumstance that contributes to the happiness of childhood. As spring commences, the young leaves on the trees are similar in color and much the same in shape; and in the first years of life we all resemble one another and harmonize very well. But with puberty divergence begins; and, like the radii of a circle, we go further and further apart.

The period of youth, which forms the remainder of this earlier half of our existence (and how many advantages it has over the later half!) is troubled and made miserable by the pursuit of happiness, as though there were no doubt that it can be met with somewhere in life, a hope that always ends in failure and leads to discontent. An illusory image of some vague future bliss—born of a dream and shaped by fancy—floats before our eyes; and we search for the reality in vain. So it is that the young man is generally dissatisfied with the position in which he finds himself, whatever it may be; he ascribes his disappointment solely to the state of things that meets him on his first introduction to life, when he had expected something very different; whereas it is only the vanity and wretchedness of human life everywhere that he is now for the first time experiencing.

It would be a great advantage to a young man if his early training could eradicate the idea that the world has a great deal to offer him. But the usual result of education is to strengthen this delusion; and our first ideas of life are generally taken from fiction rather than from fact.

In the bright dawn of our youthful days, the poetry of life spreads out a gorgeous vision before us, and we torture ourselves by longing to see it realized. We might as well wish to grasp the rainbow! The youth expects his career to be like an interesting romance; and there lies the germ of that disappointment which I have been describing. What lends a charm to all these visions is just the fact that they are visionary and not real, and that in contemplating them we are in the sphere of pure knowledge, which is sufficient in itself and free from the noise and struggle of life. To try and realize those visions is to make them an object of will—a process which always involves pain.

If the chief feature of the earlier half of life is a never satisfied longing after happiness, the later half is characterized by the dread of misfortune. For, as we advance in years, it becomes in a greater or less degree clear that all happiness is chimerical in its nature, and that pain alone is real.

Accordingly, in later years, we, or, at least the more prudent among us, are more intent upon eliminating what is painful from our lives and making our position secure, than on the pursuit of positive pleasure. I may observe, by the way, that in old age, we are better able to prevent misfortunes from coming, and in youth better able to bear them when they come.

In my young days, I was always pleased to hear a ring at my door: ah! thought I, now for something pleasant. But in later life my feelings on such occasions were rather akin to dismay than to pleasure: heaven help me! thought I, what am I to do? A similar revulsion of feeling in regard to the world of men takes place in all persons of any talent or distinction. For that very reason they cannot be said properly to belong to the world; in a greater or less degree, according to the extent of their superiority, they stand alone. In their youth they have a sense of being abandoned by the world; but later on, they feel as though they had escaped it. The earlier feeling is an unpleasant one, and rests upon ignorance; the second is pleasurable, for in the meantime they have come to know what the world is.

The consequence of this is that, as compared with the earlier, the later half of life, like the second part of a musical period, has less of passionate longing and more restfulness about it. And why is this the case? Simply because, in youth, a man fancies that there is a prodigious amount of happiness and pleasure to be had in the world, only that it is difficult to come by it; whereas, when he becomes old, he knows that there is nothing of the kind; he makes his mind completely at ease on the matter, enjoys the present hour as well as he can, and even takes a pleasure in trifles.

The chief result gained by experience of life is clearness of view. This is what distinguishes the man of mature age, and makes the world wear such a different aspect from that which it presented in his youth or boyhood. It is only then that he sees things quite plain, and takes them for that which they really are: while in earlier years he saw a phantom world, put together out of the whims and crotchets of his own mind, inherited prejudice and strange delusion: the real world was hidden from him, or the vision of it distorted. The first thing that experience finds to do is to free us from the phantoms of the brain—those false notions that have been put into us in youth.

To prevent their entrance to all would, of course, be the best form of education, even though it were only negative in aim: but it would be a task full of difficulty. At first the child's horizon would have to be limited as much as possible, and yet within that limited sphere none but clear and correct notions would have to be given; only after the child had properly appreciated everything within it, might the sphere be gradually enlarged; care being always taken that nothing was left obscure, or half or wrongly understood. The consequence of this training would be that the child's notions of men and things would always be limited and simple in their character; but, on the other hand, they would be clear and correct, and only need to be extended, not to be rectified. The same line might be pursued on into the period of youth. This method of education would lay special stress upon the prohibition of novel reading; and the place of novels would be taken by suitable biographical literature—the life of Franklin, for instance, or Moritz' Anton Reiser.

In our early days we fancy that the leading events in our life, and the persons who are going to play an important part in it, will make their entrance to the sound of drums and trumpets; but when, in old age, we look back, we find that they all came in quite quietly, slipped in, as it were, by the side door, almost unnoticed.

From the point of view we have been taking up until now, life may be compared to a piece of embroidery, of which, during the first half of his time, a man gets a sight of the right side, and during the second half, of the wrong. The wrong side is not so pretty as the

right, but it is more instructive; it shows the way in which the
threads have been worked together.

Intellectual superiority, even if it is of the highest kind, will
not secure for a man a preponderating place in conversation until
after he is forty years of age. For age and experience, though they
can never be a substitute for intellectual talent, may far outweigh
it; and even in a person of the meanest capacity, they give a certain
counterpoise to the power of an extremely intellectual man, so
long as the latter is young. Of course I allude here to personal
superiority, not to the place a man may gain by his works.

And on passing his fortieth year, any man of the slightest
power of mind—any man, that is, who has more than the sorry
share of intellect with which Nature has endowed five-sixths of
mankind—will hardly fail to show some trace of misanthropy.
For, as is natural, he has by that time inferred other people's
character from an examination of his own; with the result that he
has been gradually disappointed to find that in the qualities of the
head or in those of the heart—and usually in both—he reaches a
level to which they do not attain; so he gladly avoids having
anything more to do with them. For it may be said, in general, that
every man will love or hate solitude—in other words, his own
society—just in proportion as he is worth anything to himself.
Kant has some remarks upon this kind of misanthropy in his
Critique of the Faculty of Judgment.

In a young man, it is a bad sign, as well from an intellectual as
from a moral point of view, if he is precocious in understanding the
ways of the world, and in adapting himself to its pursuits; if he at
once knows how to deal with men, and enters upon life, as it were,
fully prepared. It argues a vulgar nature. On the other hand, to be
surprised and astonished at the way people act, and to be clumsy
and cross-grained in having to do with them, indicates a character
of the nobler sort.

The cheerfulness and vivacity of youth are partly due to the
fact that, when we are ascending the hill of life, death is not
visible: it lies down at the bottom of the other side. But once we
have crossed the top of the hill, death comes in view—death,

which, until then, was known to us only by hearsay. This makes our spirits droop, for at the same time we begin to feel that our vital powers are on the ebb. A grave seriousness now takes the place of that early extravagance of spirit; and the change is noticeable even in the expression of a man's face. As long as we are young, people may tell us what they please! We look upon life as endless and use our time recklessly; but the older we become, the more we practice economy. For towards the close of life, every day we live gives us the same kind of sensation as the criminal experiences at every step on his way to be tried.

From the standpoint of youth, life seems to stretch away into an endless future; from the standpoint of old age, to go back but a little way into the past; so that, at the beginning, life presents us with a picture in which the objects appear a great way off, as though we had reversed our telescope; while in the end everything seems so close. To see how short life is, a man must have grown old, that is to say, he must have lived long.

On the other hand, as the years increase, things look smaller, one and all; and Life, which had so firm and stable a base in the days of our youth, now seems nothing but a rapid flight of moments, every one of them illusory: we have come to see that the whole world is vanity!

Time itself seems to go at a much slower pace when we are young; so that not only is the first quarter of life the happiest, it is also the longest of all; it leaves more memories behind it. If a man were put to it, he could tell you more out of the first quarter of his life than out of two of the remaining periods. Nay, in the spring of life, as in the spring of the year, the days reach a length that is positively tiresome; but in the autumn, whether of the year or of life, though they are short, they are more genial and uniform.

But why is it that to an old man his past life appears so short? For this reason: his memory is short; and so he fancies that his life has been short too. He no longer remembers the insignificant parts of it, and much that was unpleasant is now forgotten; how little, then, there is left! For, in general, man's memory is as imperfect as his intellect; and he must make a practice of reflecting upon the lessons he has learned and the events he has experienced, if he does not want them both to sink gradually into the gulf of oblivion. Now, we are unaccustomed to reflect upon matters of no importance, or, as a rule, upon things that we have found disagreeable, and yet that is necessary if the memory of them is to be preserved. But the class of things that may be called insignificant is continually receiving fresh additions: much that wears an air of importance at first, gradually becomes of no consequence at all from the fact of its frequent repetition; so that in the end we actually lose count of the number of times it happens. Hence we are better able to remember the events of our early than of our later years. The longer we live, the fewer are the things that we can call important or significant enough to deserve further consideration, and by this alone can they be fixed in the memory; in other words, they are forgotten as soon as they are past. Thus it is that time runs on, leaving always fewer traces of its passage.

Further, if disagreeable things have happened to us, we do not care to ruminate upon them, least of all when they touch our vanity, as is usually the case; for few misfortunes fall upon us for which we can be held entirely blameless. So people are very ready to forget many things that are disagreeable, as well as many that are unimportant.

It is from this double cause that our memory is so short; and a man's recollection of what has happened always becomes proportionately shorter, the more things that have occupied him in life. The things we did in years gone by, the events that happened long ago, are like those objects on the coast which, to the seafarer on his outward voyage, become smaller every minute, more unrecognizable and harder to distinguish.

Again, it sometimes happens that memory and imagination will call up some long past scene as vividly as if it had occurred only yesterday; so that the event in question seems to stand very near to the present time. The reason of this is that it is impossible to call up all the intervening period in the same vivid way, as there is no one figure pervading it which can be taken in at a glance; and besides, most of the things that happened in that period are forgotten, and all that remains of it is the general knowledge that we have lived through it—a mere notion of abstract existence, not a direct vision of some particular experience. It is this that causes some single event of long ago to appear as though it took place but yesterday: the intervening time vanishes, and the whole of life looks incredibly short. Nay, there are occasional moments in old age when we can scarcely believe that we are so advanced in years, or that the long past lying behind us has had any real existence—a feeling which is mainly due to the circumstance that the present always seems fixed and immovable as we look at it. These and similar mental phenomena are ultimately to be traced to the fact that it is not our nature in itself, but only the outward presentation of it, that lies in time, and that the present is the point of contact between the world as subject and the world as object.

Again, why is it that in youth we can see no end to the years that seem to lie before us? Because we are obliged to find room for all the things we hope to attain in life. We cram the years so full of projects that if we were to try and carry them all out, death would come prematurely though we reached the age of Methuselah.

Another reason why life looks so long when we are young, is that we are apt to measure its length by the few years we have already lived. In those early years things are new to us, and so they appear important; we dwell upon them after they have happened and often call them to mind; and thus in youth life seems replete with incident, and therefore of long duration.

Sometimes we credit ourselves with a longing to be in some distant spot, whereas, in truth, we are only longing to have the time back again which we spent there—days when we were younger and fresher than we are now. In those moments, Time mocks us by wearing the mask of space; and if we travel to the spot, we can see how much we have been deceived.

There are two ways of reaching a great age, both of which presuppose a sound constitution as a *conditio sine quâ non*. They may be illustrated by two lamps, one of which burns a long time with very little oil, because it has a very thin wick; and the other just as long, though it has a very thick one, because there is plenty of oil to feed it. Here, the oil is the vital energy, and the difference in the wick is the manifold way in which the vital energy is used.

Up to our thirty-sixth year, we may be compared, in respect of the way in which we use our vital energy, to people who live on the interest of their money: what they spend today, they have again tomorrow. But from the age of thirty-six onwards, our position is like that of the investor who begins to entrench upon his capital. At first he hardly notices any difference at all, as the greater part of his expenses is covered by the interest of his securities; and if the deficit is but slight, he pays no attention to it. But the deficit goes on increasing, until he awakes to the fact that it is becoming more serious every day: his position becomes less and less secure, and he feels himself growing poorer and poorer, while he has no expectation of this drain upon his resources coming to an end. His fall from wealth to poverty becomes faster every moment—like the fall of a solid body in space, until at last he has absolutely nothing left. A man is truly in a woeful plight if both the terms of this comparison—his vital energy and his wealth—really begin to melt away at one and the same time. It is the dread of this calamity that makes love of possession increase with age.

On the other hand, at the beginning of life, in the years before we attain majority, and for some little time afterwards—the state of our vital energy puts us on a level with those who each year lay by a part of their interest and add it to their capital: in other words, not only does their interest come in regularly, but the capital is constantly receiving additions. This happy condition of affairs is sometimes brought about—with health as with money—under the watchful care of some honest guardian. O happy youth, as sad old age!

Nevertheless, a man should economize his strength even when he is young. Aristotle observes that among those who were victors at Olympia only two or three gained a prize at two different periods, once in boyhood and then again when they came to be men; and the reason of this was that the premature efforts which the training involved, so completely exhausted their powers that they failed to last on into manhood. As this is true of muscular, so it is

still more true of nervous energy, of which all intellectual achievements are the manifestation. Hence, those infant prodigies *ingenia
praecocia,* the fruit of a hot-house education, who surprise us by
their cleverness as children, afterwards turn out very ordinary folk.
Nay, the manner in which boys are forced into an early acquaintance with the ancient tongues may, perhaps, be to blame for the
dullness and lack of judgment which distinguish so many learned
persons.

I have said that almost every man's character seems to be
specially suited to some one period of life, so that on reaching it the
man is at his best. Some people are charming so long as they are
young, and afterwards there is nothing attractive about them;
others are vigorous and active in manhood, and then lose all the
value they possess as they advance in years; many appear to best
advantage in old age, when their character assumes a gentler tone,
as becomes men who have seen the world and take life easily. This
is often the case with the French.

This peculiarity must be due to the fact that the man's character has something in it akin to the qualities of youth or manhood or
old age—something which accords with one or another of these
periods of life, or perhaps acts as a corrective to its special failings.

The mariner observes the progress he makes only by the way
in which objects on the coast fade away into the distance and
apparently decrease in size. In the same way, a man becomes
conscious that he is advancing in years when he finds that people
older than himself begin to seem young to him.

It has already been remarked that the older a man becomes,
the fewer are the traces left in his mind by all that he sees, does or
experiences, and the cause of this has been explained. There is thus
a sense in which it may be said that it is only in youth that a man
lives with a full degree of consciousness, and that he is only half
alive when he is old. As the years advance, his consciousness of
what goes on about him dwindles, and the things of life hurry by
without making any impression upon him, just as none is made by
a work of art seen for the thousandth time. A man does what his
hand finds to do, and afterwards he does not know whether he has
done it or not.

As life becomes more and more unconscious, the nearer it approaches the point at which all consciousness ceases, the course of time itself seems to increase in rapidity. In childhood all the things and circumstances of life are novel; and that is sufficient to awake us to the full consciousness of existence: hence, at that age, the day seems of such immense length. The same thing happens when we are traveling: one month seems longer than four spent at home. Still, though time seems to last longer when we are young or on a journey, the sense of novelty does not prevent it from now and then in reality hanging heavily upon our hands under both these circumstances, at any rate more than is the case when we are old or staying at home. But the intellect gradually becomes so rubbed down and blunted by long habituation to such impressions that things have a constant tendency to produce less and less impression upon us as they pass by; and this makes time seem increasingly less important, and therefore shorter in duration: the hours of the boy are longer than the days of the old man. Accordingly, time goes faster and faster the longer we live, like a ball rolling down a hill. Or, to take another example: as in a revolving disc, the further a point lies from the center, the more rapid is its rate of progression, so it is in the wheel of life; the further you stand from the beginning, the faster time moves for you. Hence it may be said that as far as concerns the immediate sensation that time makes upon our minds, the length of any given year is in direct proportion to the number of times it will divide our whole life: for instance, at the age of fifty the year appears to us only one-tenth as long as it did at the age of five.

This variation in the rate at which time appears to move, exercises a most decided influence upon the whole nature of our existence at every period of it. First of all, it causes childhood— even though it embraces only a span of fifteen years—to seem the longest period of life, and therefore the richest in reminiscences. Next, it brings it about that a man is apt to be bored just in proportion as he is young. Consider, for instance, that constant need of occupation—whether it is work or play—that is shown by children; if they come to an end of both work and play, a terrible feeling of boredom ensues. Even in youth people are by no means free from this tendency, and dread the hours when they have nothing to do. As manhood approaches, boredom disappears; and old men find the time too short when their days fly past them like arrows from a bow. Of course, I must be understood to speak of men, not of decrepit brutes. With this increased rapidity of time, boredom mostly passes away as we advance in life; and as the passions with all their attendant pain are then laid asleep, the burden of life is, on the whole, appreciably lighter in later years than in youth, provided, of course, that health remains. So it is that period immediately preceding the weakness and troubles of old age, receives the name of man's best years.

That may be a true appellation, in view of the comfortable feeling which those years bring; but for all that the years of youth, when our consciousness is lively and open to every sort of impression, have this privilege—that then the seeds are sown and the buds come forth; it is the springtime of the mind. Deep truths may be perceived, but can never be excogitated—that is to say, the first knowledge of them is immediate, called forth by some momentary impression. This knowledge is of such a kind as to be attainable only when the impressions are strong, lively, and deep; and if we are to be acquainted with deep truths, everything depends upon a proper use of our early years. In later life, we may be better able to work upon other people—upon the world, because our natures are then finished and rounded off, and no more a prey to fresh views; but then the world is less able to work upon us. These are the years of action and achievement; while youth is the time for forming fundamental conceptions, and laying down the groundwork of thought.

In youth it is the outward aspect of things that most engages us; while in age, thought or reflection is the predominating quality of the mind. Hence, youth is the time for poetry, and age is more inclined to philosophy. In practical affairs it is the same: a man shapes his resolutions in youth more by the impression that the outward world makes upon him; whereas, when he is old, it is thought that determines his actions. This is partly to be explained by the results of outward observation are present in sufficient numbers to allow of their being classified according to the ideas they represent—a process which in its turn causes those ideas to be more fully understood in all their bearings, and the exact value and amount of trust to be placed in them, fixed and determined; while at the same time he has grown accustomed to the impressions produced by the various phenomena of life, and their effects on him are no longer what they were.

Contrarily, in youth, the impressions that things make, that is to say, the outward aspects of life, are so overpoweringly strong, especially in the case of people of lively and imaginative disposition, that they view the world like a picture; and their chief concern is the figure they cut in it, the appearance they present; nay, they are unaware of the extent to which this is the case. It is a quality of mind that shows itself—if in no other way—in that personal vanity, and that love of fine clothes, which distinguish young people.

There can be no doubt that the intellectual powers are most capable of enduring great and sustained efforts in youth, up to the age of thirty-five at latest; from which period their strength begins to decline, though very gradually. Still, the later years of life, and even old age itself, are not without their intellectual compensation. It is only then that a man can be said to be really rich in experience or in learning; he has been able to compare one thing with another, and to discover points of contact and connecting links, so that only then are the true relations of things rightly understood. Further, in old age there comes an increased depth in the knowledge that was acquired in youth; a man has now many more illustrations of any ideas he may have attained; things which he thought he knew when he was young, he now knows in reality. And besides, his range of knowledge is wider; and in whatever direction it extends, it is thorough, and therefore formed into a consistent and connected whole; whereas in youth, knowledge is always defective and fragmentary.

A complete and adequate notion of life can never be attained by anyone who does not reach old age; for it is only the old man who sees life whole and knows its natural course; it is only he who is acquainted—and this is most important—not only with its entrance, like the rest of mankind, but with its exit too; so that he alone has a full sense of its utter vanity; whilst the others never cease to labor under the false notion that everything will come right in the end.

On the other hand, there is more conceptive power in youth, and at that time of life a man can make more out of the little that he knows. In age, judgment, penetration, and thoroughness predominate. Youth is the time for amassing the material for a knowledge of the world that shall be distinctive and peculiar—for an original view of life, in other words, the legacy that a man of genius leaves to his fellow men; it is, however, only in later years that he becomes master of his material. Accordingly, it will be found that, as a rule, a great writer gives his best work to the world when he is about fifty years of age. But though the tree of knowledge must reach its full height before it can bear fruit, the roots of it lie in youth.

Every generation, no matter how paltry its character, thinks itself much wiser than the one immediately preceding it, let alone those that are more remote. It is just the same with the different periods in a man's life; and yet often, in the one case no less than in the other, it is a mistaken opinion. In the years of physical growth, when our powers of mind and our stores of knowledge are receiving daily additions, it becomes a habit for today to look down with contempt upon yesterday. The habit strikes root, and remains even after the intellectual powers have begun to decline—when today should rather look up with respect to yesterday. So it is that we often unduly depreciate the achievements as well as the judgments of our youth.

This seems the place for making the general observation, that, although in its main qualities a man's *intellect* or *head*, as well as his *character* or *heart*, is innate, yet the former is by no means so unalterable in its nature as the latter. The fact is that the intellect is subject to very many transformations, which, as a rule, do not fail to make their actual appearance; and this is so, partly because the intellect has a deep foundation in the physique, and partly because the material with which it deals is given in experience. And so, from a physical point of view, we find that if a man has any peculiar power, it first gradually increases in strength until it reaches its acme, after which it enters upon a path of slow decadence, until it ends in imbecility. But, on the other hand, we must not lose sight of the fact that the material which gives employment to a man's powers and keeps them in activity—the subject matter of thought and knowledge, experience, intellectual attainments, the practice of seeing to the bottom of things, and so a perfect mental vision, form in themselves a mass which continues to increase in size, until the time comes when weakness shows itself, and the man's powers suddenly fail. The way in which these two distinguishable elements combine in the same nature—the one absolutely unalterable, and the other subject to change in two directions opposed to each other—explains the variety of mental attitude and the dissimilarity of value which attach to a man at different periods of life.

The same truth may be more broadly expressed by saying that the first forty years of life furnish the text, while the remaining thirty supply the commentary; and that without the commentary we are unable to understand aright the true sense and coherence of the text, together with the moral it contains and all the subtle application of which it admits.

Towards the close of life, much the same thing happens as at the end of a *bal masque*—the masks are taken off. Then you can see who the people really are, with whom you have come into contact in your passage through the world. For by the end of life, characters have come out in their true light, actions have borne fruit, achievements have been rightly appreciated, and all shams have fallen to pieces. For this, Time was in every case requisite.

But the most curious fact is that it is also only towards the close of life when a man really recognizes and understands his own true self—the aims and objects he has followed in life, more especially the kind of relation in which he has stood to other people and to the world. It will often happen that as a result of this knowledge, a man will have to assign himself a lower place than he formerly thought was his due. But there are exceptions to this rule; and it will occasionally be the case that he will take a higher position than he had before. This will be owing to the fact that he had no adequate notion of the *baseness* of the world, and that he set up a higher aim for himself than was followed by the rest of mankind.

The progress of life shows a man the stuff of which he is made.

It is customary to call youth the happy, and age the sad part of life. This would be true if it were the passions that made a man happy. Youth is swayed to and fro by them; and they give a great deal of pain and little pleasure. In age, the passions cool and leave a man at rest, and then forthwith his mind takes a contemplative tone, the intellect is set free and attains the upper hand. And since, in itself, intellect is beyond the range of pain, and man feels happy just in so far as his intellect is the predominating part of him.

It need only be remembered that all pleasure is negative, and that pain is positive in its nature, in order to see that the passions can never be a source of happiness, and that age is not the less to be envied on the ground that many pleasures are denied it. For every sort of pleasure is never anything more than the quietive of some need or longing; and that pleasure should come to an end as soon as the need ceases, is no more a subject of complaint than that a man cannot go on eating after he has had his dinner, or fall asleep again after a good night's rest.

So far from youth being the happiest period of life, there is much more truth in the remark made by Plato, at the beginning of the *Republic,* that the prize should rather be given to old age, because then at last a man is freed from the animal passion which has hitherto never ceased to disquiet him. Nay, it may even be said that the countless and manifold humors which have their source in this passion, and the emotions that spring from it, produce a mild state of madness; and this lasts as long as the man is subject to the spell of the impulse—this evil spirit, as it were, of which there is no riddance—so that he never really becomes a reasonable being until the passion is extinguished.

There is no doubt that, in general, and apart from individual circumstances and particular dispositions, youth is marked by a certain melancholy and sadness, while genial sentiments attach to old age; and the reason for this is nothing but the fact that the young man is still under the service, nay, the forced labor, imposed by that evil spirit, which scarcely ever leaves him a moment to himself. To this source may be traced, directly or indirectly, almost all and every ill that befalls or menaces mankind. The old man is genial and cheerful because, after long lying in the bonds of passion, he can now move about in freedom.

Still, it should not be forgotten that, when this passion is extinguished, the true kernel of life is gone, and nothing remains but the hollow shell; or, from another point of view, life then becomes like a comedy, which, begun by real actors, is continued and brought to an end by automata dressed in their clothes.

However that may be, youth is the period of unrest, and age of repose; and from that very circumstance, the relative degree of pleasure belonging to each may be inferred. The child stretches out its little hands in the eager desire to seize all the pretty things that meet its sight, charmed by the world because all its senses are still so young and fresh. Much the same thing happens with the youth, and he displays greater energy in his quest. He, too, is charmed by all the pretty things and the many pleasing shapes that surround him; and forthwith his imagination conjures up pleasures which the world can never realize. So he is filled with an ardent desire for he knows not what delights—robbing him of all rest and making happiness impossible. But when old age is reached, all this is over and done with, partly because the blood runs cooler and the senses are no longer so easily allured; partly because experience has shown the true value of things and the futility of pleasure, whereby illusion has been gradually dispelled, and the strange fancies and prejudices which previously concealed or distorted a free and true view of the world, have been dissipated and put to flight; with the result that a man can now get a juster and clearer view, and see things as they are, and also in a measure attain more or less insight into the nullity of all things on this earth.

It is this that gives almost every old man, no matter how ordinary his faculties may be, a certain tincture of wisdom, which distinguishes him from the young. But the chief result of all this change is the peace of mind that ensues—a great element in happiness, and, in fact, the condition and essence of it. While the young man fancies that there is a vast amount of good things in the world, if he could only come to them, the old man is steeped in the truth of the Preacher's words, that *all things are vanity*—knowing that, however gilded the shell, the nut is hollow.

In these later years, and not before, a man comes to a true appreciation of Horace's maxim: *Nil admirari*. He is directly and sincerely convinced of the vanity of everything and that all the glories of the world are as nothing: his illusions are gone. He is no more beset with the idea that there is any particular amount of happiness anywhere, in the palace or in the cottage, any more than he himself enjoys when he is free from bodily or mental pain. The worldly distinctions of great and small, high and low, exist for him no longer; and in this blissful state of mind the old man may look down with a smile upon all false notions. He is completely undeceived, and knows that whatever may be done to adorn human life and deck it out in finery, its paltry character will soon show through the glitter of its surroundings; and that, paint and bejewel it as one may, it remains everywhere much the same—an existence which has no true value except in freedom from pain, and is never to be estimated by the presence of pleasure, let alone, then, of display.

Disillusion is the chief characteristic of old age; for by that time the fictions are gone which gave life its charm and spurred on the mind to activity; the splendors of the world have been proved null and vain; its pomp, grandeur, and magnificence are faded. A man has then found out that behind most of the things he wants, and most of the pleasures he longs for, there is very little after all; and so he comes by degrees to see that our existence is all empty and void. It is only when he is seventy years old that he quite understands the first words of the Preacher; and this again explains why it is that old men are sometimes fretful and morose.

It is often said that the common lot of old age is disease and weariness of life. Disease is by no means essential to old age; especially where a really long span of years is to be attained; for as life goes on, the conditions of health and disorder tend to increase—*crescente vita, crescit sanitas et morbus*. And as far as weariness or boredom is concerned, I have stated above why old age is even less exposed to that form of evil than youth. Nor is boredom by any means to be taken as a necessary accompaniment of that solitude, which, for reasons that do not require to be explained, old age certainly cannot escape; it is rather the fate that awaits those who have never known any other pleasures but the gratification of the senses and the delights of society—who have left their minds unenlightened and their faculties unused. It is quite true that the intellectual faculties decline with the approach of old age; but where they were originally strong, there will always be enough left to combat the onslaught of boredom. And then again, as I have said, experience, knowledge, reflection, and skill in dealing with men, combine to give an old man an increasingly accurate insight into the ways of the world; his judgment becomes keen and he attains a coherent view of life: his mental vision embraces a wider range. Constantly finding new uses for his stores of knowledge and adding to them at every opportunity, he maintains uninterrupted that inward process of self-education, which gives employment and satisfaction to the mind, and thus forms the due reward of all its efforts.

All this serves in some measure as a compensation for decreased intellectual power. And besides, Time, as I have remarked, seems to go much more quickly when we are advanced in years; and this is in itself a preventive of boredom. There is no great harm in the fact that a man's bodily strength decreases in old age, unless, indeed, he requires it to make a living. To be poor when one is old, is a great misfortune. If a man is secure from that, and retains his health, old age may be a very passable time of life. Its chief necessity is to be comfortable and well off; and, in consequence, money is then prized more than ever, because it is a substitute for failing strength. Deserted by Venus, the old man likes to turn to Bacchus to make him merry. In the place of wanting to see things, to travel and learn, comes the desire to speak and teach. It is a piece of good fortune if the old man retains some of his love of study or of music or of the theater—if, in general, he is still somewhat susceptible to the things about him; as is, indeed, the case with some people to a very late age. At that time of life *what a man has in himself* is of greater advantage to him than ever it was before. . . .

Chapter 14

THE LIFE REVIEW: AN INTERPRETATION OF REMINISCENCE IN THE AGED

Robert N. Butler

This paper postulates the universal occurrence in older people of an inner experience or mental process of reviewing one's life. I propose that this process helps account for the increased reminiscence in the aged, that it contributes to the occurrence of certain late-life disorders, particularly depression, and that it participates in the evolution of such characteristics as candor, serenity, and wisdom among certain of the aged.

Allusions to a life-reviewing process are common in the literature of various historical periods:

> They live by memory rather than by hope, for what is left to them of life is but little compared to the long past. This, again, is the cause of their loquacity. They are continually talking of the past,

From Robert N. Butler, "The Life Review: An Interpretation of Reminiscence in the Aged," *Psychiatry, Journal for the Study of Interpersonal Processes,* Vol. 26 (1963). Copyright 1963 by The William Alanson White Psychiatric Found., Inc. Reprinted with special permission.

because they enjoy remembering.—Aristotle, *Rhetoric* [367–347 B.C.].[1]

Mem'ry's pointing hand, that calls the past to our exact review.—Cowper, *Task* [1784].[2]

What makes old age hard to bear is not a failing of one's faculties, mental and physical, but the burden of one's memories.—Maugham, *Points of View* [1959].[3]

Intimations of the existence of a life review in the aged are also found in psychiatric writings—notably in the emphasis upon reminiscence—and the nature, sources, and manifestations of the life review have been studied in the course of intensive psychotherapeutic relationships.[4] But often the older person is experienced as garrulous and "living in the past," and the content and significance of his reminiscence are lost or devalued. Younger therapists especially, working with the elderly, find great difficulties in listening.[5]

The prevailing tendency is to identify reminiscence in the aged with psychological dysfunction and thus to regard it essentially as a symptom. One source of this distorted view is the emphasis in available literature on the occurrence of reminiscence in the mentally disordered and institutionalized aged. Of course, many of the prevailing ideas and "findings" concerning the aged and aging primarily stem from the study of such samples of elderly people. Since the adequately functioning community-resident aged have only recently been systematically studied[6] and intensive study of the mentally disturbed aged through psychotherapy has been comparatively rare,[7] these important sources for data and theory have not yet contributed much to an understanding of the amount, prevalence, content, function, and significance of reminiscence in the aged.

Furthermore, definitions and descriptions of reminiscence—the act or process of recalling the past[8]—indicate discrepant interpretations of its nature and function. Reminiscence is seen by some investigators as occurring beyond the older person's control: It happens to him; it is spontaneous, nonpurposive, unselective, and unbidden. Others view reminiscence as volitional and pleasurable, but hint that it provides escapism. Thus, purposive reminiscence is interpreted only as helping the person to fill the void of his later life. Reminiscence is also considered to obscure the older person's awareness of the realities of the present. It is considered of dubious reliability, although, curiously, "remote memory" is held to be "preserved" longer than "recent memory." In consequence, reminiscence becomes a pejorative, suggesting preoccupation, musing, aimless wandering of the mind. In a word, reminiscence is fatuous. Occasionally, the constructive and creative aspects of reminiscence are valued and affirmed in the autobiographical accounts of famous men,[9] but it must be concluded that the more usual view of reminiscence is a negative one.

In contrast, I conceive of the life review as a naturally occurring, universal mental process characterized by the progressive return to consciousness of past experiences, and, particularly, the resurgence of unresolved conflicts; simultaneously, and normally, these revived experiences and conflicts can be surveyed and reintegrated. Presumably, this process is prompted by the realization of approaching dissolution and death, and the inability to maintain one's sense of personal invulnerability. It is further shaped by contemporaneous experiences and its nature and outcome are affected by the life-long unfolding of character.

THE SIGNIFICANCE OF DEATH

The life review mechanism, as a possible response to the biological and phychological fact of death, may play a significant role in the psychology and psychopathology of the aged.

The following dream, related by a 70-year-old man, illustrates the awareness of approaching death:

> I dreamt that I had died and my soul was going up and when I did reach the top I saw a great, huge statue—or living man—sitting there, and then a second man came over to me and asked, "What do you want?" I answered, "I want to get in here." So the big man said,

"Let him in." But then the second man asked, "What did you do in the other world?" I told him a great deal about myself and was asked, "What else?" I told of an occasion in which I helped an old lady. "That's not enough. Take him away." It was God judging me. I was very afraid and woke up.

The interrelationship of awareness of impending death and recall of past inadequacies is shown in the following case history.

A 70-year-old retired and widowed mother came from another city to visit her son and showed no inclination to return home. Six months later, the son, anxious about his depressed, irritable mother, brought her to me. She reluctantly accepted a psychotherapeutic relationship: Frightened and guarded, overly suspicious, she continually described her worthlessness; she considered herself so unworthy that she was not able to attend church. I had two impressions—that she was wrestling with guilt concerning past wrongs, acts both committed and avoided, and that she was afraid of death and judgment.

In one interview, she suddenly appeared to confirm these impressions, which up to then had not been presented to her. She asked about privileged communication—that is, whether I would testify in a court of law against her if she were indicted for her past misdeeds, an unlikely event. Later in the hour she said, "I am worried about my granddaughter—that something does not happen to her." She did not explain but added, "I wonder if she will be able to face her final examinations and graduation day." [Since her granddaughter is an excellent student, she had little reason to worry.] Still later in the hour she said, "My doctor referred to these black spots on my head as God's subpoenas." [She was referring to brown, not black, senile freckles on her scalp.] She went on to explain that she had been having difficulties getting her hair done properly and perhaps this was because she was contagious.

The significance of death is often inappropriately minimized by psychiatric writers, reflecting the universal tendency to deny its reality; it is also sidestepped by some writers through the use of such psychoanalytic constructs as castration anxiety, which has been held to be the basic fear. Fear of death is often conceptualized as merely manifest and not authentic.[10]

The relation of the life-review process to thoughts of death is reflected in the fact that it occurs not only in the elderly but also in younger persons who expect death—for example, the fatally ill[11] or the condemned. It may also be seen in the introspection of those preoccupied by death, and it is commonly held that one's life passes in review in the process of dying. One thinks of the matador's "moment of truth" during the *faena*. The life review, Janus-like, involves facing death as well as looking back. Lot's wife, in the Bible, and Orpheus, in Greek mythology, embodied an association of the ideas of looking death in the face and looking back.

But the life review is more commonly observed in the aged because of the actual nearness of life's termination, and perhaps also because during retirement not only is time available for self-reflection, but also the customary defensive operation provided by work has been removed.

In extreme cases, severe consequences of the life review seem to be quantitatively related to the extent of actual or psychological isolation. The writings of Cannon, Richter, Adland, Will, and others,[12] suggest a relationship between isolation, or loneliness, and death. "The feeling of unrelatedness is incompatible with life in the human being," writes Will.[13]

Reviewing one's life, then, may be a general response to crises of various types, of which imminent death seems to be one instance. It is also likely that the degree to which approaching death is seen as a crisis varies as a function of individual personality. The explicit hypothesis intended here, however, is that the biological fact of approaching death, independent of—although possibly reinforced by—personal and environmental circumstances prompts the life review.

MANIFESTATIONS OF THE LIFE REVIEW

The life review, as a looking-back process that has been set in motion by looking forward to death, potentially proceeds toward personality reorganization. Thus, the life review is not synonymous with, but includes reminiscence; it is not alone either the unbidden return of memories, or the purposive seeking of them, although both may occur.

The life review sometimes proceeds silently, without obvious manifestations. Many elderly persons, before inquiry, may be only vaguely aware of the experience as a function of their defensive structure. But alterations in defensive operations do occur. Speaking broadly, the more intense the unresolved life conflicts, the more work remains to be accomplished toward reintegration. Although the process is active, not static, the content of one's life usually unfolds slowly;[14] the process may not be completed prior to death. In its mild form, the life review is reflected in increased reminiscence, mild nostalgia, mild regret; in severe form, in anxiety, guilt, despair, and depression. In the extreme, it may involve the obsessive preoccupation of the older person with his past, and may proceed to a state approximating terror and result in suicide. Thus, although I consider it to be a universal and normative process, its varied manifestations and outcomes may include psychopathological ones.

The life review may be first observed in stray and seemingly insignificant thoughts about oneself and one's life history. These thoughts may continue to emerge in brief intermittent spurts or become essentially continuous, and they may undergo constant reintegration and reorganization at various levels of awareness. A 76-year-old man said:

> My life is in the background of my mind much of the time; it cannot be any other way. Thoughts of the past play upon me; sometimes I play with them, encourage and savor them; at other times I dismiss them.

Other clues to its existence include dreams and thoughts. The dreams and nightmares of the aged, which are frequently reported,[15] appear to principally concern the past and death. Imagery of past events and symbols of death seem frequent in waking life as well as dreams, suggesting that the life review is a highly visual process.[16]

Another manifestation of the life review seems to be the curious but apparently common phenomenon of mirror-gazing, illustrated by the following:

> I was passing by my mirror. I noticed how old I was. My appearance, well, it prompted me to think of death—and of my past—what I hadn't done, and what I had done wrong.

One hospitalized 80-year-old woman, whose husband had died five years before her admission, had been discovered by her family berating her mirror image for her past deeds and shaking her fist at herself. She was preoccupied by past deeds and omissions in her personal relationships, as evidenced by this excerpt from nursing notes:

> Patient in depths of gloom this morning—looking too unhappy for anything. Patient looked angry. I asked her with whom. She replied, "Myself." I asked, "What have you done that merits so much self-anger so much of the time?" She replied, "Haven't you ever looked yourself over?" In the course of conversation I suggested she might be too harsh with herself. At this she gave a bitter laugh and stuck out her chin again.

Later in her hospitalization she purposely avoided mirrors.

Another patient, 86 years old and periodically confused, often stood before the mirror in his hospital room and rhythmically chanted either happily or angrily. He was especially given to angry flare-ups and crying spells over food, money, and clothes. When angry he would screech obscenities at his mirror image, so savagely beating his fist upon a nearby table that the staff tried to protect him by covering the mirror. But in contrast to the first patient he denied that the image was himself, and when an observer came up beside him and said, "See, this is me in the mirror and there you are in the mirror," he smiled and said, "That's you in the mirror all right, but that's not me."

Adaptive and Constructive Manifestations

As the past marches in review, it is surveyed, observed, and reflected upon by the ego. Reconsideration of previous experiences and their meanings occurs, often with concomitant revised or expanded understanding. Such reorganization of past experience may provide a more valid picture, giving new and significant meanings to one's life; it may also prepare one for death, mitigating one's fears.[17]

. The occasions on which the life review has obviously been creative, having positive, constructive effects, are most impressive. For example:

> A 78-year-old man, optimistic, reflective, and resourceful, who had had significantly impairing egocentric tendencies, became increasingly responsive in his relationships to his wife, children, and grandchildren. These changes corresponded with his purchase of a tape recorder. Upon my request he sent me the tapes he had made, and wrote: "There is the first reel of tape on which I recorded my memory of my life story. To give this some additional interest I am expecting that my children and grandchildren and great-grandchildren will listen to it after I am gone. I pretended that I was telling the story directly to them."

Ingmar Bergman's very fine, remarkable Swedish motion picture, *Wild Strawberries,* provides a beautiful example of the constructive aspects of the life review. Envisioning and dreaming of his past and his death, the protagionist-physician realizes the nonaffectionate and withholding qualities of his life; as the feeling of love reenteres his life, the doctor changes even as death hovers upon him.

Although it is not possible at present to describe in detail either the life review or the possibilities for reintegration that are suggested, it seems likely that in the majority of the elderly a substantial reorganization of the personality does occur. This may help to account for the evolution of such qualities as wisdom and serenity, long noted in some of the aged. Although a favorable, constructive, and positive end result may be enhanced by favorable environmental circumstances, such as comparative freedom from crises and losses, it is more likely that successful reorganization is largely a function of the personality—in particular, such vaguely defined features of the personality as flexibility, resilience, and self-awareness.

In addition to the more impressive constructive aspects of the life review, certain adaptive and defensive aspects may be noted. Some of the aged have illusions of the "good past"; some fantasy the past rather than the future in the service of avoiding the realities of the present; some maintain a characteristic detachment from others and themselves. Although these mechanisms are not constructive, they do assist in maintaining a status quo of psychological functioning.

Psychopathological Manifestations

As indicated earlier, the many and varied behavioral and affective states resulting from the life review can include severe depressions, states of panic, intense guilt, and constant obsessional rumination; instead of increasing self-awareness and flexibility, one may find increasing rigidity. The more severe affective and behavioral consequences apparently tend to occur when the process proceeds in isolation in those who have been deeply affected by increasing contraction of life attachments and notable psychosocial discontinuities, such as forced retirement and the death of the spouse. But, again, while environmental circumstances are important, it is in character and its life-long unfolding that the unfortunate manifestations of the life review mainly originate.

In a recent series of articles on the aged appearing in a national magazine, a 70-year-old woman in a mental hospital is quoted, "Some nights when I can't sleep, I think of the difference between what I'd hoped for when I was young and what I have now and what I am."[18] The most tragic situation is that of the person whose increasing—but only partial—insight leads to a sense of total waste: the horrible insight just as one is about to die of feeling that one has never lived, or of seeing oneself realistically as in some sense inadequate.[19]

Because the affective consequences are not all readily attributable to definitive losses, the painful accompaniments of the life review are often hard for the observer to understand. It is often extremely difficult for the reviewer to communicate his insights because of their unacceptability to him. When he can communicate them, it is also extremely difficult for the observer to comprehend and face them. The more tragic manifestations are the most difficult—at times impossible—to treat. I believe that this situation is one contribution to the increased suicide rate found in old age.[20]

One group of persons who seem to be especially prone to anxiety, despair, depression, or the extreme kind of total catastrophe outlined above, consists of those who always tended to avoid the present and to put great emphasis on the future. These people made heavy investments in and commitments to the future: The future would bring what they struggled to achieve, and it would be free of that which they dislike but have tolerated in the present. This places a considerable strain upon old age, which cannot often deliver; the wishes cannot be met. The poet Adah I. Menken clearly stated this idea in the line, "Where is the promise of my years, once written on my brow?"[21]

Another group that appears to be especially prone to some of the more severe manifestations and outcomes of the life review consists of those who have consciously exercised the human capacity to injure others. These people, in whom guilt is real, can see no way of reversing the process; they do not imagine forgiveness and redemption. Still another group that appears especially vulnerable to the consequences of the life review may be best described as characterologically arrogant and prideful. This group may overlap with the previous group, but not all its members necessarily have undertaken directly hurtful actions. Their narcissism is probably particularly disturbed by the realization of death.

The following case illustration concerns a person whose life and personality probably involves a merger of all of the factors predisposing one toward psychopathological complications resulting from the life review.[22]

Mrs. G, a 69-year-old married woman, developed a depression six months prior to hospitalization; her depression had been unsuccessfully treated by electroshock, tranquilizers, and heeded recommendations that she take vacations and move to a new environment. She was agitated, suspicious, delusional, nihilistic ("This is the end of the world"), self-derogatory, and self-accusatory, and revealed suicidal ideas. She was embittered and hostile, particularly toward her husband, with whom she was often combative. She was preoccupied with thoughts of death. She had lived for nearly 20 years across the street from a hospital morgue; her physician had sensed this to be disturbing to her and had therefore recommended moving, which she did. She refused psychological testing, explaining, "Why should I be uncomfortable during the little time remaining?" She had a fear of cancer, and once stated, "You can see your funeral go by but still not believe it." She viewed her situation as futile and increasingly refused to talk in any detail about herself to others, including members of her family.

She was in good physical health although she showed increasing preoccupation with her gastrointestinal tract. Upon admission, symptoms suggesting the possibility of a malignancy required investigation. The examinations were all negative, but the patient became increasingly "fixated" upon her lower bowel.

There was no evidence of organic mental changes, including confusion. She became essentially mute several weeks after her admission; she refused to recognize her psychotherapist as a therapist and refused to cooperate with nursing personnel or the ward administrator. She felt no one "could understand." She assaulted others and herself; she would smash her fist at her head and body until she was a frightful sight to behold, with extensive eccymoses and hematomas all over her body. She refused to eat or drink and continued to lose weight; she rarely slept, day or night. Upon the firm insistence of the administrator that she would be sedated and fed intravenously or by tube, she responded by maintaining a minimum intake of food and fluid. Occasional sedation interrupted her sleeplessness. Otherwise, she did not materially change at that time, and continued to be assaultive toward family members and staff, and to be self-abusive. Because of her years and the remarkable amount of self-destructiveness, she created considerable anxiety and despair in the staff, which eventually was reflected in terms of considerable anger and rage at her. It was exceedingly difficult to break through this kind of bind. Her threat of suicide made the situation for the professional staff even more difficult. During the course of a year, however, she improved to the extent that she was no longer as self-punitive or assaultive.

On one occasion she communicated to the Director of Psychotherapy her concern with "God's wrath" and at various times gave intimations of her severe and intense sense of guilt about both past actions and past omissions. Her wish to kill herself seemed quite clear in both direct and indirect statements.

Her past history strongly suggested that she had never realized her potentialities as a person and had never achieved an individual sense of identity. Her premorbid personality was characterized by dependency, indecisiveness, self-centeredness, stubbornness, and a lack of generosity, despite the fact that she had stayed home to care for her mother and father after the other siblings had married. An attractive woman, she did not marry until a year and half after her mother's death, when she was 47; her husband was then 60. Behind a dignified and passive façade lay a formidable character. She was the quiet but potent center of opposing family forces; her gift was the masterly regulation of these forces. Moreover, she had become increasingly isolated in the three years prior to admission.

In addition to whatever irrational and unconscious feelings of guilt the patient may have experienced, it appeared quite clear that she had in fact done or omitted to do things that justified her sense of guilt. From indirect intimations and direct communications, it became apparent that she was engaged in a process of reviewing her past life but that despite the presence of professional people she was unwilling to review her life with them.

Her therapist concluded that "all of these changes, especially the more restricted life, might have brought on an opportunity for the patient to inquire about herself; that is, to do some introspective thinking. Such introspection might have led to some thoughts about the uncertainty of her future, as well as some unpleasant traits of her personality, and it is this kind of inquiry that might have led to her depression."

The terrifying nature of some of the insights accompanying aging can also be seen in the following illustration from James's *The Beast in the Jungle*.[23] In it James delineated the nature of the "beast" of insight, and of detached, egotistic, intellectualizing John Marcher, upon whom the beast descended. In this profoundly disturbing creation, Marcher's illumination grows to the point of "gazing at [what] was the sounded void of his life," and "leaving him stupefied at the blindness he had cherished."[24]

John Marcher had earlier been reminded by his friend, Mary Bartram:

> You said you had had from your earliest time, as the deepest thing within you, the sense of being kept for something rare and strange, possibly prodigious and terrible, that was sooner or later to happen to you.

She theorized,

> Isn't what you describe perhaps but the expectation—or at any rate the sense of danger, familiar to so many people—of falling in love?[25]

As the story progressed, and life passed by,

> He felt in these days what, oddly enough, he had never felt before, the growth of a dread of losing her by some catastrophe—some catastrophe that yet wouldn't at all be *the* catastrophe.[26]

They aged:

> He had been struck one day, after an absence exceeding his usual measure, with her suddenly looking much older to him than he had ever thought of her being; then he recognized that the suddenness was all on his side—he had just simply and suddenly noticed. She looked older because inevitably, after so many years, she *was* old, or almost; which was of course true in still greater measure for her companion.
>
> His surprises began here; when once they had begun they multiplied; they came rather with a rush. It was as if, in the oddest way in the world, they had all been kept back, sown in a thick cluster, for the late afternoon of life, the time at which for people in general the unexpected had died out.[27]

The possibility of losing Mary through death troubled him.

It would represent, as connected with his past attitude, a drop of dignity under the shadow of which his existence could only become the most grotesque of failures. What did everything mean—what, that is, did *she* mean, she and her vain waiting and her probable death and the soundless admonition of it all—unless, that, at this time of day, it was simply, it was overwhelmingly too late?[28]

Since it was in Time that he was to have met his fate, so it was in Time that his fate was to have acted; and as he waked up to the sense of no longer being young, which was exactly the sense of being stale, just as that, in turn, was the sense of being weak. . . .[29]

He had in this later time turned nervous, which was what he in all the other years had never been; and the oddity was that his nervousness should have waited till he had begun to doubt, should have held off so long as he was sure.[30]

When his friend died, he found he had no special position or admission to the social situation of mourning. He didn't have:

. . . the distinction, the dignity, the propriety, if nothing else, of the man markedly bereaved. It was as if in the view of society he had not *been* markedly bereaved . . . he found himself wondering if he oughtn't to have begun, so to speak, further back.[31]

He visited her grave monthly.

It thus grew for him, in the oddest way, a positive resource; he carried out his idea of periodical returns, which took their place at last among the most inveterate of his habits. What it all amounted to, oddly enough, was that in his finally so simplified world this garden of death gave him the few square feet of earth on which he could still most live. It was as if, being nothing anywhere else for anyone, nothing even for himself, he were just everything here, and if not for a crowd of witnesses or indeed for any witness but John Marcher, then by clear right of the register that he could scan like an open page. The open page was the tomb of his friend, and *there* were the facts of the past, there the truth of his life, there the backward reaches in which he could lose himself. He did this from time to time with such effect that he seemed to wander through the old years with his hand in the arm of a companion who was, in the most extraordinary manner, his other, younger self; and to wander, which was more extraordinary yet, round and round a third presence—not wandering she, but stationary, still, whose eyes, turning with his revolution, never ceased to follow him, and whose seat was his point, so to speak, of orientation. Thus in short he settled to live—feeding all on the sense that he once *had* lived, and dependent on it not alone for a support but for an identity.[32]

But the realizations increased.

No passion had ever touched him, for this was what passion meant; he had survived and maundered and pined, but where had been *his* deep ravage? . . . He had seen *outside* of his life, not learned it from within, the way a woman was mourned when she had been loved for herself. . . . Now that the illumination had begun, however, it blazed to the zenith, and what he presently stood there gazing at was the sounded void of his life. He gazed, he drew breath, in pain; he turned in his dismay, and, turning, he had before him in sharper incision than ever the open page of his story. The name on the table smote him as the passage of his neighbor had done, and what it said to him, full in the face, was that *she* was what he had missed. This was the awful thought, the answer to all the past, the vision at the dread clearness of which he grew as cold as the stone beneath him. Everything fell together, confessed, explained, overwhelmed; leaving him most of all stupefied at the blindness he had cherished.[33]

This remarkable story was written in 1903 when James was 60. Other writings of James's contain similar content. *The Ambassadors* is about a man superbly equipped to react to the experiences which came to him too late.[34] The titles of his two unfinished novels are also pertinent to the life review: *The Sense of the Past* and *The Ivory Tower*. As Van Wyck Brooks has written, James's fiction became increasingly tragic with age.[35]

Discussion

It is evident that there is a considerable need for the intensive detailed study of aged persons in order to obtain information concerning their mental functioning, the experience of aging, approaching death, and dying. Behavior during aging may be clarified by the revelations of subjective experience. Because of the garulity, repetitiveness, and reminiscence of the aged, it is not always easy for investigators or therapists to listen; but for those who will listen there are rewards. The personal sense and meaning of the life cycle are more clearly unfolded by those who have nearly completed it. The nature of the forces shaping life, the effects of life events, the fate of neuroses and character disorders, the denouement of character itself may be studied in the older person. Recognition of the occurrence of such a vital process as the life review may help one to listen, to tolerate and understand the aged, and not to treat reminiscence as devitalized and insignificant.

Of course, people of all ages review their past at various times; they look back to comprehend the forces and experiences that have shaped their lives. The principal concern of most people is the present, however, and the proportion of time younger persons spend dwelling on the past is probably a fair, although by no means definite, measure of mental health. One tends to consider the past most when prompted by current problems and crises. The past also absorbs one in attempts to avoid the realities of the present. A very similar point has been made by others in connection with the sense of identity: One is apt to consider one's identity in the face of life crisis; at other times the question of "Who and what am I?" does not arise.

At present, not enough is known about the mental disorders of the aged and how they differ from the manifestly similar disorders of younger age groups. It is known, however, that late life is the period when people are most likely to develop mental disorders—specifically, organic disorders and depressions. The question arises as to whether the life review is related to the increased occurrence as well as the character and course of these disorders.

The current nosology distinguishing the so-called exogenous or reactive depressions from the endogenous depressions may be clarified and explained in part by the concept of the life review. Endogenous depressions, which operationally are those which are least easily comprehended in terms of environmental variables, may owe their existence to the inner process of life review. The relationships of and distinctions between depression and despair need study. The role of guilt especially requires investigation. Recently, Busse suggested, in connection with "so-called normal elderly persons," that "guilt as a psychodynamic force of import-ance is infrequently seen in our subjects of elderly persons living in the community. It appears that old people become involved in very little guilt-producing behavior."[36] This sanguine idea seems ques-tionable. Not only do older people appear to maintain the capaci-ties to undertake hurtful actions and to feel guilt but also they have not lost the past, which, indeed, comes back forcibly. It is essential to accept the occurrence of reality-based as well as imagined guilt.[37]

The oft-stated impression that the aged have relatively greater impairments of recent than remote memory—an impression not substantiated by any experimental data since "remote memory" is difficult to test—may reflect the older person's avoidance of the present as a consequence of the life review.

Other writers have offered constructs pertinent to the aged that probably relate to the life review process. The atrophy of the capacity to project oneself into the future, described by Drapf,[38] may be another way of discussing the life review; here stress is upon the absence of a process rather than upon the presence of another, active, substitutive process. Balint has written of the *Torschlusspanik* (literally, the panic at the closing of the gate),[39] which may be related to the state of terror already described in the extreme unfolding of the life review and may also be germane to the "time panic" which has been described by Krapf.

Intimations of the life review are also found in the literature of psychotherapy; indeed, the dangers involved when an older person reviews his life have been cited as either a contraindication to, or a basis for modification of technique for, psychotherapy in this age group. Rechtschaffen wrote, "also to be seriously considered in this regard is the emotional price paid when a patient reviews the failures of his past. It must be exceedingly difficult for a person nearing death to look back upon the bulk of his life as having been neurotic or maladjusted."[40] It is this consideration that led Grotjahn to suggest that it was important for the aged person to integrate his past life experiences as they have been lived, not as they might have been lived.[41] It is curious, and probably reflective of psychiatrists' own countertransference concerns, that the dangers of reviewing one's life in psychotherapy should be emphasized; underlying is the implication that truth is dangerous.[42] The existence of a life review occurring irrespective of the psychotherapeutic situation suggests that the aged particularly need a participant observer, professional or otherwise, and that the alleged danger of psychotherapy should be reevaluated.

Past and current forms of, or views about, the psychotherapy of the aged might well be evaluated in terms of their relation to the life review. The "Martin Method," for example, may have been successful because of the enthusiasm, interest, and support provided in this inspirational catechismic form of therapy, but perhaps also because the client was asked to relate his life history in detail, including the seemingly irrelevant side thoughts or images, which might help in understanding "subconscious complexes."[43]

Goldfarb and his associates, on the other hand, propose a technique based upon illusion—namely, creating the illusion of mastery in the patient. Goldfarb's brief therapy is oriented neither toward insight nor toward discharge, but rather toward amelioration of disturbed behavior.[44]

One might also speculate as to whether there is any relationship between the onset of the life review and the self-prediction and occurrence of death. Another question that arises is whether the intensity of a person's preoccupation with the past might express the wish to distance himself from death by restoring the past in inner experience and fantasy. This may be related to human narcissism or sense of omnipotence, for persons and events can in this way be recreated and brought back. At the same time a constructive reevaluation of the past may facilitate a serene and dignified acceptance of death.[45]

The phenomenon of mirror-image gazing is of both practical

and theoretical interest. In addition to affording one a diagnostic clue to the existence of the life-review, it may provide an unusually excellent experimental basis for the study and further elucidation of the changing concepts of self- and body-image, and the phenomenon of depersonalization, that accompany the rapid, profound, and multiple bodily and mental changes in the aged.[46]

Certain schizophrenic and neurotic patients are also known to seek out and gaze at their images in the mirror, talk to their images, and reveal many similar behavioral manifestations. The French psychiatrist Perrier has stated flatly that the schizophrenic does not recognize himself in the mirror; he considers that this symptom shows that the patient has neglected and lost his ego.[47] Schulz has described a 25-year-old female patient whose depersonalization—she felt her right arm was not connected to her body—ceased when she was reassured about her body integrity by looking in the mirror.[48] The experience of a probably paranoid schizophrenic observing himself in mirrors is also excellently described in a novel by Simenon.[49]

Shulz also reported a neurotic patient who would examine himself in the mirror while shaving and experience the recurring inner questions, "Is that me?" and "Who am I", probably illustrating his concern about his identity.[50] In this connection, one observes that adolescents frequently spend time examining themselves in mirrors; and analysands, especially female, often report mirror-gazing in their childhood, especially during pubescence. Persons of certain narcissistic character-types describe disrobing before a mirror and deriving great pleasure in self-observation; occasionally there are reports of actual or wished-for orgastic experiences. The theme of the mirror as revealing character is ancient, ranging from the stories of Narcissus and Snow White to the use of the mirror as a chastity test in the *Arabian Nights* tales.

Memory is an ego function whose neurophysiological mechanisms remain hypothetical and inconclusively demonstrated. It serves the sense of self and its continuity; it entertains us; it shames us; it pains us. Memory can tell us our origins; it can be explanatory and it can deceive. Presumably it can lend itself

toward cure. The recovery of memories, the making the unconscious conscious, is generally regarded as one of the basic ingre-
dients of the curative process. It is a step in the occurrence of
change. Psychotherapists tend to associate self-awareness with
health, and lack of awareness with morbidity.

Probably at no other time in life is there as potent a force
toward self-awareness operating as in old age. Yet, the capacity to
change, according to prevailing stereotype, decreases with age.
"Learning capacity" falters with time, and it is fair to say that the
major portion of gerontological research throughout the country is
concerned almost enthusiastically with measuring decline in various cognitive, perceptual, and psychomotor functions.[51] Comparable attention toward studies of the individual, of growing wisdom, of the meaning of experience, is not ordinary. It is therefore
of interest to notice the positive, affirmative changes reported by
the aged themselves as part of their life experience,[52] and to find
constructive alterations in character, possibly as a consequence of
the life review. The relationships of changed functions to aging per
se and to diseases, psychosocial crises, and personality remain
obscure.[53] There is at least reason to observe that personality
change can occur all along the life span, and that old age is no
exception. Change obviously cannot be attributed only to professional effort, and changes in behavior outside of professional
effort and beyond professional understanding should not be
casually categorized as either unreal or "spontaneous." It is necessary to study the changes wrought in life by experience, eventful or
uneventful, by brief or enduring relationships with other human
beings, or even through images evoked by hearing or reading of
the experiences or efforts of others.

In the course of the life review the older person may reveal to
his wife, children, and other intimates, unknown qualities of his
character and unstated actions of his past; in return, they may
reveal heretofore undisclosed or unknown truths. Hidden themes
of great vintage may emerge, changing the quality of a lifelong
relationship. Revelations of the past may forge a new intimacy,
render a deceit honest; they may sever peculiar bonds and free

tongues; or they may sculpture terrifying hatreds out of fluid, fitful antagonisms.

Sameness and change may both be manifestations of the active process of ego identity. Erikson writes, ". . . identity formation neither begins nor ends with adolescence: it is a lifelong development largely unconscious to the individual and to his society."[54] He also writes that "early development cannot be understood on its own terms alone, and that the earliest stages of childhood cannot be accounted for without a unified theory of the whole span of pre-adulthood."[55] Similarly, it may be argued that the entire life cycle cannot be comprehended without inclusion of the psychology of the aged.

Notes

[1]Aristotle, *Selections,* ed. W. D. Ross (New York: Scribner's, 1927; p. 324).

[2]William Cowper, *Task.* (Boston, Thomas Badger, 1819; p. 113).

[3]Somerset Maugham, *Points of View.* (Garden City, N.Y., Doubleday, 1959, p. 70).

[4]Robert N. Butler, "Intensive Psychotherapy for the Hospitalized Aged," *Geriatrics,* Vol. 15, 1960, pp. 644–653.

[5]Robert N. Butler, "Re-awakening Interests," *Nursing Homes; Journal of American Nursing Home Association,* Vol. 10, 1961, pp. 8–19.

[6]Ewald W. Busse, Robert H. Barnes, and Albert J. Silverman, "Studies in the Processes of Aging: I. Behavioral Patterns in the Aged and Their Relationship to Adjustment," *Diseases of the Nervous System* (1954) 15:22–26. Ewald W. Busse and others, "Studies in the Process of Aging: Factors That Influence the Psyche of Elderly Persons," *American Journal of Psychiatry* (1954) 110:897–903. Seymour Perlin and Robert N. Butler, "Psychiatric Aspects of Adaptation to the Aging Experience," in *Human Aging: Biological and Behavioral Aspects,* National Institute of Mental Health; Washington, D.C., Government Printing Office, in press.

[7]Allan Rechtschaffen, "Psychotherapy with Geriatric Patients: A Review of the Literature," *Journal of Gerontology,* Vol. 14, 1959, pp. 73–84. See also footnote 4.

[8]See, for example: Horace B. English and Ava Champney English, *A Comprehensive Dictionary of Psychological and Psychoanalytical Terms.* (New

York: Longmans, Green, 1958). *The Oxford English Dictionary;* Oxford, Clarendon Press, 1933. Leland E. Hinsle and Robert J. Campbell, *Psychiatric Dictionary,* 3rd ed. (New York, Oxford University Press, 1960).

[9]*Felix Frankfurter Reminisces,* recorded in talks with Harlan B. Phillips; New York, Reynal, 1960.

[10]Martin Grotjahn, "Psychoanalytic Investigation of a Seventy-One-Year-Old Man with Senile Dementia," *Psychoanalytic Quarterly,* Vol. 9, 1940, pp. 80–97.

[11]The recent Japanese motion picture *Ikiru* describes the salvation of a man whose thirty unproductive years as a governmental bureau chief were interrupted by cancer; he undertook a new and constructive activity following acceptance of his impending death and review of his past.

[12]Walter B. Cannon, "'Voodoo' Death," *American Anthropologist,* Vol. 44, 1942, pp. 169–181. Curt P. Richter, "On the Phenomenon of Sudden Death in Animals and Man," *Psychosomatic Medicine,* Vol. 19, 1957, pp. 191–198. Marvin L. Adland, "Review, Case Studies, Therapy and Interpretation of Acute Exhaustive Psychoses," *Psychiatric Quarterly,* Vol. 21, 1947, pp. 38–69. Otto Allen Will, Jr., "Human Relatedness and the Schizophrenic Reaction," *Psychiatry,* Vol. 22, 1959, pp. 205–223. Frieda Fromm-Reichmann also wrote about loneliness in her old age in "On Loneliness," pp. 325–336, in *Psychoanalysis and Psychotherapy,* ed. Dexter M. Bullard (Chicago, University of Chicago Press, 1959).

[13]See Will, in footnote 12; p. 218.

[14]The term *life review* has the disadvantage of suggesting that orderliness is characteristic. The reminiscences of an older person are not necessarily more orderly than any other aspects of his life, and he may be preoccupied at various times by particular periods of his life and not the whole of it.

[15]See Perlin and Butler, in footnote 6.

[16]Various sensory processes are involved. Older people report the revival of the sounds, tastes, smells of early life, as: "I can hear the rain against the window of my boyhood room."

[17]For example, Joyce Cary's *To Be a Pilgrim.* (London: Michael Joseph, 1942.) concerns an insightful old man "deep in his own dream, which is chiefly of the past," (p. 7) and describes the review of his life, augmented by the memories stimulated by his return to his boyhood home.

[18]"Old Age: Part IV," *Life,* August 3, 1959, pp. 67–74; p. 67.

[19]Samuel Beckett's one-act play *Krapp's Last Tape* dramatically illustrates the life review (*Krapp's Last Tape and Other Dramatic Pieces.* New York, Grove Press, 1960).

[20]One may compare this with Durkheim's concept of anomie (Emile Durkheim, *Suicide,* translated from *Le Suicide* [1897] by John A. Spaulding and George Simpson; Glencoe, Ill.: Free Press, 1951).

[21]Adah I. Menken, *Infelicia*. London: Chatto and Wincus, 1888; p. 37.

[22]See footnote 4. I am indebted to Dr. Ping-nie Pao for making available these clinical data.

[23]Henry James, "The Beast in the Jungle (1903)," pp. 548–602, in *The Short Stories of Henry James*, ed. Clifton Fadiman (New York, Modern Library, 1945).

[24]Footnote 23; p. 596.

[25]Footnote 23; p. 556.

[26]Footnote 23; p. 572.

[27]Footnote 23; p. 573.

[28]Footnote 23; p. 574.

[29]Footnote 23; p. 575.

[30]Footnote 23; pp. 576–577.

[31]Footnote 23; p. 589.

[32]Footnote 23; p. 593.

[33]Footnote 23; pp. 595–596.

[34]Henry James, *The Ambassadors*. (Garden City, N.Y., Doubleday, 1958).

[35]Van Wyck Brooks, *The Pilgrimage of Henry James*. (New York, Dutton, 1925).

[36]Ewald W. Busse, "Psychopathology," pp. 364–399, in *Handbook of Aging and the Individual*, ed. James E. Birren (Chicago, University of Chicago Press, 1959; p. 390).

[37]Martin Buber, "Guilt and Guilt Feelings," *Psychiatry*, Vol. 20 , (1957,) pp. 114–129.

[38]E. Eduardo Krapf, "On Aging," *Proceedings of the Royal Society of Medicine* [London], Vol. 46, 1953, pp. 957–964.

[39]Michael Balint, "The Psychological Problems of Growing Old," pp. 69–85, in *Problems in Human Pleasure and Behavior*. (London, Hogarth, 1951).

[40]See footnote 7; p. 74.

[41]Martin Grotjahn, "Some Analytic Observations About the Process of Growing Old," pp. 301–312, in *Psychoanalysis and Social Science*, Vol. 3, ed. G. Roheim. (New York, International Universities Press, 1951).

[42]In the atmosphere of hospital units for the mentally disturbed aged are to be found the notions that the aged "can't stand the truth," must be protected from "bad news," and need to be reassured about their "conditions," and, curiously, that therapy may prove too "disturbing." (See footnote 4.) I submit that the hospitalized aged, already disturbed, need honesty.

[43]See footnote 7.

[44]Alvin I. Goldfarb, "The Rationale for Psychotherapy with Older Persons," *American Journal of Medical Science*, Vol 232, 1956, pp. 181–185.

[45]However, I do not intend to imply that a "serene and dignified acceptance of death" is necessarily appropriate, noble, or to be valued. Those who die screaming may be expressing a rage that is as fitting as dignity.

[46]Martha M. Werner, Seymour Perlin, Robert N. Butler, and William Pollin, "Self-Perceived Changes in Community-Resident Aged," *Archives of General Psychiatry* Vol. 4, 1961, pp. 501–508.

[47]F. Perrier, "The Meaning of Transference in Schizophrenia," *Acta Psychotherapy*, [Basel] Vol. 3 (suppl), 1955, pp. 266–272. Translation by M.A. Woodbury.

[48]Clarence Schulz, personal communication.

[49]Georges Simenon, *The Man Who Watched the Trains Go By*. (New York, Berkley, 1958).

[50]See footnote 48.

[51]See footnote 4.

[52]See footnote 46.

[53]National Institute of Mental Health, *Human Aging: Biological and Behavioral Aspects*. (Washington, D.C., Government Printing Office, in press).

[54]Erik H. Erikson, "The Problem of Ego Identity," in *Identity and the Life Cycle, Psychological Issues*, Vol. 1, 1959, pp. 101–164.

[55]See footnote 54.

Chapter 15

AGING, CATASTROPHE, AND MORAL REASONING

John B. Orr

For centuries—perhaps eons—there have been claims that elderly people enjoy a special wisdom denied to youth. Although Simone de Beauvoir calls these claims "mystical twaddle," and points to the fact that the more typical condition of old age is hunger, isolation, poverty, and disease,[1] the image of the elderly sage repeatedly surfaces. In our own period it is implicit in the efforts of the enormously popular *Foxfire Book* to discover and preserve the wisdom of elderly Appalachia; in self-flagellating protests against the manner in which our society excludes the elderly; and in feelings that the disappearance of extended family patterns is creating a generation of deprived children.

In this essay, I am going to view this recurring image of the elderly sage as a problem for the phenomenology of moral development. More concretely, I intend (1) to develop a concept of

From John B. Orr, "Aging, Catastrophe, and Moral Reasoning," *Soundings, An Interdisciplinary Journal,* vol. 57, 1974. Reprinted by permission of the editor.

age-related "stages" of moral reasoning, based largely on the work of Jean Piaget; (2) to consider the utility of this concept for the analysis of adult moral reasoning; and (3) to view the image of the elderly sage as a case in point.

The problem of discovering the relationship between aging and moral reasoning is awkward, because aging is not a category that has typically structured the Western perception of adult morals. Ethics as an intellectual discipline has given substantial attention to the structure of moral identity, but, as James Gustafson repeatedly observes, it has given far too little attention to the forces that shape the moral self—to ways in which moral reasoning emerges out of people's experience of their social worlds.[2] Ethics, for example, has assumed an ageless self, or at least one whose intellectual capacities and moral sensibilities grow out of a full-flowered (but unacknowledged) middle age. Thus, the image of the elderly sage is an embarrassing intrusion, reminiscent as it is of birthdays and of the real conditions imposed by the facts of age.

AGE-RELATED "STAGES" OF MORAL REASONING

Any effort to deal with moral reasoning among elderly adults is almost forced to start at the opposite end of the spectrum—in childhood—and to do so in the company of developmental psychologists. Developmental psychologists have had remarkable success in describing sequential patterns of moral reasoning among children and youth, and they have dominated what little discussion there has been about moral development in general. They have virtually been awarded squatters' rights, perhaps in just compensation for the tedious hours spent listening to children argue about rules and the makers of rules.

The reasons for starting with developmental psychologists are also more substantive, particularly when those developmental psychologists have been identified with the cognitive-structural tradition. This tradition has been thoroughly radicalized in the past few decades under the leadership of Jean Piaget, and the fortunate consequence is a body of data that is immediately interesting within the phenomenological study of moral development. Piaget's training in philosophy led to an early fascination with the work of Edmund Husserl, and his rejection of Husserl was not so much a rejection of his broad phenomenological method as it was an expression of disenchantment with Husserl's refusal to consider concrete evidence. Bluntly stated, Piaget accused Husserl of being an armchair scientist who would not recognize that the descriptive enterprise requires an empirical foundation.[3] In choosing to be a scientist rather than a philosopher, however, Piaget chose a model of science profoundly influenced by Husserl. He addressed problems of moral development as a developmental epistemologist, looking for experiential origins of concepts utilized in ethics. His concept of developmental stages in moral judgment represented an essential intuition of the lifeworlds of children—an intuition that had consciously bracketed issues related to the correspondence of these lifeworlds to those of adults. Piaget thus constructed a phenomenology of moral change—a first step in articulating a broad theory as to how age relates to moral judgment within the human consciousness.

In two books that deserve to be regarded as classics,[4] Jean Piaget carefully maps the evolution of the child's word and demonstrates the importance of this map for understanding the child's developing moral judgment. He traces the child's pilgrimage through an animistic world, explainable in terms of moral necessity, into a dualistic social world dominated by the authority of Fathers, and finally into a highly differentiated world in which the child is both an object among objects and a moral equal. The pilgrimage through these lifeworlds is also one in which the child moves from egocentric morality to "annunciatory" patterns of moral reflection (i.e., in which he submits to the mystical power of the world of the adult), and finally to a concern for reciprocity and principles of justice.

In delineating the parallelism between moral and intellectual development, Piaget appears to be impressed with the explanatory powers of biological-maturational metaphors, but at the same time he resists letting them dominate. Neither logical nor moral norms are innate in the human organism, and their emergence should not be interpreted as a process of self-fulfillment in any narrow sense. "The control characteristic of sensorimotor intelligence is of external origin," Piaget argues. "Similarly, it is persons external to him who canalize the child's elementary feelings; those feelings do not tend to regulate themselves from within."[5] Piaget will have no part in doctrines that assign necessity to patterns of moral development in particular cases, and he provides no justification at all for projecting images of maturity that necessarily belong to any age population.

Conversely, however, Piaget claims that "not everything in the a priori view should be rejected,"[6] and he refuses to relinquish the idea of moral evolution, at least among children. In both the sensorimotor operations and the parallel experience of moral reasoning, there is a search for coherence and organization directed toward an ideal equilibrium, indefinable as structure but implied in the functioning that is at work.[7] This a priori is not a principle from which concrete patterns of moral reasoning can be inferred, nor is it a structure of consciousness. Rather "it is the sum total of functional relations implying the distinction between existing states of disequilibrium and an ideal equilibrium yet to be realized."[8]

These careful qualifications concerning the use of maturational metaphors in the analysis of moral development have been played down by some of Piaget's colleagues, who speak much more rigidly about invariant patterns or "stages" of moral development. Piaget does indeed assume a logic of development, but this logic strains the explanatory utility of growth metaphors. The child's movement toward a highly differentiated universe, and thus his movement toward moral reciprocity, takes place by way of what Aaron Gurswitsch calls "thoroughgoing reorganizations and restructurations."[9] The process is catastrophic. The child must confront a sequence of worlds, each different from the other in its principle of organization, and each responsive to a new situation that makes previous world images and patterns of moral reasoning untenable.

Changes in moral reasoning among children appear to support a concept of "stages," according to Piaget, in part because transformations in the child's concept of his social world and of himself as a social being are heavily influenced by such cognitive factors as general mental age or general intellectual maturity. The intrusion of new cognitive capacities acts as shocks[10] that threaten less differentiated images of the world and introduce the need for patterns of moral reasoning more appropriate to the new perceptions of the social world. The shocks represent situations for which the child must account—conditions that throw routinized modes of moral reflection into question.

Such shocks within the process of early cognitive development are not capricious, however. They are sedimentary in structure, their "layering" reflecting the progressive development of psychomotor systems. Shocks are experienced by the child, not as the unfolding or expansion of a mysterious wad of capacities, but as problems of community, especially as problems that emphasize the tension between relations of constraint and relations of cooperation. The child is buffeted by experiences that threaten his routine styles of understanding, feeling, and acting within the social world. His egocentrism is attacked. He must renegotiate relations with law-giving personalities and institutions. And he must restructure his understanding of the sources and authority of rules. In short, the shocks that give rise to new patterns of moral reasoning are thoroughly coincident with and embedded in the process of social comparison, opposition, discussion, and mutual control. Shocks are experienced as occasions for taking better account of situations and for responding more effectively on the basis of sharpened or more highly differentiated images of the world.

Piaget's understanding of a developmental stage does indeed lead to a hierarchical ordering of lifeworlds, and Lawrence Kohlberg's later attempts to find Platonic implications are not misplaced. Although Piaget could easily be interpreted in a more flexibly pluralist fashion in justification of multiple realities with multiple life styles, he has moralized the notion of intellectual age and has thereby equated such terms as *latest, most mature,* and *best*. Lifeworlds that are more highly differentiated are better, and a Platonic vision of justice as the highest ideal is morally superior to individual social forms of hedonism. In a tantalizing way that begs for closer analysis, Piaget has placed systematic ethical options on a time-continuum and has suggested that these might be graded in terms of their tendencies toward a Platonic concept of maturity.

Of more immediate interest, though, is Piaget's suggestion that aging and moral reasoning merge in the experience of constructing and sharing lifeworlds. His point is simply that aging *is* a source of human community, because persons share a network of age-related shocks that elicit common images of the world and common moral meanings. Of course, persons live in a number of communities, e.g., religious, national, cultural, economic, racial, familial. These provide stocks of moral precedents, axioms, heroes, stories, and patterned styles of the moral life. But Piaget's contribution is to point out what common sense affirms: that people also share moral styles within age communities. At least among children, the population to which he has limited his investigations, Piaget sees that persons can understand each other within age groups, in spite of the fact that their particular styles of moral argument are not reinforced by authorities. Age communities function invisibly; they appear to structure the medium for moral discourse among children. The shocks that give rise to shared images and meanings may go unacknowledged; but the consequent sense of being understood by one's age group is testimony to their force.

Piaget thus turns his study of the stages of moral judgment into a study of rhetoric—the rhetoric that structures moral reflection and argument within age-related communities. Whether or not moral obligation is finally relative to these communities, or to any other community, is of course a deeper issue. But Piaget is suggesting that among children moral discourse is enabled by the fact that childish worlds are widely enough shared that they allow for meaningful argument. Moral argument proceeds because there is broad agreement concerning fundamentals of the moral life, and because a fund of shared perceptions and images is available for the mutual legitimation of feelings and courses of action.

In his analysis of the moral rhetoric of childhood communities, which is also his analysis of age-related stages of moral judgment, Piaget parallels the Christian ethicist H. Richard Niebuhr and the philosopher Paul Ricoeur in their suggestion that moral rhetoric in communities is structured by synecdoches—i.e., key ideas, key images, key relationships, or central tasks that represent or express the spirit of a community's style of life.[11] Piaget demonstrates that the rhetoric of "stages" is dominated by synecdoches, e.g., managing the spirits of an animistic world, obeying the father, trading things, making a contract. These key images grow from the child's experience of community and in turn guide the child in his efforts to shape desired forms of community. Each key image or synecdoche stands for a complete *logos,* an order which provides not only principles of reasoning but also a perspective, a world view in terms of which particular issues are interpreted and argued.[12]

THE MORATORIUM OF ADULTHOOD

Growing up is very different from growing old, and the age-related communities of childhood reflect this difference. To grow up is to be in a position where patterns of thought, feeling, and behavior are evaluated in terms of their tendencies, or at least in terms of their relation to supposedly more mature models. Although the worlds of the child provide for perceptions and judgments that are as self-validating as those available in adult worlds, the childhood realities are always viewed as instrumental to other possibilities. The traditional structure of childhood education dramatizes this fact. There are grade levels, promotions, and achievement tests, which perennially direct the child's attention to what he will become. Parents speak to their children about going through stages. And children view persons who are older as embodiments of future possibilities. Whether or not the experience of childhood proceeds by way of "thoroughgoing reorganizations and restructurations," as Piaget suggests, biological-maturational metaphors seem helpful in illumining the whole process of growing up. The metaphors are synecdochal for the overall life styles of childhood.

But growing old is very different from growing up. The maturational metaphors are foreign to adult experience. They are not synecdochal. If adults are told that they are maturing, or growing up, something is wrong; they have not completed a process that, all things being equal, they should have completed. To be accused of the need to grow up is to be stained, to be found to be morally insufficient. In adulthood, there are indeed age-related stereotypes, such as images of the brash and idealistic styles of early adulthood, the compromising character of middle age, the mellow yet crisis-laden character of the forties. But stereotypical images are hardly stages, and these images do not suggest that adulthood is a period of growth toward moral enlightenment. Even the boundaries that have been established within the discipline of psychology distinguish between growing up and growing old. There appears to be a frustrating barrier between the study of child development and the study of adult personality—a barrier that has much to do with the fact that child psychology is consistently grounded in the imagery of evolving organisms, while the psychology of adult personality is not.

Following Piaget's general understanding of age-related worldviews, Lawrence Kohlberg and Richard Kramer have attempted to apply the concept of developmental stages to the study of adult moral reasoning and have concluded that after early adulthood no further age-related increases in moral maturity can be expected. In childhood, they argue, the timing and onset of new stages, including moral stages, is heavily affected by such factors as general mental age or individual maturity. After about age twenty-five, although individual differences in intelligence affect the adult's life styles, such differences do not explain the patterns of further development or change. There will be changes, but they cannot be explained by theories of cognitive transformation because such transformations do not seem to occur.[13]

Thus, Kohlberg and Kramer picture adulthood as an indefinitely extended moratorium in which persons are caught at the level of moral maturity they were able to achieve in earlier years. Adulthood brings stabilization, i.e., "a greater consistency of structure with itself (greater 'stage purity') and a greater consistency between thought structure and action."[14] Important moral conflicts continue to occur, and it may even be possible for persons to appreciate or to move into more highly differentiated, justice-sensitive worlds. But Kohlberg's and Kramer's conclusions offer little basis for arguing that after twenty-five aging brings wisdom or that elderly people can claim a level of moral insight denied to youth.

The image of adulthood as an extended moral moratorium, repulsive as it may be to persons who are enchanted by the rhetoric of personal growth, is helpful in illumining dimensions of everyday experience. A phenomenology of moral development, of course, has no room for the denial of possibilities implied by the moratorium image, because adult moral consciousness assumes the ability of persons to choose among life-options. Still, among adults the lifeworlds associated with differences among styles of moral judgment are not commonly viewed as being arranged in any hierarchical order of ascending maturity, nor are they understood as unstable tendencies toward an ideal equilibrium. If adults were ever aware of age-related patterns of moral judgment among children, they do not relate these to analogous patterns among adults. What might earlier have been regarded as a developmental stage becomes an "ethical option," and therefore adults view other adults as persons who are older or younger in their styles of moral judgment. Other styles are sometimes viewed as being immature, but such perceptions are hardly intended as developmental judgments. They are accusations.

Even adults who see their moral task as "self-fulfillment" or "growth" do not regard themselves as moving through a hierarchy of stages of moral judgment. "Self-fullfillment" and "growth" are synecdoches for a style of life that emphasizes affectivity, sensitivity, and self-in-body; the terms do not elicit associations with anything like Kohlberg's or Piaget's stages of moral judgment. The synecdoches evoke images of a life option, an either/or.

The aptness of the moratorium metaphor is further established in the simple fact that the age-related lifeworlds of later childhood and youth function quite adequately in shaping perceptions and moral judgments among adults. Their synecdoches constitute root metaphors, or what Stephen Pepper calls world hypotheses,[15] and as such they are powerfully self-reinforcing. In the context of adult relations, they have proved themselves historically to be capable of filtering and shaping experience and of enabling communication among large groups of people over extended periods of time. As in childhood and youth, the synecdoches and their related lifeworlds are continually assaulted by shocks that have to be handled; but our experience in adulthood is that these shocks are generally destructive of patterns of moral reasoning. Adult worlds *are* more stable, because for political, economic, and social reasons adults develop an investment in particular synecdoches. Support for these is provided by friends, family, and economic associates who pattern relationships and expectations in terms of synecdoches and who, in effect, tell people that they like their choices. A persons's system of self-images is structured in terms of the synecdoches, and to call them into question is to attack the adult's fundamental identity. To convert too often to other styles is to lose interest in one's own moral stability.

The self-verifying, self-reinforcing character of moral synecdoches does not imply that the moral moratorium of adulthood is complete. Kohlberg and Kramer are correct when they observe that moral change is a focal point for adult life, even though cognitive change may not be; and they are correct when they affirm the seriousness of the adult's moral reflection. But for Kohlberg and Kramer adult moral change usually happens in the context of a *formal* moratorium, i.e., the relative stability of the larger patterns or gestalts within which moral reasoning proceeds. Adults change their minds, they argue, but they do not normally repent of their lifeworlds. Adults change their substantive commitments, but usually they do not change their moral life styles.[16]

In the intriguing symposium *Moral Education: Five Lectures,* however, Kenneth Keniston criticizes this image of formal stability and substantive flux for being unhistorical, i.e., for seeing formal moral development as a mechanical ritual, reenacted in the life of each individual. What Kohlberg does not see, Keniston claims, is that in our own society new images of selfhood with related styles of moral judgment are in the making, and that persons currently are experiencing these as cultural strains within their lifeworlds. Such tendencies are formal as well as substantive. They represent the emergence of new possibilities for what it means to be moral, or at least the surfacing of a new synecdoche not acknowledged by Piaget, Kohlberg, or Kramer in their developmental scheme.[17]

For our purposes, Keniston's point is well taken. One must be as guarded in speaking about an adult moratorium (or, to use Kohlberg's own term, adult stabilization) as Piaget was in speaking about developmental stages. Piaget insisted that a priori concepts of moral development are both helpful and not helpful. There are patterns or sequences that can be discerned in the life history of persons, but these are not imposed from within as necessary patterns of development. As in childhood and youth, adult synecdoches come from and are sustained by people's participation in the process of social comparison, argument, opposition, and role-taking, and they function as long as correlated perceptions and judgments are adequate to the task of accounting for experience and providing for satisfying relational styles in the social world. Piaget's image of the developmental function of catastrophe remains valid. Catastrophe always constitutes the temptation and the condition for formal as well as substantive moral change. Adulthood cannot provide guarantees against disillusionment or the need for radical readjustments in patterns of perception, feeling, and behavior.

THE ELDERLY SAGE

The recurrent image of the elderly sage in cultural lore suggests that the patterns of catastrophe peculiar to adulthood may drive people toward higher levels of moral equilibrium, but instances from everyday experience are only sporadically available. Adults are aware of a few elderly persons whose age seems to be a dimension of their charismatic authority and who seem to have reached a plane qualitatively above that achieved even by persons typically recognized as "successful agers." Simone de Beauvoir suggests that certain professions encourage the charisma and contributions of the aged, particularly professions in which the ability to synthesize and/or to be creative is valued.[18] One is more likely to find elderly sages, for example, in the company of philosophers and artists than in the company of engineers. But the lot of the few cannot be regarded as a developmental stage. If the conditions of old age are capable of propelling a limited number of the truly gifted into a period of professional excellence, that may be an occasion for muted celebration, but not for ecstasy. To speak about elderly wisdom as a broad possibility, when only the elite can achieve it, appears to be a cruel and self-deceptive practice.

In fact, the catastrophes or shocks peculiar to old age seem more commonly to lead to experiences of moral regression—to episodic repetitions of childhood's narcissistic stages. Persons over sixty-five, according to Kohlberg and Kramer, are drawn to styles of moral judgment characteristic of an "underworld" of incarcerated criminals, schizophrenics, and college sophomores.[19] They move toward forms of perceptions and moral judgment that are characteristic of Kohlberg's stage 2, where judgments are naively egoistic and where right actions are viewed as instrumental to the satisfaction of one's own (and only occasionally others') desires.[20] Narcissism—the preoccupation with the self, with one's own opinions, with the body, with isolation and loneliness—is the threat, the extreme case, the terrible possibility of old age, its frightening prospects more real than the possibilities of achieving elderly wisdom.

The threat of narcissism belongs to the experience of growing old in ways that are foreign to growing up. The college sophomore, for example, experiences his so-called identity crisis in the context of his discovery of moral relativism, and the shock may easily send him into narcissistic life styles for a short while. But he knows that he is in a state of transition and that he can and should aspire to higher forms of idealism that at the moment he is tempted to reject. Growing old, though, is more definitive of boundaries; and the threat of narcissism is experienced as more permanently overwhelming.

According to Simone de Beauvoir, narcissism arrives with old age as a surprise—as a defeat that has already been inflicted (often in the absence of an awareness that a battle has ever been in progress). It is experienced as an attack from outside, something that is crudely imposed, and therefore something that is foreign and undeserved.[21] Beauvoir[22] writes:

> When we are grown up we hardly think about our age any more. We feel that the notion does not apply to us; for it is one which assumes that we look back toward the past and draw a line under the total, whereas in fact we are reaching out toward the future, gliding on imperceptibly from day to day, from year to year. Old age is particularly difficult to assume because we have always regarded it as something alien, a foreign species: "Can I have become a different being while I still remain myself?"

When a person first is told that he is old, his sense of self may hardly be able to comprehend the fact. The catastrophe is that the self is caught in a kind of deception. It had previously considered age and adulthood casually. It had lived unaware within the moratorium of adulthood. Now, however, the self is exposed as aged, a member of a population whose status in the social world is increasingly suspect. The self from now on must turn in on itself and be preoccupied in a new way with the problematic condition of being old.

What Beauvoir poetically describes is a catastrophic system of shocks, the correlate of which may be expulsion from adulthood and reinsertion into an age-related community. Within our culture, to be an adult is to be in the age-heterogeneous moratorium, where being moral is choosing among life options. To be a child, to be a youth, to be an old person: these are age-related "stages" that do not belong to adulthood. Intuitively, adults recognize this fact. They institutionally isolate the nonadult; they treat him with an air of paternalism; they qualify his legal rights; and they discriminate against him economically. To be identified with an age community is to become a member of a peculiar minority group, whose precarious social status is made even more problematic by the fact that it is not one that historically has been identified as disenfranchised.

Richard H. Williams and Claudine Wirths, among others, speak about the parallel social-psychological process in which old persons are expelled from adulthood. "Intrinsic to aging," they say, "is a process of mutual severing of ties between the individual and the social system in which he lives, reduced normative control by his social system, and reduced obligation to it."[23] Persons who have developed self-images in adulthood that are satisfying and that have been reinforced over years of time by family, friends, co-workers, and others whose opinions are valued suddenly find themselves in a position of social isolation. Their self-images are attacked through the loss of employment, the death of life partners, and the withdrawal of approval for espoused values. The process is tantamount to the shattering of the adult moratorium, simply because that moratorium rested on the ability of persons to participate as valued members of the social world, not as generalized old-age selves. Moral narcissism is the threat of old age, because, as Piaget pointed out, more mature forms of moral reasoning depend upon participation in a social world where persons are roughly equal. When elderly people are stripped of valued social roles, more is potentially taken from them than activities that previously had filled their time. A lifeworld, with its system of supports for mature perceptions and moral judgments is withdrawn; and the styles of childhood become appropriate. Narcissism belongs to that world where the Fathers reign, and that is the world which unthinkingly we offer old people. Piaget's and Kohlberg's concept of regression is in this case both appropriate and cruel. It is appropriate because being old does indeed often involve ejection from worlds that grown-up people value; and it is cruel because the return to narcissistic lifeworlds is not like a process of becoming senile or of losing one's grip on reality. The process is far more commonsensical. Narcissism constitutes a pattern of perceiving, feeling, and behaving that makes sense when one has to live in paternalistic situations. It is a fitting lifestyle, even though it makes younger adults impatient (perhaps because in the narcissism of the elderly they hazily see the terrible political deeds they have wrought).

Curiously, at least one way that the image of the elderly sage has been formed reinforces this attack on the adulthood of old people. I am thinking, for example, of the *Family of Man* photographs, where the aged are pictured as stoic, deeply wrinkled and rich in character; but they are also pictured consistently as passive and beyond the pettiness of adult pragmatic responsibilities. The elderly sage is a seer, and not a doer—an unhappy option in an industrial society, where wisdom has seldom been generously rewarded. Indeed, the celebration of elderly character may subtly become a way in which the social isolation of old people is solidified, just as the nostalgic enjoyment of Uncle Remus stories dulled the ability to recognize the more painful condition of the black minority.

Some elderly people apparently intuit this plot that would rob them of their adulthood and refuse to call themselves old. Tuckman and Lorge found, for example, that within a population of ninety-nine elderly persons (whose mean age was seventy-four), "except for the 80's and older with its bare majority classifying themselves as old, the 60's and 70's primarily classify themselves as middle-aged and young rather than old."[24] Robert Kastenbaum found that between thirty percent and eighty percent of persons in the retirement range do not consider themselves as old.[25] In a more graphic fashion, one resident of a retirement community, aged seventy-three, interpreted her own refusal to accept the identity of an old lady: "An 'old lady' often won't wear a brassiere; she won't listen to anyone else; and she is too interested in what she eats. I'm not old."[26] Whether or not the denial of old age is an element in adjustment during the retirement years is debatable. But the denial is certainly a sign that in old age moral identity is once again (as in childhood and youth) considered in relation to an age community with its characteristic set of synecdoches and that for some this relation is intolerable.

This refusal to grow old should not be dismissed as quixotic. It is one way (certainly not the only way)[27] of building defenses, of refusing to give up the synecdoches belonging to adulthood, in spite of the fact that supportive adult roles are being withdrawn. The shocks of growing old do not have to drive persons back to narcissistic patterns of moral judgment; they merely constitute the temptation and condition for such change. Old people have already developed a significant investment in their self-images, their perceptions of the social world, and their patterns of moral judgment; and these will not usually be surrendered without a struggle. To refuse to grow old is to raise the first, i.e., to symbolize the depth of commitment that one has to an adult lifeworld. The refusal says, in effect, that the old person chooses to fight narcissism while accepting the risk of appearing to be overly rigid and anachronistic.

Why it is that the shocks of growing old can be resisted by some and not by others is an issue that does not fall within the scope of this essay. It is enough to say that disengagement from adult roles places significant moral strains on old people; and short of heroism, effective resistance to regression would require conditions that are only occasionally available in our culture. Situations are needed that would provide roles and self-images for the elderly as satisfying as those enjoyed in early adulthood. These in turn would require the nurturing of social groups among the elderly that function to reinforce the value of these roles and self-images. Isolation breeds narcissism, and alternatives to narcissistic patterns are associated with efforts to energize social worlds among old people.

In this context the usual image of the elderly sage might make better sense. The elderly sage was valued not because he was developmentally superior but because he was needed as a repository of social values and community knowledge—adult roles in a traditional society. If these particular roles have been eliminated or disqualified by rapid change and knowledge-technology, that does not mean that elderly wisdom is gone forever or that elderly wisdom is anachronistic. Wisdom is inseparable from adult reposibility among the aged, and it is encouraged when old people are needed and valued. It is a healthy thing, then, that images of the sage continue to surface in our culture. They remind us of injustices, and even of the fact that with justice can come the possibility of guarding the most mature forms of reason we have been able to achieve.

Notes

[1] Simone de Beauvoir, *The Coming of Age*. (New York: Putnam, 1972, p. 469).

[2] See, for example, James Gustafson, *Christ and the Moral Life* (New York: Harper and Row, 1968), p. 263.

[3] Jean Piaget, *Insights and Illusions of Philosophy*. (New York: World Publishing, 1968); *Psychology and Epistemology*. (New York: Grossman, 1958).

[4] Jean Piaget, *The Child's Conception of the World*. (Totowa, N.J.: Littlefied, Adams, 1969); *The Moral Judgment of the Child*. (New York: Free Press, 1965).

[5] Jean Piaget, *The Moral Judgment of the Child*, pp. 98–99.

[6] *Ibid.*, p. 399.

[7] *Ibid.*

[8] *Ibid.*

[9] Aaron Gurswitsch, "The Phenomenology of Perception," in *An Invitation to Phenomenology*, ed. James M. Edie (Chicago: Quadrangle Books, 1965), p. 28.

[10]The term *shocks* comes from Alfred Schutz; it is used here only as a convenient abbreviation for the concept developed more lengthily by Piaget.

[11]See, for example, H. Richard Neibuhr, *The Responsible Self.* (New York: Harper & Row, 1963), especially pp. 159–160; Paul Ricoeur, *The Symbolism of Evil.* (Boston: Harper & Row, 1967).

[12]This concept is also developed at some length by Ian T. Ramsey, "Moral Judgments and God's Commands" and "Toward a Rehabilitation of Natural Law," *Christian Ethics and Contemporary Philosophy,* ed. Ian T. Ramsey (New York: Macmillan & Co., 1966), pp. 172–180, 382–396.

[13]Lawrence Kohlberg and Richard Kramer, "Continuities and Discontinuities in Childhood and Adult Moral Development," *Human Development,* Vol. 12, Summer, 1961, p. 95.

[14]*Ibid.,* p. 118.

[15]Stephen Pepper, *World Hypotheses.* (Los Angeles: University of California Press, 1961).

[16]Kohlberg and Kramer, p. 113.

[17]Kenneth Keniston, "Youth and Violence: The Contexts of Moral Crisis," *Moral Education: Five Lectures,* eds. James Gustafson, et al. (Cambridge, Mass.: Harvard University Press, 1970), pp. 109–131.

[18]Simone de Beauvoir, Chap. 5.

[19]Kohlberg and Kramer, p. 109ff.

[20]*Ibid.,* p. 100.

[21]Simone de Beauvoir, p. 420.

[22]*Ibid.*

[23]Richard H. Williams and Claudine G. Wirths, *Lives through the Years.* (New York: Atherton Press, 1965), p. 3.

[24]Cited in Robert Kastenbaum and Nancy Durkee, "Elderly People View Old Age," *New Thoughts on Old Age.* ed. Robert Kastenbaum (New York: Springer Publishing Co., 1964), p. 251.

[25]*Ibid.*

[26]Interview with resident of Leisure World, Seal Beach, California.

[27]Richard H. Williams' and Claudine G. Wirths' *Lives through the Years* describes in a large number of case studies how adult roles have been stabilized by persons in the process of disengagement from the social system. A few of these studies, however, speak of certain life styles as "successful" for aging because they have *always* been narcissistic, not because they protect more mature options.

Chapter 16

TOWARD A STAGE THEORY OF ADULT COGNITIVE DEVELOPMENT

K. Warner Schaie

INTRODUCTION

Throughout my scientific career, perhaps with the exception of a very minor transgression, I have taken a strictly empiricist position and have devoted myself to the description of cognitive change over the adult life span, utilizing what seemed to be the best available techniques for such description. Having become older, and if not wiser, at least less defensive about admitting to the possible utility of armchair speculation, I am now ready to confess agreement with the dialectic position, that taking no position, takes a position as well, albeit not an explicated position. Indeed, in my previous theoretical exposition I took a regression view of aging, while in my more recent integrative writing I have opted in essence for a stability model of cognitive development.

Adapted from K. Warner Schaie, "Toward a Stage Theory of Adult Cognitive Development," *The International Journal of Aging and Human Development*, Vol. 8, 1977–78.

Further, positions such as mine, or those of writers such as Bayley, Horn, or Comalli, imply a continuity position for age changes in adult cognitive development regardless of the empirical findings as to decrement or stability of cognitive function. That is, no matter what we say, when we assess cognitive function by means of procedures found valid for young adults, we assume quantitative change in cognitive structures that remain qualitatively uniform throughout life.

In my own work, I have assiduously tried to show that most apparent differences in cognitive function between young and old are not ontogenetic in nature. Instead, such differences are often found because individuals are compared who belong to generations differing in the asymptotic level of acculturated materials acquired by them in young adulthood. But even if there is little change over age within individuals on measures validated for the young, this does not tell us that the young and the old are cognitively alike. Indeed, simple observation requires the admission, if only in terms of simple face validity, that there ought to be some qualitative age differences. And, what I may have done over the past decades is to show, first, that old people do not necessarily show intellectual decrement on certain tasks developed for the young; second, that the old are obsolete rather than decrepit; but also fortunately that this does not help as much to understand fully intellectual functioning in old age.

My first clues regarding the problems posed by continuity models of cognitive development in adulthood came with my more appreciative digestion of review of changes in factor structure of intelligence across age. Some of this material is certainly not new, since Cohen almost two decades ago reported changes both in the number and composition of factors derived from the Wechsler tests. But more recent discussions have made it quite clear that it may be overly simplistic to interpret developmental change in adulthood to be straightforward quantitative change.

A further persuasive argument was presented to me by an interesting study by Alpaugh who investigated creativity in a group of school teachers sampled over the adult age range but equated for education and performance on the WAIS vocabulary test. In this group, creativity decreased with age, even though vocabulary performance did not. This finding would be explained by a continuity model of cognitive function only if there were cohort differences in creativity that are independent from those found for intelligence. But the latter possibility is of a low order of probability and I would rather believe that once again qualities are measured in ways appropriate for the young but not necessarily for the old.

I feel compelled, then, to argue now that the processes that have been documented for the acquisition of cognitive structures and functions in childhood and during the early adult phase may not be relevant to the maintenance of functions and reorganization of structures required to meet the demands of later life. But if I adopt this position, I feel I must go a step further and begin to articulate an alternative model for adult cognitive development that might provide a blueprint for the development of new descriptive strategies. This is what I shall now propose to do.

ARE THERE ADULT COGNITIVE STAGES?

It seems to me that all previous models for intellectual development are narrowly confined to what we might denote as the acquisition of problem solving skills. In a sense, Piaget merely describes successive modes of increased efficiency in the solution of problems that involve the acquisition of new information.[2] Within such a sequence of increasingly efficient acquisitional processes, it is quite possible to describe the extent to which different classes of problem solving have been mastered by a structure of intellect model. But what happens when the young adult has reached some kind of asymptote in this acquisitional process?

Flavell claims that childhood cognitive modifications involve formal "morphological" properties that result from the biological-maturational growth process underlying these changes. In contrast, he argues that "no such underlying process constrains and directs adult cognitive changes . . . the most important adult cognitive changes are probably the result of life experiences, and would for the most part be expected to lack the across-subjects uniformity that characterizes the child's intellectual growth."

I think Flavell is wrong on the first count; that is, the morphological basis of children's cognitive development has never been fully documented, at least not to my satisfaction. Children's cognitive growth then is likely to reflect experiential factors as well, but is experience relevant to the acquisition of both process and substance? The adult experience, on the contrary, is likely to be relevant to quite different goals.

If we conceptualize cognitive growth as the stage of acquisition and postulate an asymptote for such growth in young adulthood, I believe, we have then by definition set forth a requirement for further adult stages. For if it be the purpose of the first part of life to acquire the intellectual tools needed to fully participate in the human experience, it then becomes necessary to postulate, if only on teleological grounds, that such preparation must have some further goals.

Now, it may be argued that survival into adulthood may be solely determined by the need for species reproduction. Even if this be so, in a species endowed with a prolonged period of immaturity, adult cognitive skills would as a minimum have evolutionary significance in their contribution to the survival, protection and acculturation of the next generation.

I would like to suggest then that the period of acquisition described, for example, by Piagetian models, whether mediated primarily by biological or experiential events, in the main ends in young adulthood, and is replaced by other life stages, requiring different models.

What is the Nature of Adult Stages?

If we accept the notion that adult development stages occur in response to experiential phenomena, we must next consider the attributes of such phenomena. Let me suggest that our search should lead us to an analysis of changes in cognitive requirements posed by environmental press. Here the work of social psychologists and anthropologists (and most noteworthy, that of the Langley-Porter group under the leadership of Marjorie Lowenthal and her associates) concerned with the analysis of adult life transitions gives us important cues.[3]

A tentative scheme involving five possible adult cognitive stages is sketched in Figure 16–1. These sequential stages are noted as *acquisitive, achieving, responsible, executive* and *reintegrative*.

Throughout the period characterized by us as *acquisitive*, the young organism has typically functioned in a protected environment. We believe that an important qualitative change in the environmental press occurs when the young adult is required to establish his own independence. For one thing, his problem-solving behavior no longer can be an isolated phenomenon, the consequences of which can be blunted by societal and/or parental protection. From now on, the adult will be held responsible fully and individually, and he must therefore embed his cognitive struc-

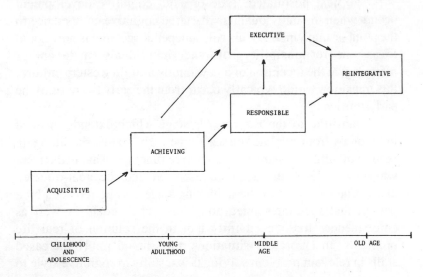

Figure 16–1.

tures in a broader network, whose goal is no longer mere acquisition, but is now concerned with the achievement of competence.

I would like to suggest that the *achieving stage* (which age-wise may occur anywhere from the late teens to the early twenties) requires further progress beyond the processes associated with the level of formal operations described by Piaget and his disciples as occurring in adolescence. That is, we are now concerned with much more goal-directed formal operations; task resolution is embedded in the consequences of the solution for achieving independent social function of the organism. As a consequence, we would predict more efficient and effective cognitive function with respect to tasks that have role-related achievement potential, while the peak may indeed have passed for problem-solving activities that are task-limited. Adolescence may see peak function in behaviors that are task-specific, respectively where the task, no matter how trivial, is important for the organism in the sense of the acquisition of skills regardless of their social implications. Young adulthood, in contrast, requires goal orientation. Different peak ages found on the Primary Mental Abilities would fit this contention.

The next postulated stage of adult cognitive development occurs when the individual has mastered cognitive competence to the point of implementing his role independence, and is now about to assume responsibility for other individuals (mate and/or offspring) at the inception of a new family unit. In western culture, this transition would typically occur from the early twenties to the early thirties.

Transition to the *responsible* stage which extends in most individuals from the late thirties to the early sixties should again require qualitative changes in cognitive function. That is the free-wheeling style of the acquisitive period and the goal-directed entrepreneurial style of the achieving stage will be replaced by a pattern that facilitates integrating long-range goals as well as consequences for one's family unit in the solution of real life problems. In laboratory situations, this should imply increased skills in relevant problem solving tasks, shifts in cognitive style to greater flexibility and lessened field dependence, gain in what has been described as the crystallized, but loss in the fluid abilities, the latter being of lowered relevance to the experiential demands upon the individual.

For some individuals, in the thirties and into the early forties, another stage may be reached which has been described by Neugarten in terms of the *executive* abilities of the middle-aged.[4] The elicitative experiential press here would seem to be the assumption of responsibility for societal systems, instead of simple units, with the corresponding need to develop cognitive strategies that are efficient at integrating complex and high level hierarchical relationships. Here we should expect further gains on laboratory tasks such as pattern recognition, inductive thinking, and complex problem solving tasks, with corresponding lowering of skills in task specific situations as well as possibly some increase in difficulty in dealing with new bits of information as contrasted to the retrieval of past data.

For both the "responsible" and the "executive" stages, common psychometric tests of intelligence are likely to prove quite inadequate. The "building blocks" of intelligence are, of course, most important during the "acquisitive" and "achieving" stages, but they fail to tell us the whole story, when the emphasis of cognitive function changes to organizational, integrative, and interpretive roles. Now it may be possible that a variety of task measuring problem solving skills and cognitive styles may be suitable vehicles for measuring intellectual competence at these stages of cognitive development. I fear, however, that it will be necessary to develop new measurement technologies that will borrow heavily on the information processing and systems analysis literature.

We have now described levels of cognitive development whose common mode is the need for the integration of acculturated intellectual skills at increasing levels of role complexity. It remains to consider a further stage or stages that will account for cognitive behavior during that part of life when the extent of societal involvement and responsibility relaxes and when biological changes may indeed once again impose constraints upon cognitive function.

I believe that the final phase of cognitive development, which I have elected to denote as the *reintegrative* stage, completes the transition from the "what should I know," through the "how should I use what I know," to the "why should I know" phase of life. Adaptive cognitive processes at this level of development may well operate in an orthogonal fashion to a young adult structure of intellect model. Cognitive processes here are most certainly moderated by motivational and attitudinal variables to a much larger degree than would be true at any other life stage, an intuitive recognition, which up to now has received only limited attention.

The transition of the "reintegrative" stage occurs at a time when the complexity of the adult cognitive structure has reached an overload stage, and consequently demands simplification, and where environmentally programmed role requirements are reduced due to occupational retirement, relinquishment of responsibilities for children and family, and other role restrictions previously described as "disengagement" phenomena. But the cognitive response is not that of disengagement at all, it is one of achieving more selective attention to cognitive demands that remain meaningful or attain new meaning. Thus, problem solving now no longer occurs as a simple response to a competence-motivation linked stimulus situation, but requires meaning and purpose within the immediate life situation of the individual, or within the more cosmic interests of selected older individuals who exemplify what folk myth describes as the "wisdom of old age."[5]

Completely new strategies for the measurement of intellectual competence of the elderly will obviously be required. Such strategies will first of all require an analysis of criterion variables relevant to the life experience and life roles of both the recently retired (or young) old and the very aged. Some of the pioneering work of Deming and Pressey may be illustrative, but the network of item content will have to be wide and the processes to be investigated need yet to be identified. The task will be no less than that faced by Binet in initially measuring the intelligence of school children.

SOME UNFINISHED BUSINESS

I have now sketched some very gross outlines of my thinking on the characteristics of adult stages of cognitive development and the kind of operations that might be suitable for the differential investigation of such stages. I am quite aware of the fact that I have not addressed myself to the question of how my scheme related to models of adult development such as those suggested by Erikson[6] or by Kohlberg,[7] some of whose stages may sound quite similar to mine. More importantly, I have not addressed other implicit issues in the construction of developmental paradigms. For example, attention will have to be given to the question of what might be necessary and sufficient conditions for transition from one adult stage to the next, or whether such transitions imply substitutive or superimposed behavior patterns.

Significant progress in the study of intellectual competence in adulthood and old age will not be made until we turn to ecologically valid criteria and develop a technology predicated upon the life context of the population under study rather than populations at other life stages. Hopefully, specifications such as those offered here will encourage movement towards the new models and operations required in this direction.

Other issues yet to be dealt with concern the manner in which the increasing complexity of environmental press interacts with the individual's cognitive structure such that a change in shifting from one stage to the next is required. And, finally, we need to specify just how a hierarchical model of cognitive complexity can be related to the motivational parameters that I have suggested may become predominant in moderating cognitive behavior in old age.

NOTES

[2]See J. H. Flavell, *The Developmental Psychology of Jean Piaget*. (Princeton, N.J.: Van Nostrand, 1963).

[3]M. F. Lowenthal, M. Thurnher, D. Chiriboga, et al., *Four Stages of Life*. (San Francisco: Jossey-Bass, 1975).

[4]B. L. Neugarten, "Continuities and Discontinuities of Psychological Issues Into Adult Life," *Human Development*, Vol. 12, 1969, pp. 121–130.

[5]See also L. Kohlberg, "Continuities in Childhood and Adult Moral Development," in *Life-Span Developmental Psychology: Personality and Socialization*, eds. P. B. Baltes and K. W. Schaie (New York: Academic Press, 1973).

[6]E. H. Erikson, *Childhood and Society*. (New York: Norton, 1963).

[7]W. R. Birkhill and K. W. Schaie, "The Effect of Differential Reinforcement of Cautiousness in the Intellectual Performance of the Elderly," *Journal of Gerontology* Vol. 30, 1975, pp. 578–583.

Chapter 17

THE COMING OF AGE

Simone de Beauvoir

A limited future and a frozen past: such is the situation that the elderly have to face up to. In many instances it paralyzes them. All their plans have either been carried out or abandoned, and their life has closed in about itself; nothing requires their presence; they no longer have anything whatsoever to do. This is what happened to Michel Leiris after the success of *Biffures*. "It seemed to me that my life had reached a kind of horrible culmination. As I saw it, this ending of life was rather like the last days of my stay in Florence. We had done the Tuscan capital from top to bottom, and all we had left to see was a few trifles: in just the same way I had only a few trifles left to do in the time that still remained for me to live," he says in *Fibrilles*. In the same book he explains why his future had become so depopulated.

From Simone de Beauvoir, *The Coming of Age*, trans. Patrick O'Brian (New York: G. P. Putnam's Sons, 1972, London: Andre Deutch, Ltd. 1972). Reprinted by permission of the editors.

When one no longer looks upon being wiped out by death or senility as a fate but expects it as an evil that is about to strike, then—and this was the case with me—one loses even the smallest wish to undertake any new thing: one reckons the very small amount of time that still lies ahead—a throttled time that has no relation with that of the days when it was unthinkable that any undertaking should not have space enough to develop freely; and this puts out one's fire entirely. In the same way, when a man has been accustomed to it for many years, as I have been, it is hard to tell oneself each day that the night, now cluttered with weariness and sleep, will not be that limitlessly open time in which—supposing that nothing has weakened him—he may make love, spending his strength without counting the cost. It may be that I am clearer-minded than others, more vulnerable or more graspingly concerned with my own person, but it seems to me that a man whose life has thus moved from the boundless to the bounded lives in a kind of asphyxia. . . . Art and poetry, those last resources, stand there as a means of breaking the strangle-hold. But surely it is a pity to climb down so far as to treat them as a substitute, something that will allow one to soothe the heartbreaking poverty of old age?

In fact, the project of writing had such deep roots in this case that it stood firm against the crisis; indeed, his very anguish provided Leiris with new themes and he wrote *Fibrilles*. But it may happen, either for reasons of health or because of outside difficulties, that the old person is utterly and finally disheartened: either he sees nothing more to do, or he gives up his undertakings, supposing he has no time to carry them through to the end.

Yet there are also cases where the categorical imperatives arising from the past retain all their strength: this piece of work must be finished, that book written, these interests safeguarded. When this is so, the elderly man starts a race against time that leaves him not a moment's respite. "My most painful experience as old age came nearer, was that of losing all sense of leisure," said Berenson at seventy. It is even more painful to be unable to finish that which one longs to finish: as we have seen, Papini was bitterly distressed at not being able to reach the end of his greatest book, *Le Jugement Dernier*.

Our projects may aim at goals that lie beyond our death: it is common knowledge that most people attach great importance to their wills and to the carrying out of their last wishes. In repetitive societies and those in which history moves slowly, a man has not only his own future at his disposal but also that of the world in which he takes it for granted that the results of his labor will continue to exist. When this is so, an eighty-year-old may take pleasure in building or even in planting trees. When the majority of undertakings, whether they were agricultural, commercial, financial, or run by craftsmen, were of a family nature, forming part of an economically stable society, the father could hope that his sons would carry on with his task and hand it down in their turn to their children. He thus avoided "touching the boundary-stone"—the estate or firm in which he had given himself an objective state would last indefinitely. He would survive himself: his labor was not lost.

At present, the aged man can no longer reckon upon an eternity of this kind: the pace of history has increased. Tomorrow it will destroy what was built yesterday. The trees the old man has planted will be cut down. Almost everywhere the family unit has fallen apart. Small firms are either taken over by monopolies or they fail. The son will not relive his father's life, and the father knows it. Once he has gone, the estate will be abandoned, the shop sold, the business wound up. All that he has achieved and all that gave a meaning to his life lies under the same threat that menaces him. If he has a generous love for his children and if he approves of the course they have chosen he may be happy to think that he lives on in them. But because of the chasm that usually divides the generations, this does not happen very often. Generally speaking, the father does not see himself in his son. The void swallows him entirely.

Modern society, far from providing the aged man with an appeal against his biological fate, tosses him into an outdated past, and it does so while he is still living. The acceleration of history has caused an immense upheaval in the relationship between the aged man and his activities. Formerly, it was supposed that with the progress of the years a treasure piled up within him—experience. A certain knowledge of things, a certain knowledge of life that was not to be learned from books gradually accumulated in his mind and body, much as crystals are deposited on twigs plunged into petrifying springs. Hegelian philosophy puts forward a rational justification for this idea, according to which every past instant is enfolded in the present instant, which necessarily prepares a still more perfected future, even failures being put right in the end: old age, the final stage of a continual advance, is life's highest pitch of perfection. But in fact this is not how life progresses at all. Its line of advance is perpetually broken by the falling back of our projects into practico-inert reality. At every given moment it provides its own sum, but this summation is never completed: "Human action amounts both to the whole and to the destruction of the whole."* That is why our motion is not a firm advance, but rather that reeling, staggering movement that Montaigne speaks of. Sainte-Beauve observed, "We harden in some places and rot in others: we never ripen." Old age is not the *summa* of our life. As time gives us the world so with the same motion it takes it from us. We learn and we forget; we enrich ourselves and we lose our wealth.

The eighty-year-old Mauriac wrote, "Neither lessened nor fallen nor made richer—but the same: that is how the old man sees himself. Let no one talk to him about life's acquisitions: it is unbelievable how little we retain of all that which has poured in throughout all these years. Facts are forgotten or have grown muddled. And what am I to say about ideas? Fifty years of reading: and what remains of it?"

The notion of experience is sound when it refers to an active apprenticeship. Some arts and callings are so difficult that a whole lifetime is needed to master them. As we have seen, manual workers manage to cloak their physical deficiencies by means of their experience: it allows them to organize the field of their activities. From the intellectual point of view, Herriot used to say that "culture was what was left when everything else was forgotten"; and indeed, something does remain—a greater skill in

*Sartre, *Critique de la raison dialectique*.

relearning what was known, method in work, resistance to error, safeguards. In many fields, such as philosophy, ideology, and politics, the elderly man is capable of a synthetic vision forbidden to the young. In order to be able to appreciate the importance or unimportance of some particular case, to reduce the exception to the rule or allot it its place, to subordinate details to the whole, and to set anecdote aside in order to isolate the general idea, one must have observed an enormous number of facts in all their aspects of likeness and difference. And there is one form of experience that belongs only to those who are old—that of old age itself. The young have only vague and erroneous notions of it. One must have lived a long time to have a true idea of the human condition, and to have a broad view of the way in which things happen: it is only then that one can "foresee the present"—the task of the statesman. That is why, in the course of history, elderly men have been entrusted with great responsibilities.

Yet it is in scarcely any but repetitive or at least stable societies that age can confer a qualification. If he has taken care to move forward, the elderly man is more advanced in an unchanging world than those who have set off after him. This is not the case in the changing world of today. Individual development or "becoming" exists in the context of a social development with which it does not coincide: this difference of rhythm is harmful to the elderly man, who necessarily finds himself out of date. To move forward he must perpetually be tearing himself free from a past that holds him with an ever-tighter grasp: his advance is slow. Yet mankind is not all of a piece; when confronted with that past which weighs down the former generations, the new are free; they take up the torch and carry it on until they too are crushed by the weight of the practico-inert, and they in their turn are outstripped by the young. It is not in the power of an individual to keep up in this race, in which the project is perpetually reborn in all its freshness. He is left behind. In the midst of change he remains the same; he condemns himself to supersession.

As far as knowledge is concerned he necessarily falls behind. I see this clearly from my own example. I have learned a great deal since I was twenty, but year by year I become relatively more ignorant because there are more and more discoveries; the sciences grow richer, and in spite of my efforts to keep abreast at least in some fields, the number of things I do not know increases.

For a more exact understanding of this disqualifying process, we must leave generalities and consider the particular aspect of various activities. But let us first observe that it is insofar as he wishes to be a factor in the evolution of society that the old person is behind the times; as a consumer he takes advantage of technical progress without being worried by it at all—indeed, he welcomes it eagerly. In theory, Tolstoy loathed novelty, yet he was wonder-struck by the gramophone and the cinema, and he thought of writing film-scripts. He went to watch car-racing and he longed to see airplanes. Andersen, at sixty-five, was charmed by the speed of the new forms of transport: the journey across Sweden had taken a week in the old days; now it could be done in twenty-four hours. "We old people are affected by the unpleasant side of a transitional period straddling two generations; but it is very interesting." When he was seventy, Wells was extremely enthusiastic about all modern inventions, particularly the cinema.

Morin studied the commune of Plodemet and published the results of his research in *Commune en France:* here there were some infirm, sick, decrepit, and abandoned old people who said of themselves that all they were good for was to guard the house like a dog. Although they were physically fit, a few others shut themselves up in the past: they could not read or write, and they refused running water, gas, and electricity. "What's the use? It's not suitable for people of our age," said one of them. But most were amazed and delighted by the modern world. "Now we shall have seen everything, from the bicycle to men on the moon," said an eighty-year-old joiner. They could remember their astonishment at the sight of the first cars and the first airplanes; they were enchanted by oil heating and the televison. In their opinion the past was a barbaric age. "A hundred years ago they were real savages, here in these parts, indeed they were. Now we're civilized: everyone can at least read and write. It was a wretched life in the old day's; now it's fine." They are pleased that the young men use machines and radar for fishing. They are subjectively proud that the world has objectively advanced. Insofar as their own interests, their past and their activities are not called into question, and there is no antagonism cutting them off from mankind as a whole: they see themselves as part of it with delight. Its evolution is a magnificent spectacle, one that they watch from a distance without feeling that their way of life is in dispute.

In Plodemet there is a striking contrast between the attitude of the very old and inactive men and that of the men between fifty and sixty who work. The latter come into conflict with the present age because it endangers their economic and ideological interests. They are against the modernization of farming, which would require an apprenticeship that they are unwilling to undergo. They cling to the routine that has formed their lives; they do not want to give up the advantages of their experience and find themselves on a lower footing than the young, who are cleverer at handling the new machines than they. Many grow pig-headed in their refusal: when this happens the sons go off to work in the town and the fathers feel that they have been betrayed. "So many old parents are deserted by their children!" said one fifty-five-year-old farmer. "They have based their whole lives on setting something up, and then there is no one to carry on."

The following piece of police-court news comes from an issue of *France-Soir* of October 1968.

> "There was an explosion in the yard—my father-in-law had just killed Wolf, our Alsatian. Jean, my husband, opened the door. His father rushed in. He was holding a grenade in his hand. Jean threw himself on him: they fought. The grenade fell to the ground and went off." This was Dominique's evidence. Albert Rouzet, sixty-five, a farmer at Chinay (Côte d'Or), suffered from neurasthenia, and the day before he made up his mind to do away with the whole family, beginning with his twenty-five-year-old son Jean, whom he blamed for running the farm on modern lines. "In my days we got up at dawn to get the day's work ready, and there was no need to spend all the money on buying machines to work the land," he used to say. The explosion killed both father and son.

As far as farmers are concerned, society does allow a choice between traditional methods and progress; but there are other cases where the advance of industry or commerce condemns the eldely craftsman or shopkeeper without appeal. Towards the end of the nineteenth century the rise of the big stores ruined many small traders. It is their story that Zola tells in *Au Bonheur des Dames*. He describes the older generation's struggle against the future that is taking away their living; he describes their despair. Baudu, a yellow-faced, white-haired, authoritarian patriarch, is the owner of Au Vieil Elbeuf, a little hundred-year-old shop with a low ceiling and deep, sombre, dusty windows; on the other side of the street there is the big store in all its splendor, and the gleaming windows of its drapery department seem to defy him. When his niece, just arrived from Paris, sees him, he is standing in the doorway, his mouth twisted, his eyes bloodshot, staring furiously at the display of Au Bonheur des Dames. The old-fashioned little shop with its worn, polished oak counters, its drawers with massive handles, its dark bales of cloth rising to the ceiling, has almost no customers left. Baudu is eaten up with rage and hatred. "Oh God, oh God," he groans, glaring at the store where his niece is going to work. He is outraged and he foretells the ruin of the new establishment: a draper's shop ought not to sell goods outside their line of business—it is a "bazaar." "Draper's assistants selling furs—how ridiculous!" He cannot accept the overturning of all the traditions by which he has lived. He eats his heart out. In former days his old shop had more customers than any other in his part of the town, and he was proud of it. And now, like all its small neighbors, it is dying. "It was a slow death, with no sudden shock—business continually dwindling, customers lost one by one." The Bonheur des Dames does well, and Baudu is compelled to admit it. "They are succeeding: so much the worse for them! As for me, I protest. That's all: I protest." To pay his bills, he sells his house in the country. He is ruined, and endlessly he complains of these modern times—everything is falling to pieces; there is no such thing as the family any more. And at the same time he is humiliated; he feels that he has been beaten. "The knowledge of his defeat stripped him of his former assurance, the assurance of a respected patriarch." In the end he is offered a job at the Bonheur des Dames; but he refuses it and shuts himself up in his despair. Here we see the relationship established between biological and social time. If Baudu had been younger he would have wanted to modernize his shop, and he would have done so. But this shortness of his future and the weight of his past close all outlets to him. His shop was the reality in which he had his objective being: once it is ruined he no longer exists—he is a dead man under suspended sentence. Blind to the rest of the world, to the end he stubbornly preserves the man he has been by means of his refusals and his memories. Tragedies of this kind happen today when the big stores set up branches in little towns, ruining the local shopkeepers. In capitalist countries, the phenomenon is all the more frequent because of concentration.

There are many occupations in which advancing years are no real disqualification—they do not prevent the worker from doing his job: nevertheless, age does affect the individual who is engaged in them. As we have seen, at a given moment workers, office staff, executives, and civil servants are retired. Society takes an ambiguous view of aging in doctors, barristers, and professional men in general. This is particularly striking in the case of doctors. For a certain length of time, age adds to their value; it is thought to bring experience, and a man with a long career behind him is preferred to a novice. Later the picture changes. The old doctor is looked upon as worn out, in biological decline, and as one who has therefore lost much of his ability. And above all he is thought to be out of date; people imagine that he is not familiar with modern discoveries. Patients leave him: his waiting room empties. In almost every field, the elderly man, even supposing that he is not compulsorily retired and that he is still up to his job, is condemned to idleness because of this prejudice.

In those callings that require great physical qualifications, old age is decisive. Very early the athlete is debarred from competition. He often carries out a reconversion in his own branch—the skiing champion becomes a trainer; the professional boxer is a manager: but he may also turn to quite a different area, and this often happens—Carpentier opened a bar, Killy sells sports-cars, Marielle Goitschel has moved to films. There is a break in their lives; they foresaw it, but nevertheless many of them have difficulty in finding other jobs and they grow bitter. There is a similar break for dancers and singers—the dancers lose their suppleness and the singers' voices fail. Many take to teaching the art they no longer practice, and in this way they may still transcend themselves through the success of their pupils. Others, either from necessity or from choice, retire altogether. Actors have to reckon on change in both their voices and their appearance. Some prefer to deny it altogether: I saw De Max playing the role of the young Nero when he was eighty. When it is a question of "holy cows" the public love this stubborn perseverance: they applauded the eighty-year-old Sarah Bernhardt when she played Athalie with a wooden leg. Actors usually change their roles; but there are not many parts for elderly people on the stage and still fewer in films. On the stage, if the text is important, there is the danger of a lapse of memory. Here again, actors try to find a new career without moving too far from their past; but the possibilities are few, and most of them are condemned to retirement and poverty. The *chansonniers,* who sing their own songs in cabarets and night-clubs, are more fortunate; no extraordinary technical skill is required of them, and they can adapt their acts to their capacity. Indeed, in their case the very fact of being old may be an asset: when he was eighty Maurice Chevalier gave a show whose immense success was largely due to the fact that he was an octogenarian. Even so, this calls for excellent health and the ability to keep the favor of the novelty-loving public for years and years. It is the executive musicians, the pianists, violinists, and cellists, who most usually overcome their physical decline, in spite of the body's importance in their careers. They may retain their fame and talent to the age of eighty, always supposing that they are not struck by an illness that would destroy their skill and that they go on practicing. If they resist biological aging, social aging does not affect them adversely, because all they are asked to do is to maintain their standard. Though there are cases where musicians surpass themselves towards the end of their lives, because of their ever-deepening comprehension of what they play.

Brain-workers are less troubled by their physiological decline than the rest. A certain number enjoy a unique autonomy in their relationship with society: these are the creators. There are not a great many of them, but because of their privileged position they are, as it were, touchstones or detectors—by them we may judge what is practically possible for an elderly man when he is given the maximum of opportunity. They help us to see the nature of the relationship between age and fruitfulness in the various intellectual and artistic fields, and they tell us how we are to understand it.

It is most unusual for a scientist to make discoveries in his old age. Euler did carry out important mathematical work when he was seventy-one and seventy-two. Galileo was seventy-two when he finished his best book, the *Dialogues concerning the New Sciences*, and he was seventy-four when he wrote his *Mathematical Disquisitions and Demonstrations*. Buffon wrote the last seven volumes of his *Histoire naturelle* between the ages of sixty-seven and eighty-one, and they contain the best of his work. Between seventy-eight and eighty Franklin invented bifocal lenses and studied lead poisoning. Laplace finished his *Mécanique céleste* at the age of seventy-nine. Herschel was reading important papers to the Royal Society when he was eighty and more. Michelson was seventy-seven when he published the results of the experiment on the speed of light that he carried out with Morley. Gauss and Pavlov continued the work of their youth when they were old men, adding much to it. But all these are exceptions. Lehman* tried to establish a correlation between age and human accomplishment in his book *Age and Achievement;* and basing himself upon Professor Hildich's *Brève histoire de la chimie* he shows that the most important discoveries in chemistry have been made by men be-

---

*Lehman's statistical method is utterly erroneous when it is applied to art and literature. In science it is easier to evaluate the number and value of the discoveries.

tween twenty-five and thirty, and the most in number by those between thirty and thirty-five: out of 993 examples of outstanding work, only three are due to men of over seventy. In physics, the most favorable age seems to be between thirty and thirty-four; in astronomy, between forty and forty-four. Lehman observes that Edison was productive all his life, but that his best period was at thirty-five. Chevreul lived to be 103 and he went on working far into old age; but he is chiefly known for the discoveries on animal fat that he made when he was thirty-seven.

It is above all in mathematics that late discoveries are so very rare. There is one brilliant exception. Elie Cardan was sixty-seven when he published an epoch-making paper that was completely new in relation to his earlier work; in this paper he solved problems that he had himself propounded at the age of twenty-eight and that the greatest mathematicians had been unable to answer. Some other cases of this kind may be quoted; but they are very few. The eldely mathematicians' sterility is so notorious that Bourbaki's group would not accept anyone over fifty.

Aging in the scientist is not of a biological nature. Here there is no question of overwork, nervous wear and tear or mental fatigue; some scientists remain in excellent health to the end of their days. Why is it that once they have passed a certain age they no longer make discoveries?

In order to find the answer, we must first understand the nature of the choice that a man makes when he decides to devote himself to science. The object of his study is the universal as it can be grasped by means of abstract symbols and concepts. This implies that he makes the universal part of himself. He does away with his subjectivity in order to think along the lines of a universally valid rational system. Even if he works by himself, he is not alone: he is taking part in a collective work that tries to reach a common goal, though by different paths. In any case, nowadays he is usually one of a team, all of whose members are on the same footing. The scientist is not a lone wolf; he inherits from those who have gone before him; the path he follows has already been opened to some degree, and he travels in the company of other workers;

they meet with the same difficulties, and it may happen that the means of overcoming them is discovered simultaneously in several different places—it is science as a whole that prepares the individual discovery and calls it into being. To be sure, however much the worker may be ruled by the object of his research, he nevertheless remains a unique subject, almost in spite of himself; he has his own vision of the world, his own imagination, his own way of making decisions. It is for this reason that he sometimes emerges from the general body and discovers an original idea. But his option in favor of the universal means that these flashes neither come often nor last long. It is understandable that they should be most frequent in youth or at the beginning of maturity, for that is the time at which the scientist is mastering the body of knowledge that forms his particular study; he sees it with a new eye, and this allows him to perceive its gaps and contradictions. He has the courage to attempt to repair them because he has his whole life before him to correct his errors and to develop the truths whose existence he divines. Later, a considerable amount of work has to be done to verify, organize, and exploit his discovery. Once more the research becomes collective, and it is not necessarily the discoverer who is best qualified for carrying it through. Most often he remains the man of that moment, of that idea; whereas what the evolution of science requires is a fresh break with the past.*

A great mathematician of fifty-five has told me that he reads mathematical works with greater ease and profit than he did when he was young: his power of comprehension, his experience, and ability to synthesize have increased. But his curiosity has grown somewhat dull. When he was twenty-five and the victim of that youthful illusion that stretches the future indefinitely, he formed the plan of knowing everything in all the branches of mathematics. Now he is resigned to reading only those works that have a direct bearing on his speciality, and to leaving many others to one side.

*Nearly all the exceptions I have mentioned date from a time when scientists worked alone: some of these discoveries made late in life are of an almost craftsmanlike nature.

He explains that in modern mathematics specialization is so highly developed, and the various branches so shut off from one another, that he would find it easier to follow a biologist maintaining his thesis than a fellow-mathematician lecturing on some foreign area of his own science. In his opinion a worker who is not cut off from research retains the possibility of making discoveries from a considerable period: but he is hampered by epistemological obstacles of which the young know nothing. In our day an Evariste Galois* would be impossible: a man must be twenty-five or thirty to master the whole mathematical edifice in all its complexity, and that is the most favorable period for discovery. Later there is often a sense of inhibition. When a man knows that no one has been able to prove the truth or the falsity of a given proposition, and when he has done all he can without success, he decides that it would be wasting his time to persist and he gives up. This happened to my friend eleven years ago. Then a Russian mathematician told him that he had solved the problem. My friend returned to it; and since he knew that the solution could be found, there was no longer any question of letting go. And he did find it; he found it very quickly, by the simple juxtaposition of two other theorems that were perfectly familiar to him. He told me that this was a very frequent occurrence. Here the young are at a great advantage: they are often unaware that others have struggled in vain with the question that occupies them, and try to tackle it with the utmost confidence. They have time and to spare before them, and they are not tempted to economize their energy.

Above all, said my informant, it is the past that weighs upon the elderly scientist, the past in the form of habits of mind and ideological interest. All present mathematics is being renewed at a dizzying speed, and the change calls the whole structure in question. With every alteration an entirely new form of language has to be learned; and clearly the reason that it is preferred to the old form is that it is quicker and more suitable, and that it makes discovery

*Evariste Galois died when he was nineteen.

easier. The mathematician who cannot make up his mind to adopt it is obliged to translate the new truths into the terms he is familiar with, and this slows down his work very seriously. It may happen that a forty-year-old professor is unable to comprehend a statement of his own theories explained by a twenty-five-year-old mathematician to his contemporaries in the new language, commom to them but unknown to their older colleague. The older man can never hope to outstrip those who are in possession of the more precise instrument. Yet after a certain stage it is both hard and discouraging to learn Hebrew or Chinese, and many aging scientists recoil. The mathematician has as it were a withdrawal, a shrinking from his line of thought. "If I have the intuition of a new theorem," said my friend, "I realize that it will compel me to revise everything I had hitherto taken as established, and I hesitate." Then again he said, "In growing older one becomes both more and less free. Freer in relation to others, since one is not afraid of surprising them, or of ignoring certain prejudices or of challenging established ideas. But less free in relation to oneself." Last year he wrote a mathematical book that is now going through the press. But since then he has written an article that makes the book out of date; it was painful for him to have to inflict this contradiction upon himself, but he disregarded it. And now this very article itself is called into question by still more recent work that he has just finished. The progress of mathematics is not a placid, smooth advance. It is a series of arguments and disputes that results in a perpetual modification. A great deal of enthusiasm and of time and energy is called for if everything that one has learnt hitherto is to be turned upside down: it is a process more suited to young men than others.

This particular case confirms my general remarks upon the activities of the elderly man: the weight of the past slows him down or even brings him to a halt, whereas the young generations break free from the practico-inert and move forward.

We can come to a more exact definition of what holds the elderly scientist back. In the first place, he has ideological interests: he is "alienated," transferred to his work, that "aggregation of inert meanings based on verbal material"* in which he has built up his being outside himself. All this is imperilled in the world, since it exists for others, who transcend it by the light of their own projects. Its author does his utmost to defend it, opposing theories and systems that tend to discredit it. He is quite willing to correct and to enrich, but not to deny it, although at a given point a denial might be necessary for progress. For him it contains inert requirements with which he must comply, and this may lead him into blind alleys. Some research workers are so alienated to their ideological interests that they will falsify the results of experiments that contradict their theories. Darwin was aware of this danger and he made it a rule to make an immediate note of facts and ideas that ran counter to his doctrine, "for I knew by experience that ideas and facts of this kind vanish more easily from the memory than those which are in our favour." Yet it is said that in his old age he would not listen to the reading of anything written in opposition to his views: and August Comte did the same. Obstinacy of this sort makes it impossible to review a work in the light of fresh knowledge, so as to detect errors and attempt to correct them. Lévy-Bruhl was an exceptional case: in his notebooks for 1938 and 1939, he renounces all his former ideas on the prelogical mental patterns, participation, and nonconceptualization that he thought he had observed among primitive peoples. Yet he made no new discoveries.

Even if he is truly disinterested the scientist still comes up against inner resistances. He has habits of mind that make him obstinately persist in out-of-date methods. That same specialization which made his successes possible prevents him from keeping abreast of work that runs parallel to his; and it might happen that a knowledge of this work would be necessary for fresh discovery on his part. The more clear-sighted among them are aware of these gaps. Shortly after he had been awarded the Nobel prize, Professor Kastler spoke of going back to the students' benches to follow a

*Sartre, *Critique de la raison dialectique.*

course of lectures on the quantum theory. And above all the elderly scientist is so familiar with some ideas that he looks upon them as self-evident and therefore never thinks of questioning them: but they have to be discarded for any advance to be possible. When Bachelard spoke of "epistemological obstacles," old age seemed to him one of the most important.

In order to defend his outdated concepts, the aged scientist will often deliberately block the progress of science; and the standing he enjoys makes it possible for him to do this. As Bachelard says, "The great scientists are useful to science in the first half of their lives and harmful in the second." Arthur Clarke has made a survey of a very large number of discoveries that were said to be impossible by scientists, not because they lacked the necessary knowledge, but because they did not possess the necessary imagination and daring: this he puts down to their age, and for him a scientist is old as soon as he has reached his fortieth year. Some eighty years ago, the notion that electric light could be used in homes was hooted down by all the experts; nevertheless, the thirty-one-year-old Edison worked on the incandescent bulb, making it a practical reality. But later in his life he too was just as backward, setting himself against the introduction of alternating current. Newcomb, the American astronomer, wrote a very well-known essay proving that it was impossible for objects heavier than air to fly. When the Wright brothers actually took off, Newcomb stated that their machine would never be capable of carrying more than a single person, and that it therefore had no practical application. Another astronomer, W. H. Bickering, was of the same opinion. By this time the principles of flight were understood; but the two scientists refused to draw the obvious conclusions. In 1926 Professor Bickerlow advanced proofs of his assertion that no projectile could ever be sent to the moon: the only source of energy that he took into consideration was nitroglycerin, and his calculations assumed that the fuel had to form an integral part of the missile. In 1938 a Canadian astronomer, J. W. Campbell, worked out that it would need a million tons of fuel to remove a weight of one or two pounds from the gravitational pull of the earth; and from this he drew the same conclusions as Bickerlow. His calculations were based on the supposition that the rocket would have to be endowed with a fabulous speed and that the acceleration would be so slow that the fuel would be exhausted at a low altitude. Rutherford was sixty-six when he died in 1937: he stated that it would never be possible to set free the energy contained in matter. Five years later the first chain-reaction began to operate in Chicago. When Pontecorvo said that the highly penetrating particles called neutrinos would allow the observation of the interior of stars, those astrophysicists who were qualified to utter an opinion laughed him to scorn: a little later he carried out his experiments successfully. Clark's conclusion is that "the man who knows most facts about any given subject is not necessarily the one who will most clearly foresee the future in this field." And he condemns old scientists even more harshly than Bachelard: "Scientists over fifty are no longer good for anything but holding congresses, and they should at all costs be kept far away from laboratories."

Clark's account is not very satisfactory. He attacks men of widely differing value. He does not study the reasons for their resistance. He confines himself to saying that it is inevitable that they should have preconceived notions. "A completely open mind would be an empty mind." Yet he does emphasize one important fact: instead of being of use for foretelling the future, knowledge can be a hindrance. Thus, when Auguste Comte was thirty-five he asserted that it would never be possible to know the composition of the sun. I might also quote the declaration on the subject of traveling by train, made by the Lyons Academy of Medicine in 1835: this prophesied that the human frame would be unable to bear the dizzy speed. "The vibration will bring about nervous diseases . . . while the rapid succession of images will cause inflammation of the retina. The dust and smoke will give rise to bronchitis and pleural adhesions. And lastly the anxiety caused by the continual danger will keep the travelers in a perpetual state of tension, and it will be the precursor of cerebral disorders. For a pregnant woman, any journey by train must inevitably bring on a miscarriage, together with all its consequences."

After a certain age even very great minds find it difficult to move with the times. In 1935, when he was fifty-five, Einstein speaking of the suicide of his friend Ehrenfest, the physicist, attributed it to the inner conflicts that attack any deeply honest scientist who has passed the age of fifty. Ehrenfest had a clear understanding of certain problems that he was unable to solve in a constructive manner. "During these last years," said Einstein, "the strangely turbulent development of theoretical physics made the situation worse. It is always hard to learn and to teach things that one cannot fully accept in one's heart. And to this there is added the ever-increasing difficulty of adapting oneself to new ways of thought, a difficulty that always confronts any man who has passed fifty."

Einstein himself had to deal with this situation, and it is interesting to look into his case. He was not alienated to any ideological interests. He had never sought to have the last word, and he was comparatively indifferent to his reputation. His love for the truth was absolutely pure. But he had so firmly anchored a view of science that it never occurred to him to give it up at any price whatsoever: it had to provide a harmonious and rational image of the world. The paradox of his career is that his theory of relativity had a great influence upon the quantum theory, and yet Einstein, when he was over forty-five, looked upon the quantum theory with an unfavorable eye. The Polish physicist Infeld, who had earlier worked with Einstein, says, "There is something ironic about the role of champion that Einstein assumed in the great revolution, since later he turned his back on that very revolution which he had helped bring about. As time goes by he moves farther and farther from the younger generation of scientists, most of whom are carrying out research on the quantum theory."

Antonina Vallentin, in whom Einstein confided on the subject of his "mathematical torments," says that this was not a question "of the usual divorce between a fresh generation, fully aware of the boldness of its thought, and an old man left over from the past like a rock in the middle of a road that runs on beyond him. His tragedy was rather that of a man who, in spite of his age, stubbornly goes on traveling a more and more forsaken path, while almost all his friends and all the young people around him assert that this path leads nowhere and that he has set out along a blind alley."

He was not sure that he was right. In March 1949, when he was seventy, he wrote to Solovine, "You suppose that I contemplate my life's work with calm satisfaction. But seen close to the whole thing has quite a different look. There is not one single notion that I am convinced will hold its ground and broadly speaking I am not certain of being on the right path. Our contemporaries look upon me both as a heretic and as a reactionary who has, as it were, outlived himself. To be sure, this is a question of fashion and of a shortsighted view; but the feeling of inadequacy comes from within."

Yet he found it impossible to modify his position. As he saw it, a theory was valid only if it possessed an "inner perfection": an abundance of "external confirmations" was not enough for him. The theory of unitary fields that he tried to perfect for thirty years did conform with these requirements: that of elementary particles did not. He understood Niels Bohr's quantic theory right away— so much so that he said, "I should probably have managed to reach something like this myself." But immediately after he added, "Yet if all this is true, then it means the end of physics." He did not choose to admit that physics might take on an unharmonious aspect. Later Bohr's results stopped looking paradoxical; they were included in a new general theory that reconciled a corpuscular and the "wave" points of view by means of the "probability wave" idea. It was an idea that Einstein would not admit, although the whole structure was built up on the basis of his own system. He was not a man to be satisfied with old truths; but, seeing that it never occurred to him to give up these criteria, he did not find the new ideas conclusive.

His theory of unitary fields was so difficult to express mathematically that he was never in a position to verify it. And on the other hand, his resistance prevented him from taking part in the advance of quantum physics. Because he was utterly devoid of egocentricity he did not experience his frustration and isolation as a subjective tragedy. But objectively it is almost universally agreed that he wasted the last thirty years of his life in pointless research. Kouznetsov, his biographer, observes that some of Einstien's ideas, dating from the forties and dealing with relativist quantum physics, have now come to fruition. He therefore concluded that Einstein's criticism "showed the limits of quantum physics, beyond which could be seen the outline of even more revolutionary theories." As science advances by repudiating the past in order to outstrip itself, in later times the laggards may always be looked upon as forerunners. But the fact is that towards the end of his life Einstein hindered rather than helped scientific progress.

SELECTED BIBLIOGRAPHY

An essay containing a conceptual analysis of cognition and supporting the thesis of emerging cognitive strengths in old age is "Categorizing and Conceptualizing Styles in Younger and Older Adults" by N. Kogan, *HD*, 1974. Gisela Labouvie and others argue against the stereotype of inevitable general cognitive decline in old age, and also argue that cognitive decline in old age is determined by social neglect and discrimination, in "Operant Analysis of Intellectual Behavior in Old Age," *HD*, 1974. A review of some recent psychological literature on cognitive development in old age, and an analytic discussion of how that literature should be interpréted, are found in "Cognitive Functions in Middle and Old Age Adults," by Diane Papalia and Denise Del Vento Bielby, *HD*, 1974. Cognitive growth related to religious knowledge is reported in David O. Moberg, "Religiosity in Old Age," *G*, 1965. An epistemological theory meant to accommodate developmental changes and drawing on recent philosophy of language is developed in "Language and Cognition: Some Life-Span Developmental Issues," by Klaus F. Riefel, *G*, 1973.

An analysis of the concept of wisdom in old age is found in Vivian Clayton, "Erickson's Theory of Human Development as It Applies to the Aged: Wisdom as Contradictive Cognition," *HD*, 1975. Old Testament perspectives on the wisdom of old age—as well as on several other aspects of old age—are cited and interpreted in Samuel I. Spector, "Old Age and the Sages," *IJAHD*, 1973.

Epistemological questions related to changes in the perception of time in old age are examined in C. Davis Hendricks and John Hendricks, "Concepts of Time and Temporal Construction Among the Aged, With Implications for Research," in Jaber F. Gubrium (ed.), *Time, Roles and Self in Old Age* (New York: Human Sciences Press, 1976) and Michael A. Wallach and Leonard R. Green, "On Age and the Subjective Speed of Time," *JG*, 1961. Somewhat more generally philosophical discussion of the same topic are found in the early chapters of Robert W. Kleemeier (ed.), *Aging and Leisure: A Research Perspective Into the Meaningful Use of Time* (New York: Oxford University Press, 1961). Several analyses of changes in the experience of time over the entire life span, primarily psychological but with occasional insights and arguments of philosophical interest, are contained in Part Two, "Time as Continuity and Intrusion," in Marjorie Fiske Lowenthal, Majda Thurnher and David Chiriboga, *Four Stages of Life* (San Francisco: Jockey-Bass, 1975). A philosophically sophisticated analysis of the experience of time in old age is given by David Tracy in his essay "Eschatological Perspectives on Aging," in Seward Hiltner (ed.), *Toward a Theology of Aging* (New York: Human Sciences Press, 1975). See also Robert Kastenbaum, "The Structure and Function of Time Perspective," *The Journal of Psychological Researches*, (1964). Metaphysical and epistemological aspects of the experience of time in old age are discussed in Paul Cameron, K. Desai, Darius Bahador and G. Dremel, "Temporality Across the Life Span," *IJAHD*, 1977.

Another philosophically interesting description of the perceptions, judgements, and outlook of life review is given in James Birren, *The Psychology of Aging* (Englewood Cliffs, N.J.: Prentice-Hall, 1964). Aristotle's discussion of the themes "one swallow does not make a summer" and "happiness belongs to the whole life" in *Nichomachean Ethics,* Book I, Chapters 9 and 10, has significance for the epistemology of life review. A classic literary exploration of the epistemological importance of life review, based upon the thesis that reality is accessible only through the retrospect of old age, is Marcel Proust, *The Past Recaptured,* tr. Andreas Major (New York: Random House, 1970). A recent literary effort with the same theme, which also contains a statement of a conceptual dilemma of describing life review reversals of judgment, is James Cozzens, *Morning Noon and Night* (New York: Harcourt, Brace and Co., 1968). The power of a life history perspective in interpreting experience in old age is described in Barbara Myerhoff and Virginia Tufte, "Life History as Integration," *G,* 1975. Several forms of integrative judgement and knowledge related to the life history perspective are examined in Charlotte Buhler and Fred Massarick, *The Course of Human Life* (New York: Springer, 1968), Part V. The conceptual complexity of the idea of reminiscence as a form of mentation and its relation to memory is examined in Robert Havighurst and Richard Glasser, "An Exploratory Study of Reminiscence," *JG,* 1972.

The experience of increased perception of the meaning of life emerging in old age is described with philosophical depth in David L. Norton, *Personal Destinies* (Princeton: Princeton University Press, 1976), Chap. 6, and in several places by Erik Erikson, including *Childhood and Society* (New York: Norton, 1963), chap. 7; "The Human Life Cycle" in *The International Encyclopedia of Social Sciences* (New York: Norton, 1968); *Life History and the Historical Moment* (New York, Norton, 1975), Part Two, Chapter I; *Identity and the Life Cycle* (New York: International Universities Press, 1959), and the essay "Reflections on Dr. Borg's Life Cycle" cited in the bibliography of Chapter 1 above. The emergence of a universalizing perspective in moral judgement in old age is reported in Lawrence Kohlberg, "Continuities in Childhood and Adult Moral Development Revisited," in P. Baltes and K. Warner Schaie, *Life-Span Developmental Psychology:*

Personality and Socialization (New York: Academic Press, 1973). The same topic is explored in Kohlberg's essay "Stages and Aging in Moral Development—Some Speculations," *G,* 1973. Two essays on cognitive metamorphosis in old age are Stuart Spicker, "Gerontogenetic Mentation: Memory, Dementia and Medicine in the Penultimate Years," and Kathleen Woodward, "Master Songs of Meditation: The Later Poems of Eliot, Pound, Stevens and Cumming," both in Stuart Spicker, Kathleen Woodward and David VanTassel, *AEHPG*.

Those interested in epistemological issues related to old age can profit, in a general way, from Jean Piaget's *Principles of Genetic Epistemology* (New York: Basic Books, 1972) and from Theodore Mischel, *Cognitive Development and Epistemology* (New York: Academic Press, 1971). In Matilda White Riley's "Social Gerontology and the Age Stratification of Society," *G,* 1971, she argues for the important epistemological thesis that the research activity of studying the aged itself influences and changes the process and experience of aging, thus altering the object of study in the very process of trying to find out about it. The importance of certain epistemological concepts, especially reductionism, ideas of understanding, time, and knowledge for the purpose of explaining the place of the aged in society is analyzed by Eric J. Cassell in "On Educational Changes in the Field of Aging," *G,* 1972.

Part IV

GERONTOLOGY AND PHILOSOPHY OF SCIENCE

INTRODUCTION

There is no single discipline answering to the name "gerontology." Old age is studied from the perspectives of many independent disciplines, which together make up the field of gerontology in their common application to old age. Certain problems relating to the concepts and methods of these various fields of study, as they apply specifically to old age, fall in the domain of philosophy of science. Three of these problems are represented in this part. First, there is the problem of whether the concepts, theories, and observations of scientists who study old age are neutral, as they aim to be, or "value-laden" in ways that might significantly influence our understanding of old age. Can existing sciences study the processes and experiences of human aging without presupposing implicit judgments of value about aging and old people? This problem is discussed in Michel Philibert's essay "A Phenomenological Approach to the Images of Aging." By an "image" of aging, Philibert means a complex collection of attitudes, beliefs, emotions, and perceptions that together constitute a person's "mind set" or "way of thinking" about old age. He argues that contemporary gerontology is misdirected by the influence of implicit, unexamined but strongly held images of old age that suggest that the proper objects for the scientific study of aging are the discovery of true generalizations about the experience of growing old and discovery of laws of biological decline. The first of these, Philibert suggests, is impossible, and the second is too narrow as a basis for the scientific study of aging, because it identifies the whole process of aging with one of its aspects: biological change.

An adequate basis for the study of aging, Philibert argues, would be a thorough examination and open criticism of all of the images of aging available in our cultural tradition. Such a review of available images of aging would bring the positive, compensatory images to view, such as the ideal of aging as a process of human growth toward wisdom. And this, in turn, would lead gerontology itself away from its exclusive preoccupation with models of decrement and decline toward a more constructive, life-affirming and perspicuous direction of development. It would also have the effect, Philibert believes, of unifying and ordering gerontology, a field in which progress is impeded by hidden conflicts in the underlying images that unconsciously direct the research of individual gerontologists.

A second problem of method in gerontology concerns the logic of longitudinal research. This problem exists for the empirical investigation of any complex developmental process. In the case of aging, the problem is to discriminate between changes inherent in the process of growing old and differences between age groups or generations. A classic example of how this problem vexes gerontological research is found in early attempts to study the effects of advancing age on adult intelligence. For many years, empirical investigators in many fields observed that young people scored higher on intelligence tests than old people. (These observed differences are referred to as "the textbook age gradients" and "textbook cross-sectional gradients" in the essay "Age Changes and Age Differences" by K. Warner Schaie.) In the beginning, these differences were thought to be a direct consequence of the process of growing old. But as Schaie explains, no such conclusion was warranted. The observed differences in the performances of the two age groups are often equally well explained by the different cultural and educational experiences affecting the persons in those age groups, such as the higher general level and quality of education enjoyed by members of the younger test groups.

The difficulty of disentangling effects of cultural and social conditions from the effects of the aging process itself in the behavior of test groups of old persons has emerged as a persistent problem in gerontology. A partial solution is offered in Schaie's essay.

The third problem to be examined in this part concerns the nature of the conflict between incompatible theories that give equally successful explanations of the same observed phenomena. The selection "Two Theories of Aging" by Elaine Cumming and William Henry describes what has become a notorious example of this kind of theoretical conflict in gerontology. Cumming and Henry discuss two theories, both of which seem equally able to explain certain observed phenomena in the aging process. Both of these theories, the "activity theory" and the "disengagement theory," seek to explain the increasingly withdrawn behavior that is often observed as people advance into old age. According to the activity theory, withdrawal is caused by stress-inducing environmental and circumstantial disturbances, such as illness, economic constraints, absence of public transportation, and so on. According to the disengagement theory, withdrawal is not externally caused but is a natural component of aging, an inevitable, gradual process of diminishing interest and energy, matched and encouraged by a corresponding natural withdrawal of society from the aged person. These different theoretical perspectives have been tested and retested for many years, and the literature of proof and counterproof has grown large. (It is from this literature that I adopted the phrases "philosophy of activity" and "philosophy of disengagement" in Part I.)

The rivalry of the activity and disengagement theories is an especially clear case of different, incompatible theoretical perspectives on the same observed phenomena whose differences do not seem to be resolved by experiment and observation. Reflecting on the persistence of the tension between them leads one to appreciate the need for philosophical analysis of fundamental theoretical ideas and assumptions in science.

Chapter 18

THE PHENOMENOLOGICAL
APPROACH TO IMAGES OF AGING*

Michel Philibert

GERONTOLOGY: DEVELOPMENT AND STAGNATION

In the period after World War II, the study of aging (known as "gerontology" since 1929) has expanded considerably. It has not been clear, however, that quality has materialized from quantity— a fact that has led several observers to suggest that gerontology as a field has not yet reached its full fruition.[1] It has wanted to be scientific in its methods; but it has borrowed its models and methods predominantly from the experimental natural sciences. The result, according to some, is an impasse, from which phenomenological approaches might point a way out.

*From Michel Philibert, "The Phenomenological Approach to Images of Aging," *Soundings, An Interdisciplinary Journal*, Vol. 57, 1974. Translated from the French by John Orr, Erika Georges and Suzanne de Benedittus. Reprinted by permission of the editor.

Phenomenology and Science

At first glance, phenomenology seems to turn its back on science. It wants to describe things as they appear to consciousness instead of looking for a hidden structure behind the veil of appearances, for a deeper reality, or for necessary relationships. This conspicuous neglect of scientific councerns could serve gerontology, however, to the extent that the appearance of human aging is inseparable from its reality, and to the extent that our attitude toward aging shapes our experience. What, then, is a phenomenological approach to images of aging?

Image

I will use the term *image* in a very general sense. I do not intend to limit analysis either to scientific concepts and theories of aging, or to mental pictures, schemas, dynamic sequences, or mental films. People hold opinions, beliefs, or mental attitudes toward aging that are more or less coherent and that carry images and memories together with the beginnings or outlines of knowledge. We shall call these *multiform constructions* "images." They constitute orientations or perspectives; or, to borrow Donald Evans' term, they are "onlooks" on aging.[2] As an analogy, my economic activity can be looked on as a way of earning a living or as a vocation: two perspectives. Likewise, one can look on aging as a threat or as an opportunity: two views, or two images.

Aging

The term *aging* is intended in the most neutral and most general sense. It is the advancing of age. Time passes in the movement from birth to death; we gain in age; we change irreversibly. I do not believe that the term aging should refer only to unfavorable changes that affect us proportionately with the passage of time, or to changes associated with being elderly. My bias, though, is not universally shared. For many persons, particularly in certain cultures, aging is viewed as a negative process, or a terminal one, or both of these simultaneously.

AGING AND RELATED CONCEPTS

Therefore we cannot limit our investigation to images of "aging"; we must extend it to associated images and concepts. We must examine what relations exist between *aging* as a process and *old age* as either a final period of life or as a social category. What is the relation between *aging* and *growth?* Are these distinct, successive, and antithetical phases, or are they two aspects of the same dynamic process? What continuity or discontinuity can be observed between *youth* and *old age?* Is *aging* an *illness?* Is it a victory over *death,* or is it the period when death is quickly approaching? Whether our image of aging is precise or hazy, sophisticated or naive, coherent or contradictory, it includes an image of old age, of the old, of growing, of youth, of adulthood, of the age-rank ladder.

DATA FOR THE INVESTIGATION OF AGING

Where should we look for the images of aging? The sources are extensive: (1) in popular literature and in more universally conceived forms of literature: texts, rituals, liturgies, magic formulas, poems, dramas, comedies, chronicles, essays, novels, stories, songs, hygienic and medical prescriptions; (2) in laws, customs, and shape of institutions; (3) in the arts: in paintings, mime, dancing, music, movies; (4) in the sciences: biology, demography, psychiatry, psychology, sociology, anthropology, administrative science, economics, politics; (5) in the enormous and dispersed documentation of travelers, anthropologists, geographers, lawyers, and historians of institutions, law, religion, the arts, and literature.

With the exception of Leo Simmons, most gerontologists

have neglected these data, in part because the quantity and heterogeneity of material make collection, classification, and analysis a long and difficult undertaking. More important, though, gerontologists have avoided these data because they resist classification within the scientific models which they habitually utilize. The statements and symbols that express the images of aging and that have been created by mankind in the course of its thousands of years of experience are not scientific statements or symbols. They express biases, opinions, beliefs, and fantasies, which are of interest only for the collector of folklore, the historian of ideas, and perhaps the psychologist who is interested in peculiarities of the human spirit. The gerontologist, on his part, "is not interested." He yearns to substitute a scientific language for one that is prescientific, because he is committed to discovering objective laws, not the subjective opinions that have surrounded the experience of aging.

The gerontologist will simply have to be persuaded that, as a scientist, he can be helped in understanding human aging through the examination of these images. It will not be an easy task to convince him that he needs the help of lawyers, geographers, historians, anthropologists, literary critics, and exegetes; but it is a task that humanistic scholars cannot avoid.

THE DEVELOPMENT AND DECLINE OF AN ILLUSION

Instead of taking the long detour through anthropology, history, and the analysis of texts, for over a quarter of a century gerontologists have preferred the pathway of direct observation. Fascinated by the success of the experimental natural sciences, as Hume was with Newton, they have thrown their efforts into laboratory analyses and studies dominated by cross-sectional sampling techniques. Whether they have dealt with muscular power or memory, the activity of the heart or verbal fluidity, they have observed, measured, analyzed, and compared the performances or functions of old and young subjects. They have interpreted the *differences* they found as the expression of *changes* resulting from aging. They have believed that the multiplicity of observations would generate facts, then laws, and that, in turn, the laws would generate theories. They have believed that from the juxtaposition of genetic, biochemical, physiological, psychological, demographic, sociological, and economic studies, an interdisciplinary, synthetic, integrated knowlege of human aging would emerge.

Today we are becoming aware of the naivete of this projection—even of the fragility of the hopes and convictions that nourished it. Still, for a growing number of people and institutions who are earning their living by working professionally in gerontology, the illusion of a scientific career in the field continues to retard their ability to adopt new methods.

A New Awareness

The differences between young and old subjects may represent, instead of the effects of aging, inborn differences between successive cohorts or generations, but they may also represent effects imposed by particular sociocultural, historical environments. For example, the great majority of observations accumulated during the past twenty-five years refer to only a fraction of humanity (from European or Western cultures, or from industrialized countries), a unique generation whose historical destiny seems to be exceptional. In order to evaluate properly the characteristics of the aged, it would be necessary to relate these to the circumstances of adult life, of youth and childhood, and even to the circumstances of birth and conception. And, in order not to confuse the differences as of today between the young and the old with the changes that accompany aging, it would be necessary to observe the same generation during 110 years.

Of course no researcher, team, or research institution can undertake a study of such length; no method, hypothesis, or theory can be sure to survive for such a long period. And, even if it were possible, such a study would not enable us to distinguish among changes that result from the historical circumstances peculiar to the generation studied and those that relate to universal laws of aging. To distinguish such laws would require the comparison of styles of aging within different generations (by definition, successive generations). Thus, taken seriously, gerontology's method of direct observation, far from being a shortcut, requires at least *200 years* of research.

ANOTHER METHOD

A tentative comparison among the styles of aging associated with different generations is still possible if, without waiting for the results of future observations conducted according to current scientific canons, one turns to observations accumulated for thousands of years in the literature on customs, rituals, and religion, in which prescientific humanity had already formulated its experience of life and its experience of aging. When Molière has Sganarelle say (*Don Juan,* V, ii) that "the young must obey the old," and when Plato has Socrates say the same thing, we are given two choices. We can decide, on the one hand, that the assertion does not express a scientifically demonstrated or demonstrable truth; then we may exclude the assertion from the proper domain of gerontology, since it cannot teach us anything useful about the human experience of aging or about ways to formulate our approaches to aging today. On the other hand, we may decide that the assertion has played an important role, historically, and we may want to ask literary critics and historians of philosophy (in short, the exegetes) to define this function in the context of the works where it is described. We may also want to ask historians and sociologists about how societies other than our own determine the allocation—verbal and real—of functions of authority among the young and the old. In that case, we may begin to understand something about the *norms* (rather than the "laws") of human aging, and perhaps about which norms we should denounce, modify, restore, or promote in our political life.

Toward the Definition of Criteria

One of the first tasks of a phenomenology of aging is the determination of criteria for a typology of images and concepts of aging. I am suggesting six points which, if examined, will allow us to characterize on a set of scales any image of aging, be it scientific or not, explicit or implicit, in behavior, gesture, or institution:

1. What role does the image or concept attribute to physical aging within the process of human aging? An essential or a secondary role? First cause or a part of a whole, a link in a circular chain of causality, a moment in a dialectical process?
2. Is aging regarded mainly as a decline, a process of destruction, of degradation, of deterioration, or as ambivalent and capable of furnishing man with an opportunity for an opening up, an improvement, a development of his being?
3. Is "aging" considered to be coextensive with the entire course of life, or is it limited to its final portion (which may be shorter or longer)?
4. Is aging viewed predominatly in its universality, or is its differential character stressed through an emphasis on functional, individual, and social differences?
5. Is aging presented as a necessity, i.e., as a calamity one must suffer, or as a phenomenon that can be modified by individual or collective action?
6. How is the relation between aging and death viewed? More precisely, how do the anticipation and the approach of death affect the image of old age? Do they diminish or augment the importance of old age?

Toward the Construction of a Typology

The application of these criteria to the analysis of images and concepts of aging and old age, whether they are scientific, prescientific, or nonscientific, leads to the identification of two ideal types that are opposed to each other, and in terms of which the multiple images of aging can more or less be identified. To be sure, particular images sometimes appear to be incomplete or inconsistent—a fact which in my opinion can be explained by the ambivalence of the advance in age. But, however related in their actual appearance, the two ideal types are at least logically separable: (1) images that emphasize the predominantly physical and largely negative, terminal, universal, necessary, and gruesome characteristics identified with aging; (2) images that emphasize the sociocultural features, that view aging as coextensive with the entire length of life, that stress the differentiated and controllable dimensions of aging and look on it as offering opportunities for further growth.

LITERARY EXAMPLES: AGING AS SPIRITUAL GROWTH

At this point it will be helpful to examine some concise images of aging. For this purpose, we could easily draw from the sculptures of Vigeland (Oslo), which are dominated by a preoccupation with the course of life, or from such films as *The Shameless Old Lady* by René Allio or *Wild Strawberries* by Ingmar Bergman. To do so, however, would require too long a discussion, as well as an iconography that is difficult to assemble and reproduce. Therefore we will borrow our examples from literature.

In *Conversations with Confucius,* as reported by a disciple, we find a short autobiography of the Chinese master, which runs as follows:

> At fifteen, my mind was bent on learning. At thirty, I stood firm. At forty, I was free from delusions. At fifty, I understood the laws of Providence. At sixty, there was nothing left in the world that might shock me. At seventy, I could follow the promptings of my heart without trespassing moral law.

The conception of aging underlying this quotation considers aging as a spiritual rather than a biological process. Confucius looks on his own experience in aging as a lifelong growth in creativity and wisdom. Continued growth and final fulfillment are not seen as a universal feature of man's life, nor as a gift from Fortune to the happy few, but as a kind of achievement rewarding a lifelong dedication. Living is learning, aging is learning, for those who pay the price. Development through adult and mature years is linked to lifelong self-education. Aging as spiritual growth is an opportunity that may either be enjoyed or neglected. Aging is seen as a differential and manageable process.

The same pattern appears in the following quotation from Baudelaire's *Curiosités Esthetiqués:*

> At the end of his career, Goya's eyesight had weakened to such an extent that his pencils, so it was said, had to be sharpened for him. Yet even at this time he executed some big and most important lithographs, including a number of bullfights full of swarming crowds, admirable plates, enormous features in miniature—a further proof in support of that strange law governing the destiny of great artists, according to which, since life and intelligence move in opposite directions, they make up on the savings what they lose on the roundabouts, and, following a progressive rejuvenation, they grow forever stronger, more jovial, bolder, to the very edge of the grave.[3]

LITERARY EXAMPLES: AGING AS PHYSICAL DECLINE AND AS SOCIAL DISGRACE

I put forward three passages in order to illustrate this image of growing old. The first two are borrowed from some recent French novels. Benoîte Groult relates in *La part des choses* the morose reflections of a fifty-year-old woman:

> The garish sun on this December morning does not leave a single one of these fifty years in the darkness, and her too fresh rose nylon robe is prejudicial to her dark complexion. She arrived at this distressing age at which one can topple over any time from the

experience of being a woman who is still beautiful to that of being an old woman whose looks touch without ever exciting. Little by little the second definitively would occupy the stage, leaving to the first, for some time still, a few brief and heart-rending appearances.[4]

Paul Guimard, in *L'ironie du sort,* records the reflections of a person, born in 1916, who in 1949 gathers his thoughts beside the tomb of one of his friends and contemporaries, shot down by the Germans in 1943. He at least will not grow old.

I am already catching a glimpse of the forty-year-old man waiting for me around the corner. He will appropriate all that you have known about me, all that I have been. He will make poor use of it. His hair is thinner, breath shorter, heart less lively, skin lusterless, his spirit less sure than mine. He will not make use of this heritage, which he has not deserved. He will disentangle himself from what is encumbering him, and I will not be able to help it. I am already his prisoner. Then will come the man of fifty, and the one of sixty, who will make me die a little at a time. They will take away my teeth; they will knit me with wrinkles. I hate these old men who lie in wait for me in order to beleaguer me and mutilate me.[5]

These two texts equally ascribe to older adults the inability to project themselves into old age and accept as their own the anticipated image of the old persons they will become. For them there is no conceivable continuity between what they are and what they are going to be. They cannot imagine any progress in wisdom or authority that could compensate for the irremediable physical decline. The heroine of Benoîte Groult's novel at first sees her future like the passing of the same self from one state to another: from the stage of being the still beautiful woman to that of being an old woman (beauty and age being mutually exclusive). Within the next phrase, however, her thoughts turn to a more radical formulation: it is no longer a question of successive stages, but of two distinct persons, one of whom is chasing the other—two different women who are not identical any more at all. The subject identifies herself with the present state and views her future state as another person, foreign and hostile, who will take her place and take her life away.

For the hero of Guimard's novel, there is not only a dual personality but disintegration into a series of aggressive and detestable strangers. This image of age-related periods of the personality expresses, in his own self-consciousness, the extent to which society devalues old age and the power of the segregation it structures among age groups. The individual pathology of the schizoid type, which breaks the personal unity into pieces, reflects and reinforces the social pathology, which shatters the cycle of exchange and renewal among successive generations.

For the reader who is tempted to find the term *pathology* abusive in this context, I would like to cite a clinical case, recently filmed within a hospital at Ivry, under the supervision of Professor Vignalou. Among the subjects is a sick, senile woman, who has been hospitalized for several years. She expresses the wish to leave the hospital in order to go to a retirement home—to a place where she can retire from her occupation as a concierge, which, she says, is her real identity. Her feeling of personal identity has remained attached to a situation that she has lost and a phase of her life that is already over. The actual phase which is being lived—a strange and hostile one—is purely and simply denied.

An American example will illustrate a less severe form of the difficulty that many people experience in accepting their advancing age, frightened by the image of stagnation they associate with the adult life and by the image of decay they associate with old age. At the conclusion of a recent novel by Dan Greenburg, *Scoring,* the difficulty is recognized and defined by the hero-novelist at the very moment when he overcomes it.

> My ghastly thirtieth birth had finally descended upon me. I would never again, even in my most egomaniacal moments, be able to think of myself as a boy wonder. Boy wonders become at the age of thirty merely moderately successful or even very successful men, but they are no longer boy anythings. The great promise they saw in you has either been kept or broken. You are at thirty, willy-nilly, as close as you are ever likely to get to being a genuinely grown up person. I walked through Times Square one day, . . . and I figured All Right. I figured Why Not. I figured, You've already gotten your first lousy marriage out of the way and possibly even learned a

couple of things not to do the next time. I figured, so one of the reasons you're scared of marriage is that it brings you one life process closer to death, so remaining a bachelor isn't going to keep you from aging or from dying either. I figured, so you're scared of the total commitment of marriage, so what, so everybody's scared of that, so big goddam deal. I figured, You're thirty goddam years of age, which is nearly half your life, so what are you waiting for—let's get on with it already. Let's take the next step in life. Let's do it.[6]

To place at the age of thirty, the age when the promises of childhood have been either broken or fulfilled, the middle of life, is an opinion that hardly contains anything scientific. It is the reality of a man who has only recently entered into his thirties; who lives in a society where chronology is of great importance, where chronological age has a social and symbolic significance, where one uses a decimal number system, where youth is overvalued, and where old age is devalued. Still such nonscientific statements must not be neglected by the science of aging. Indeed, they constitute primary data for a science that purportedly is interested in the human experience of aging.

THE SCIENCES OF MAN ARE NOT NEUTRAL

How does this phenomenological analysis relate to the picture of gerontology as a scientific enterprise? It seems to me that it should help to correct gerontology in general, and social gerontology in particular, by doing away with its illusory pretensions to a kind of objectivity or neutrality that cannot be attained by the sciences of man. A science of man that pretends to reject all normative considerations, to eliminate any consideration of values, to treat man as a pure object of science, becomes indeed an accomplice to the social practices that devalue man in treating him like an insect, like a tool, like a thing. Every science of man declares itself for or against man, contributes to his liberation or his enslavement, his development or his deterioration, by the methodology it uses and the theoretical status it claims. In reintegrating, via phenomenological methods, the images of aging in either of the two families of images, the sciences that cooperate within the broad field of gerontology will illumine the unacknowledged nonscientific presuppositions of so-called scientific activity and will lay bare the methodological biases that direct scientific procedures and falsify scientific results.

FROM THE PHENOMENOLOGY OF AGING TO THE PHENOMENOLOGY OF GERONTOLOGY

A phenomenological approach to aging leads to the development of a phenomenological approach to, and then to a critique of, gerontology itself. An analysis of the methodological and theoretical literature of gerontology reveals, in fact, that far from presenting a homogeneous appearance and demanding uniform research practices, the field of gerontology includes contradictions and incoherences that already afflict each of the sciences involved.

There are a number of different gerontologies, coexisting in anthologies, in congresses and conventions, in the minds of funding authorities, of students, of scholars, who ignore their radical differences and entertain the fiction that gerontology as a science is homogeneous, coherent, and sure of its protocol and its results. These gerontologies are actually irreconcilable, and indeed the future of gerontology depends on lucid choices being made among the diverse images of the field.

TWO IMAGES OF GERONTOLOGY

I will content myself here with viewing two definitions of gerontology and its object, drawn from the work of two authorities on gerontology, Nathan Shock and James Birren. My comments will deal only with two passages, and their scope is consequently limited. I do not intend to examine the context within which the definitions are developed, even though that might help to add nuances and correct my understanding of the authors' points of view.

These passages, both of which were published in roughly the same period, are at least a dozen years old. Shock and Birren have subsequently published a large number of studies; their thinking has evolved, and they might no longer quite recognize themselves in the mirror with which I am attempting to reflect their images. I am not pretending, however, to evaluate their entire work nor the quality of their spirit; gerontology owes much to both. Still, the definitions that I want to juxtapose are in the public domain, and they are contained in papers (one of which has been reedited) that continue to be utilized widely in the education of gerontologists. It seems legitimate, therefore, to show that Shock and Birren are simply not speaking about the same gerontology.

James Birren's image of gerontology as expressed in "Principles of Research in Aging," published in the *Handbook of Aging and the Individual* (1959):[7]

> Broadly speaking, the purpose of research on aging is to be able to characterize the nature of the older person and to explain how the organism changes over time, that is, to be able to make succinct statements explaining increasingly large numbers of facts about aging individuals. The role of the scientist studying aging appears to be not different from that in other fields of investigation.

Shock's definition is taken from "Some of the Facts of Aging," published in 1960.[8] Shock concludes his article with a review of hypotheses which at that time merited examination:

> In my opinion, the impairments in performance associated with advancing age are due to (a) dropping out of functional units in key organ systems, (b) some impairments in the functional capacities of cells remaining in the body of the aged, and (c) breakdown of neural and endocrine integrative functions in the individual.
>
> Although advancing age is accompanied by biological impairments that offer fertile grounds for the development of disease and pathology, there are compensatory devices which can maintain

effective behavior in the human into advanced old age. Investigation of these as yet unmeasured and little understood inner resources
over the entire life-span of the individual is the goal of research in
gerontology.

Both Shock and Birren are attempting to do the same things:
(1) to specify the object or the project of gerontological research;
(2) to link this definition with a suggestion concerning the method
or style of research.

TWO IMAGES OF AGING

It is in relation to this shared double intention that the differences between Shock and Birren can be clearly delineated.

First opposition: With reference to the third criterion that I
suggested, Birren's explication of aging (how the organism
changes over time) seems to limit the phenomenon of aging to the
last years of life. He is interested in characterizing the older
person. By contrast Shock is interested in investigating aging
"over the entire life span."

Second opposition: Although Birren utilizes the concept of
change, his attitude is much more static than Shock's (at least in
the passages under consideration). Birren appears to be concerned
with gerontology as a science whose objective is to account for
"facts," and he assumes that aging is a tangible phenomenon that
can be described and analyzed; such is the "nature" of the older
person. According to Shock, however, aging should be viewed as
development and process, to the point that even the concept of
relative stability must be understood in terms of temporal processes that can maintain (or fail to maintain) effective behavior.

It is impossible to distinguish Birren's position from Shock's
with reference to my first criterion. Birren alone speaks about the
aging of the "organism"; Shock speaks about the "body." Birren
uses the term *person* while Shock uses the term *human*. Both
discuss *individuals*. Thus, although both appear to be mainly

sensitive to biological dimensions of aging, neither rigidly limits himself to biological aspects.

The *third opposition* between the perspectives of Birren and of Shock becomes apparent from the perspective of my fourth criterion. Birren's statement underlines the universal character of aging, since he is attempting to delineate the universally shared experience of aging, the nature of the older person, and he is attempting to discover the laws of that process. Shock, on the other hand, points to devices that can compensate for the process of decline and thus maintain certain levels of behavior. For him the process of aging is relative to individual differences.

Two Conceptions of Science

It is not only the images of aging that differ in the two essays. Birren and Shock differ also in their fundamental images of scientific activity. According to Birren, research begins with the discovery and collection of facts, then moves to a second phase, the formulation of judgments that subsume these facts. He thus describes a simple model of inductive empiricism. We are provided with a model of gerontological methodology in which a scientific method, such as it is—universal, eternal—is applied to a new object, the nature of the aged person. Birren makes no allusion at all to applications (therapeutic, pedagogic, political, or other) that might be able to ameliorate the conditions of health or of life among aged persons, or to modify the manner in which persons grow old.

Admittedly, it is a delicate task to interpret the silence of a text. Let us risk, however, saying that Birren's statement postulates a theory of science that not only distinguishes its task (to account for the world, or, in this case, man) from technics (to *change* the world, or man), but draws from this distinction (wrongly) the possibility and the obligation of science's constituting itself independently from its own application. To identify science with action (praxis) is to risk, according to this conception, the contamination or the falsification of scientific observation of facts. Once scientific truth has been attained, of course, nonscientists may want to utilize the knowledge of the connection of cause and effect in order to put some sure means in the service of desired ends. But responsiblity for the utilization of science resides with the politician, the teacher, and the technician, while the scientist contents himself with objective observation and does not involve himself in the problems of application.

If it is not absolutely evident that the conception of science I have just outlined is implied in Birren's essay, at least there is no contradiction. Shock's essay, on the other hand, supposes a different conception of science.

RELATION OF THEORY AND PRAXIS

We cannot be certain whether Shock would disagree with Birren's formulation of the scientific enterprise, but his essay suggests another attitude. After enumerating "some of the facts of aging" and hypotheses concerning age-related impairments, Shock speaks about resources capable of compensating for and combating negative aspects of aging. This relation between theory and practice is not an expression of confusion. Indeed, it is an expression of the fact that gerontology is being subsidized by the public, foundations, and government not because of a love of truth but because they anticipate that gerontology will contribute to the quality of life and aging. This anticipation does not imply that the possibilities for applied knowledge should dictate the kind of conclusions sought by science. But in gerontology, as in the other sciences, progress in the development of theory will be linked to the analysis of practical difficulties and the reappraisal of current prejudices.

More precisely, we should not have to wait to care for the aged sick, to prepare for their retirement or aging, or to engage in the politics of aging, until pure gerontology has found the truth, in the meantime being forbidden any policy intervention. The conditions of aging change from year to year and from generation to generation in response to forces (some intended, others spontaneous) that affect our living conditions, our educational systems, our production of goods and services, and our social, economic, political, and cultural lives. The investigation of compensatory possibilities can result neither from pure observation nor from experimental laboratory activity alone. Compensatory actions are suggested by selective research in relation to individuals and groups—research that is informed by *norms* and that is directed toward making behavior more effective, aging more satisfying, and old age more fulfilling. The kind of research required is one in which gerontologists will engage in social experiments not under their control, pursuing it in accordance with ideological, political, or ethical norms, i.e., nonscientifically, in an "uncontrolled" way. This kind of research must often proceed tentatively, using resources whose effectiveness cannot be known until late in life, but which must be detected and cultivated in infancy and adulthood.

THE CONCEPT OF RESOURCE

The term *resource* implies in effect the idea of virtuality or potentiality; by definition it can be neither measured nor understood independently of the multiform biological, personal, and social life it attempts to affect.

We certainly want to move beyond Shock's position in not limiting gerontological investigations to "inner" resources. I believe that the quality of life and the positive or negative character of aging depend, much more broadly than Shock admits, upon the interaction of the person and his physical, social, and cultural environment. In broadening the concept of resource and consequently the objective of gerontological research, I want nevertheless to identify with Shock's inventive and evolutionary scientific attitude and with his suggestion that new scientific objectives, i.e., research on "as yet untested and little-understood resources," demand new scientific methods.

A Necessary Conversion

Gerontology as a science has everything to gain and nothing to lose by renouncing the a priori methodologies and doctrines that still dominate the greatest part of research and are leading this research to an illusory pursuit of the *nature* of the aged person and the *laws* of aging, to a definition of aging as biological decline or as a natural phenomenon, universal and necessary. Having discerned some images of old age and aging that shape the mentality of our contemporaries, our customs, and our institutions, we find that their pervasive influence extends to gerontology itself, thus impinging on its hopefully scientific attitude.

A *phenomenological* approach to gerontology could proceed fruitfully with recourse to hermeneutical and semiological methods. The sciences of man have long dreamed of attaining the rigor and fecundity of the experimental natural sciences by appropriating their methods and hypotheses. But the frustration of so many psychologies and sociologies should lead the science of man to look for some models and methods within disciplines that have accomplished the most fertile developments during the past few years: such are linguistics, exegesis, hermeneutics, semiology. Paul Ricoeur has shown that the social institutions, historical events, and human actions—through and through symbolic— should be studied as texts, by means of methods that have dramatically revitalized the analysis of texts.[9]

The Future of Gerontology

Human aging is a complex process whose biological conditions are embedded in and modified by a social and cultural, which is to say symbolic, context. One cannot study aging independently of the images, naive or sophisticated, in which it is expressed and constituted. These images require our investigation largely through the mediation of the disparate texts that express them, comment on them, or convey them. Gerontology was dominated in the first stage of its brief history by the doctors and the biologists. In a second stage a place was created for the psychologists and the sociologists, flanked by some economists and demographers. Now gerontology is at the threshold of a third stage, and a period of renewal, based upon the gathering of geographers, historians, linguists, exegetes, hermeneuticists, and semiologists around problems of aging. This new era obviously will not proceed without a period of combat.

The development is inevitable. But much depends on gerontologists. They can, of course, retard it, thus making gerontology into a rear guard discipline, breathlessly running behind physics, chemistry, and biology. Or they can hasten this new stage, opening the way for multidisciplinary approaches, and initiating and advancing a transformation of method and doctrine that psychology and sociology will recognize tomorrow.

NOTES

[1]"The knowledge produced in universities is increasingly vulnerable to the accusation of irrelevance" (Birren, Woodruff, Bergman, "Issues and Methodology in Social Gerontology," *Gerontologist,* Vol. 12, No. 2, part 2, Summer 1972.

[2]Donald Evans, *The Logic of Self-Involvement.* (London: SCM Press, 1963).

[3]Charles Baudelaire, *Curiosités Esthetiqués.* (Chauvet trans. London: Metheun, 1972).

[4]Benoîte Groult, *La Part des Choses.* (Paris: A.G. Nizet, 1972).

[5]Paul Guimard, *L'ironie du Sort.* (Paris: Denoel, 1961).

[6]Dan Greenburg, *Scoring.* (New York: Doubleday, 1972).

[7]James Birren's paper has been reproduced in Bernice L. Neugarten, ed., *Middle Age and Aging.* (Chicago: Chicago University Press, 1968), p. 545.

[8]Nathan W. Shock, *Aging: Some Social and Biological Aspects.* (Washington, D.C.: National Science Foundation, 1960).

[9]Paul Ricoeur, "The Model of the Text: Meaningful Action Considered as a Text," *Social Research,* Vol. 38, No. 3, 1971.

Chapter 19

AGE CHANGES AND AGE DIFFERENCES

K. Warner Schaie

Almost as soon as objective measures were defined which could be used to index intellectual abilities and other cognitive functions, researchers began to express interest in individual differences on such measures. One of the most persistent of such interests has been the investigation of developmental changes in cognitive behavior. Most treatments covering age changes in cognitive behavior have closely followed the prevalent approaches in the description of developmental theories. Although great attention has always been paid to early development, and maturation during childhood and adolescence is fully described, very little is said about the further development of intelligence and other cognitive variables during adulthood or senescence. In fact, the concern with age changes in cognitive behavior during adulthood did not come to be of serious interest to psychologists until it became clear that the I.Q. concept used in age scales was inapplicable for the

Adapted from *The Gerontologist*, Vol. 7, No. 2, Pt. 1, June, 1967. Copyright 1972 by the Gerontological Society. Reprinted by permission.

measurement of intelligence in adults. As a consequence of the work of Wechsler in developing social measures for the description of the intelligence of adults but also due to the earlier descriptive works of Jones and Conrad with the Army Alpha and that of the Stanford group working with Miles, it soon became clear that somewhat different conceptual models would be required for the proper understanding of adult cognitive development.

It will be noted that emphasis has been placed upon the term *age changes*. The literature on the psychological studies of aging has long been haunted by a grand confusion between the terms *age change* and *age difference*. This confusion has beclouded the results of studies involving age as a principal variable and has loaded the textbook literature with contradictory findings and what will be shown to be spurious age gradients. This presentation intends to clarify in detail the relationship between age changes and age differences and to show why past methodologies for the study of age-related changes have been inadequate.

Much of the literature on aging and cognitive behavior has been concerned with describing how older individuals differ from their younger peers at a given point in time. Such a descriptive attempt is quite worthwhile and is necessary in the standardization of measurements. This approach, however, is restricted to a description of the very real differences between organisms of various lengths of life experience at a given point in time. Unless some very strong assumptions are made, these attempts beg the issue and fail to produce relevant experiments on the question of how the behavior of the organism changes over age. This is a strong statement, and it is not made rashly since it clearly questions much of the work in the current literature. But it is required since we find ourselves increasingly puzzled about the results of our own and others' studies of age differences. Let us be explicit in clarifying the basis of our concerns and in tracing the resulting implications for the interpretation of much of the data in the developmental literature.

A general model has been developed that shows how the previously used methods of developmental analysis are simply special cases that require frequently untenable assumptions. This model has been described elsewhere in more detail.[1] At this time, however, it would be useful to state the most important characteristics of a general model required for the explanation of aging phenomena as they pertain to the relationship between age changes and age differences.

Let us begin then by clearly distinguishing between the concepts of age change and age difference. Before we can do so effectively, we must also introduce some new concepts and redefine various familiar concepts. The concept of *age* is, of course, central to our discussion. It needs to be carefully delineated, however, and whenever used will be taken to denote the age of the organism at the time of occurrence of whatever response is to be measured. Even more precisely, age will refer to the number of time-units elapsed between the entrance into the environment (birth) of the organism and the point in time at which the response is recorded.

In addition, it is necessary to introduce two concepts that are relatively unfamiliar in their relevance to developmental study. The first of these concepts is the term *cohort*. This term has frequently been used in population and genetic researches and is useful for our purpose. The term implies the total population of organisms born at the same point or interval in time. Restrictions as to the nature of the population and the latitude in defining the interval in time designated as being common to a given cohort or generation must be determined by the special assumptions appropriate to any given investigation.

The second concept to be introduced is that of *time of measurement*. It will take on special significance for us as it denotes that state of the environment within which a given set of data were obtained. In any study of aging it is incumbent upon the investigator to take pains to index precisely the temporal point at which his measurements occur. Such concern is most pertinent since changes in the state of the environment may contribute to the effects noted in an aging study.

With these definitions in mind let us now examine Figure

19–1 that will help us in understanding the distinction between age changes and age differences. Figure 19–1 contains a set of six independent random samples, three of which have a common age, three of which have been given some measure of cognitive behavior at the same point in time, and three of which have been drawn from the same cohort; i.e., whose date of birth is identical. If we compare the performance of samples 1, 2, and 3 we are concerned with *age differences*. Discrepancies in the mean scores obtained by the samples may be due to the difference in age for samples measured at the same point in time. But note that an

Time of Testing		1955	1960	1965
	1910	Sample 3 Age 45 $A_1C_3T_1$	Sample 5 Age 50 $A_2C_3T_2$	Sample 6 Age 55 $A_3C_3T_3$
Time of Birth	1905	Sample 2 Age 50 $A_2C_2T_1$	Sample 4 Age 55 $A_3C_2T_2$	
(Cohort)	1900	Sample 1 Age 55 $A_3C_1T_1$		

A - Age level at time of testing.
C - Cohort level being examined.
T - Number of test in series.

Figure 19–1. Example of a Set of Samples Permitting All Comparisons Deducible from the General Developmental Model.

equally parsimonious interpretation would attribute such discrepancies to the differences in previous life experiences of the three different cohorts (generations) represented by these samples.

If, on the other hand, comparisons were made between scores for samples 3, 5 and 6, we are concerned with *age changes*. Here the performance of the same cohort or generation is measured at three different points in time. Discrepancies between the mean scores for the three samples may represent age changes, or they may represent environmental treatment effects that are quite independent of the age of organism under investigation. The two comparisons made represent, of course, examples of the traditional cross-sectional and longitudinal methods and illustrate the confounds resulting therefrom.

Lest it be thought that there is no way to separate the effects of cohort and time differences from that of aging, we shall now consider a further set of differences which may be called *time lag*. If we compare samples 1, 4 and 6, it may be noted that the resulting differences will be independent of the organism's age, but can be attributed either to differences among generations or to differences in environmental treatment effects or both.

Any definitive study of age changes or age differences must recognize the three components of maturational change, cohort differences, and environmental effects as components of developmental change; otherwise, as in the past, we shall continue to confuse age changes with age differences and both with time lag. Hence, it may be argued that studies of age differences can bear upon the topic of age changes only in the special case where there are no differences in genetically or environmentally determined ability levels among generations and where there are no effects due to differential environmental impact. It follows, therefore, that findings of significant age differences will bear no necessary relationship to maturational deficit, nor does the absence of age differences guarantee that no maturational changes have indeed occurred.

As a further complication, it is now necessary to add the notion that differences in the direction of change for the confounded developmental components may lead to a suppression or an exaggeration of actual age differences or changes. As an example, let us suppose that perceptual speed declines at the rate of one half sigma over a five-year interval. Let us suppose further that the average level of perceptual speed for successive five-year cohorts declines by one-half sigma also. Such decrement may be due to systematic changes in experience or to some unexplained genetic drift. Whatever their cause, if these suppositions were true, then a cross-sectional study would find no age differences whatsoever because the maturational decrement would be completely concealed by the loss of ability due to some unfavorable changes in successive generations.

As another example, let us suppose that there is no maturational age decrement but that there is systematic improvement in the species. In such a case successive cohorts would do better than earlier ones, and cross-sectional studies would show spurious decrement curves, very much like those reported in the literature for many intelligence tests.

One of the most confusing facets of aging studies therefore is the fact that experimental data may reveal or fail to reveal a number of different combinations of underlying phenomena. Yet the understanding of the proper conceptual model that applies to a given set of data is essential before generalizations can be drawn. Let us illustrate the problem by considering some of the alternative models that might explain the behavior most typically represented in the literature on developmental change. Reference here is made to cross-sectional gradients such as those reported by Wechsler[2] or by Jones and Conrad.[3] These gradients typically record a steep increment in childhood with an adult plateau and steep decrement thereafter.

When we address ourselves to the question of what developmental changes are represented by such data, we face relatively little difficulty in determining whether maturational changes are contained in the age differences noted during childhood and adolescence. Our own childhood provide us with at least anecdotal evidence of the longitudinal nature of such change. Whether this portion of the developmental curve, however, is a straight line or a positive asymptotic curve is still in doubt. Also, it should be remembered that even if we agree upon the validity of evidence for maturational changes, we must still consider that such changes will be overestimated by cross-sectional data if there are positive cohort differences and/or negative environmental experience effects. Similarly, maturational growth will be underestimated in the event of cohort decrement or the effect of positive environmental influences.

For the adult and old-age portions of the developmental span, matters are much more complicated. While we can readily accept the fact of psychological maturational growth during childhood, similar evidence of maturational decline on psychological variables by means of longitudinal study remains to be demonstrated. As a consequence, we also must at least entertain models that would account for age differences in the absence of maturational age changes.

The detailed analysis of the general developmental model[4] shows that it is possible to differentiate as many as 729 models to account for developmental change if one considers the direction and slope as well as the three components involved in developmental change gradients. Of the many possible models, three will be considered now that seem to be high probability alternatives for the classical textbook age-gradients. Our three examples are models that not only would fit these textbook gradients but would furthermore predict that the cross-sectional data depicted by the gradients could not possibly be replicated by longitudinal studies.

The first of these models might be called an "improvement of the species" model. It holds that the form of the maturational gradient underlying the typical representative of the textbook gradients is positive asymptotic; i.e., that there is systematic increment in performance during childhood, slowing down during early adulthood, and that there is no further maturational change after maturity. The model further holds that the cohort gradient, or the differences between generations, should also be positive asymptotic.

Successive generations are deemed to show improved performance for some unspecified genetic or prior experience reason,
but it is also assumed that improvement has reached a plateau for
recent generations. The effect of the environment is furthermore
assumed to be constant or positive asymptotic also. When these
components are combined they are seen to provide a cross-
sectional age gradient that shows steady increment during childhood, a plateau in midlife, and accelerating decrement in old age.

The same model, however, when applied to longitudinal data
will predict steady increment during childhood, but slight improvement in midlife, and no decrement thereafter. The only
reason the cross-sectional gradient will show decrement is that the
younger generations start out at a higher level of ability and thus in
the cross-sectional study the older samples will show lower performance. Of course, this means no more than that the older
samples started out at a lower level of ability even though they
showed no decrement over their lifespan.

A second no less plausible alternative to account for the
textbook age gradients might be called the "environmental compensation" model. This model also specifies a concave maturational gradient with increment in youth and decrement in old age,
much as the cross-sectional gradient. In addition, however, this
alternative calls for a positive environmental experience gradient.
Here the effect of an environmental experience increases systematically due to a progressively more favorable environment. The
effects of cohort differences in this model are assumed to be
neutral or positive asymptotic.

If the second model were correct, then our prediction of
longitudinal age changes would result in a gradient with steep
increment in childhood but no decrement thereafter, since maturational changes would be systematically compensated for by a
favorable environment. Since the environmental component of
change over time is not measured in the cross-sectional study,
assessment would be made only of the maturational decrement
yielding information on the state of a population sample of different ages at a given point of time. But it would provide misleading

information as to what is going to happen to the behavior of this population sample as time passes.

Third, let us propose a more extreme alternative that we might label the "great society" model. This model specifies a positive asymptotic maturational gradient; i.e., increment during childhood and a plateau thereafter. The model further specifies a positive asymptotic cohort gradient; i.e., successively smaller increments in performance for successive generations. Finally the model specifies increasingly favorable environmental impact. The reason for calling this alternative the "great society" model should be readily apparent. The model implies (1) that maturity is an irreversible condition of the organism, (2) that the rapid development of our people is reaching the plateau of a mature society, and (3) that any further advance would now be a function of continually enriching the environment for us all. Note that the cross-sectional study of groups of different age at this time in our history will still conform to the textbook cross-sectional gradients. Their longitudinal replication, however, would result in a gradient that would be steep during childhood, that would level off during adulthood, but that would show continued growth until the demise of the organism.

Obviously, it is still possible that the straightforward decrement model might hold equally well for the classical gradients. The information we have on longitudinal studies let it appear that any one of the above alternatives may be a more plausible one.

It is hoped that the examples just given have alerted the reader to some of the flaws in the traditional designs used for the studies of aging phenomena. Caution is in order at this time lest the premature conclusion be reached that the increase in sophistication of our methods has indeed led to a better understanding of how and why organisms age. Thus far, it seems just as likely that all that has been investigated refers to differences among generations and thus in a changing society to differences that may be as transient as any phase of that society. Only when we have been successful in differentiating between age changes and age differences can we hope therefore that the exciting advances and methods in the more appropriate studies now in progress will truly assist us in understanding the nature of the aging process.

SUMMARY

The concepts of age change and age difference were differentiated by introducing a three-dimensional model for the study of developmental change involving the notions of differences in maturational level (age), differences among generations (cohorts), and differential environmental impact (time of measurement). It was shown that age differences as measured by cross-sectional methods confound age and cohort differences while age changes as measured by the longitudinal method confound age and time of measurement differences. Conceptual unconfounding permits specification of alternate models for the prediction of age changes from age differences and resolution of the meaning of discrepancies in the findings yielded by cross-sectional and longitudinal studies. Examples of alternative models for aging phenomena were provided.

NOTES

[1]K. Warner Schaie, "A General Model for the Study of Developmental Problems," *Psychological Bulletin*, Vol. 64, 1965.

[2]D. .Wechsler, *The Measurement of Adult Intelligence*, 2d ed. (Baltimore: Williams & Wilkins, 1944).

[3]H. E. Jones and H. S. Conrad, "The Growth and Decline of Intelligence: A Study of a Homogeneous Group between the Ages of Ten and Sixty," *Genetic Psychology Monographs*, Vol. 13, No. 3, 1933.

[4]K. Warner Schaie and C. R. Strother, I. "Models for the Prediction of Age Changes in Cognitive Behavior." Unpublished mimeographed paper, West Virginia University. Abstract in *Gerontologist*, Vol. 4, 1964.

Chapter 20

TWO THEORIES OF AGING

Elaine Cumming and William Henry

In science there is simply no way of disregarding theory. If we are not consciously using theory, we are inevitably employing instead groups of implicit assumptions because we must have anchor points for our thinking and guidelines to show us what to look for in our data. The disengagement theory of aging that we are developing here is a common sense theory, inasmuch as it arises from general observation and tends at first glance to appear rather familiar and obvious. However, it is by no means the only possible common sense theory of the aging process, and indeed it differs rather radically in its implications from another common-sense theory, which we are calling the "implicit theory" of aging. The latter is a set of assumptions about old people that appears to us to underlie a good deal of the social-scientific writing and most of the popular literature on the subject of aging and old age.

From Elaine Cumming and William Henry, *Growing Old, The Process of Disengagement*. (New York: Basic Books, 1961). Reprinted by permission.

It is quite possible for two radically opposed common sense theories to exist side by side, because they may both account for the available data, although they may emphasize different aspects of everyday observations and they may draw quite different inferences from them. It is partly to make the propositions developed in this study explicit that we are comparing them here with what appear to be those of others, and partly to sharpen the contrast between two fundamentally different ways of looking at the aging phenomenon.

DISENGAGEMENT THEORY

Starting from the common sense observation that the old person is less involved in the life around him than he was when he was younger, we can describe the process by which he becomes so, and we can do this without making assumptions about its desirability. In our theory, aging is an inevitable mutual withdrawal or disengagement, resulting in decreased interaction between the aging person and others in the social systems he belongs to. The process may be initiated by the individual or by others in the situation. The aging person may withdraw more markedly from some classes of people while remaining relatively close to others. His withdrawal may be accompanied from the outset by an increased preoccupation with himself; certain institutions in society may make this withdrawal easy for him. When the aging process is complete, the equilibrium that existed in middle life between the individual and his society has given way to a new equilibrium characterized by a greater distance and an altered type of relationship.

This theory is intended to apply to the aging process in all societies, although the initiation of the process may vary from culture to culture, as may the pattern of the process itself. For example, in those traditional cultures in which the old are valued for their wisdom, it may well be that the aging person openly initiates the process; in primitive, and especially in impoverished cultures, he may resist the process until it is forced upon him. In our own culture, the assumption implicit in writing about old age appears to be the latter rather than the former. Since our purpose here is not to make crosscultural comparisons, we will confine ourselves to delineating as many characteristics of the aging process of healthy, economically stable Americans as we can.

In any process in which the individual becomes less bound to the social systems of which he is a member, it should be possible to distinguish changes of three orders. First, changes in the number of people with whom the individual habitually interacts and changes in the amount of interaction with them should be observable. At the same time, changes may occur in the purposes of the interaction, so that shifts in the goals of the systems to which the aging member belongs should be discernible.

Second, we should find qualitative changes in the style or patterns of interaction between the individual and the other members of the system that are commensurate with the decreased involvement.

Third, we should see changes in the personality of the individual that both cause and result in decreased involvement with others and his increased preoccupation with himself. In addition, we should observe evidence, if this process is indeed the modal style of aging, of its institutionalization in society.

We will attempt to define the beginning and the end of the series of changes we will call the disengagement process, and will report evidence that bears upon the nature of the process. We will also comment on the way in which certain social institutions appear to be geared to this process. Our formulations were not thought out before the study reported here was undertaken, but were developed bit by bit as the study proceeded. Because the theory was built with the data of the study and then tested against other data from the same study, we consider it a tentative theory or a set of hypotheses about aging.[1]

Before we proceed to elaborate on our theory, however, we will discuss a theory that seems to be implicit in much of the current thinking about aging.

An Implicit Theory of Aging

When we read any "problem-oriented" publications about aging, it is possible to tease out of them a number of related themes that rest on a set of assumptions amounting to an implicit theory of the aging process. This does not mean that there is any complete expression of such a theory in the literature but, rather, widespread evidence of its various assumptions.

In the first place, investigators have often used the word "aging" misleadingly, as if it meant "old." It seems to be assumed that middle age lasts for a certain length of time and is followed abruptly by old age. Sometimes retirement is said to be the point at which this occurs, or, possibly, widowhood; more often failing health seems to be the turning point. There is no discussion of the possibility that this change from middle to old age may be adumbrated in any important way.

Available literature has sometimes suggested that every man ages alone, in the sense of being cut off, by the fact of his age, from others. Thus, people have been advised, as they get older, to start cultivating friends their own age so that they will have shared interests and problems. It seems to be assumed that the "one" who is the reference point is the only one doing any aging, and the tendency for people to think of themselves as remaining much the same has sometimes been overlooked. Most people seem to see their friends as "girls" and "boys" long after these terms have any literal meaning. There is little indication of people aging in ranks, echelons, or generations, but rather some feeling that growing old is a solitary experience, unique to each individual. This may reflect the intense individualism of middle-class intellectual scientists and their weak identity with ranks or echelons of people. These problems face all social researchers, and the reader will have to decide to what extent we have resolved them in the work reported here.

This reflection of individualism in the literature on aging is related to a projection of the standards of middle-aged behavior onto that of the old. Thus, many studies reach such doubtful conclusions as the following: the members of a group of aging people have low morale if they answer certain questions with responses other than those appropriate for a middle-aged respondent.[2] For example, an answer of "no" to the question, "Do you still feel useful to those around you?" was assumed to reflect lowered morale.

Britton and Mather[3] have been sensitive to this tendency, and in an interesting factor analysis of the content of good adjustment norms among older people they showed that the one clearly evident factor was "general activity." This is the bench mark of the young and the middle-aged. As these authors point out, "It could be theorized that adults, still clear in mind, growing into the very late years could lose their capacity for overt activity, but that they could still be well adjusted *if our criteria allowed them to be so.*"

In short, there appears to be a latent assumption that successful aging consists in being as much like a middle-aged person as possible,[4] "Feeling useful" has not been defined, however, and it has not been made clear why old people should be expected to feel that way.

An extension of this implicit theme of continuing usefulness is the feeling that the life span must, in order to be successful, undergo steady expansion. Much of what has been written advises the aging person to continue to develop new interests and to make new contacts. Although physical infirmity is acknowledged, ingenious ways have been offered of overcoming its confining effects. The individual is seen as unfolding and expanding in such a way that every time a role or a relationship is lost, a new one fills its place—perhaps even more than fills it. Studies based on such an assumption are unlikely to deal with the idea of death. As a matter of fact, death is excluded from most of the literature on aging, and it emerges only occasionally as if by accident. This is probably a direct consequence of the belief in the desirability of an ever-expanding life. It is hard to reconcile this idea with death, because the death of old people is a slipping away. If it is believed to be a good thing to remain tightly bound to the fabric of life, death must be a tearing away, and this is not a matter to which much thought has so far been given. It is assumed, but seldom talked about, that death is not an important issue for normal people—that only the morbid or perhaps the gifted think of death. Yet death is a logical preoccupation for those who are going to die, and it seems reasonable that those who are approaching death should give some thought to it, as well as to how their departure will affect the people with whom they have close ties.

Although it makes no room for death, the implicit theory does concede that while the individual is expected to continue to expand, he must overcome some resistance to doing so. This has been blamed on a society oriented to youth and to achievement, and tending to neglect the older person and to remove support from him. Much current writing,[5] whether it says so explicitly or not, recognizes that it is functional for a modern industrial society to pass on roles to the young, because it allows the young both to learn the roles *while* they are still young and to bring to them modern training and perspective. But here again is the assumption that when these roles are handed over at retirement, there is a loss of support for the older person that must be compensated for by other roles and other activites. It has seldom been suggested that people past sixty are glad to quit some of their activities. Handing over is usually described as a loss for which there must be compensation, and, indeed, studies have shown that people anticipate retirement with dread.[6] However, evidence is accumulating that suggests this is not so. Streib[7,8] and Tyhurst[9] have both reported that among a population of middle- and working-class people adjustment and satisfaction increase after retirement, and our findings, as we will report below, are in line with this.

In the implicit theory, the *quality* of interpersonal relationships among the aged is often assumed to remain unchanged. First, the old are apparently expected to maintain indefinitely a desire for instrumentality, or competence in managing the environment. Thus, "feeling wanted," a middle-aged feeling, is projected onto old people as an end in itself, because old people are believed to want to continue to be needed because of their usefulness to others. There is some doubt that this is so. Primitive people do not value feeling needed or wanted for its own sake but, rather, because such a feeling guarantees their survival. Consider Simmons' general statement about the old person in primitive society. He makes it plain that if old people strive to feel wanted, it is because they wish to be warmed, fed, and cared for in their old age:

> Social relationships have provided the strongest securities to the individual, especially in old age. With vitality declining, the aged person has had to rely more and more upon personal relations with others, and upon the reciprocal rights and obligations involved. The strongest reinforcement of these has been through continued performance of useful tasks. . . . (To) withstand the strain of obligations, social ties have had to be continuously revitalized, and for the aged, the surest move to this end has been continued execution of socially useful work.[10]

It is difficult to say why we assume that everyone desires to continue instrumental activity in a society where the performance of useful services is not inevitably tied up with being adequately care for. Why is it not suggested instead that old people may want recognition for having *been* useful, for a *history* of successful instrumentality?

When inner states are considered, the suggestion is that personality should, ideally, be immutable, that the valued "outgoingness" of middle-aged Americans should persist throughout life. Yet there is considerable evidence that increased introversion with age is ubiquitous, and this fact is at odds with a belief in an ever-expanding life. Indeed, a continuing expansion, as suggested above, does imply a persistent extroversion. Some workers have tentatively raised a question about this. Slater[11] asks, for example, if in view of the increased introversion with age, it would not be reasonable to call young introverts and old extroverts deviant, which is absurd. But on the whole the subject is not raised; it seems to be assumed that if introversion starts to increase with age, something should be done to correct the tendency.

Much current writing assumes that while older people of high morale have outgoing, rich, and satisfying relationships, these relationships are entirely free of sexuality.[12] In spite of Plato's relief at being freed of the tyrant desire, there is clinical evidence that sexual relationships are often lifelong, and Kinsey's findings certainly support this view. On this point, Kinsey says:

> The most important generalization to be drawn from the older groups is that they carry on directly the pattern of gradually diminishing activity which started with 16-year olds. Even in the most advanced ages, there is no sudden elimination of any large group of individuals from the picture. Each male may reach the point where he is, physically, no longer capable of sexual performance, and where he loses all interest in further activity; but the rate at which males slow up in these last decades does not exceed the rate at which they have been slowing up and dropping out in the previous age groups. This seems astounding for it is quite contrary to general conceptions of aging processes in sex.[13]

It is obvious that the oldest age groups contain an *accumulation* of people with no further sexual desire, but age alone by no means guarantees this.

Finally, the usual writing about aging suggests that the whole process involves a digging in of the heels and a refusal to be moved. The implication is that aging means moving away from something—the "prime of life," or "usefulness"—but there is little suggestion that it means moving toward something qualitatively different and perhaps, in its own way, equally attractive. Some writings do suggest, with various metaphors such as "the dividend years," that there are compensations in being older, but only if the aging person first achieves resignation and is able to "accept reality." Sometimes it is assumed that old people have a constant temptation to be eccentric and impulsive, or childlike, but this is believed to be a sign of failure that should be controlled. Old people who are really admired do not act like that, but keep on performing and cause the remark, "You'd never guess he was that age!" Finally, nobody, it seems, really looks forward to being old.

To summarize, the overall tone of what is written suggests that aging is an uphill affair. It seems to require much swimming against the stream for the old person to overcome the natural tendency for the world around him to withdraw its support, leaving him deserted. It is implied, however, that if the aging person is watchful and does not let his roles fall empty, and if his family and friends and community are properly oriented toward him and energetic in their convictions, he can be kept in a permanent equilibrium, differing only biologically from his middle-aged equilibrium. From this it is inferred that the middle-aged state is much preferable to the aged state, and that to remain in it indefinitely is to succeed, while to leave it and shift openly to a different stage of the lifecycle is to fail.

In interesting contrast, the writings about the maturation of the child do not indicate whether adolescence is preferable to early childhood or less desirable. Usually a transition is just described. And yet surely the loss of childhood is in some ways more poignant than the loss of middle age. Writers certainly do not make it sound so.

In some ways, we have set up a straw man here. However, we think it useful to set forth the doubts that visited us as we examined the underlying assumptions of the work we reviewed. Furthermore, as we have said above, we are substituting one common sense theory of aging for another, and it is useful to see what we are discarding when we examine what we are offering in its place. Having indicated some of the inconsistencies we have seen in the implicit theory of aging, we will try to be as critical of our own theory as we develop it.

Notes

¹This procedure is circular—we are influenced in our predictions by familiarity with the material. However, we are not so badly influenced that we can afford the luxury of new subjects every time we modify our concepts. Eventually we hope to see all of the conclusions here reported tested on other populations.

²Elaine Cumming and D. M. Schneider, "Sibling Solidarity: A Feature of American Kinship." *The American Anthropologist*, June, 1961.

³Lois R. Dean, Elaine Cumming, D. S. Newell, "Interaction Style and

Success in Aging." Paper read to the American Sociological Society meetings, Seattle, August, 1958.

[4]We are aware that the class of the investigator is often an important factor in what he assumes about his respondents, but we will not complicate the issue with this problem at this point.

[5]C. L. Stone and W. L. Slocum, *A Look at Thurston County's Older People*. Washington Agricultural Experiment Stations, Institute of Agricultural Sciences, State College of Washington, Bulletin 573, May, 1957.

[6]I. Lorge and J. Tuckman, *Retirement and the Industrial Worker*. (New York: Columbia University Press, 1953, pp. 20–37.)

[7]G. F. Streib, "Morale of the Retired," *Social Problems,* Vol. 3, 1956, p. 270.

[8]G. F. Streib, W. E. Thompson, E. A. Suchman, "The Cornell Study of Occupational Retirement" *Journal of Social Issues,* Vol. 14, 1958, p. 3.

[9]J. Tyhurst, Lee Salk, Miriam Kennedy, "Morbidity, Mortality and Retirement." Paper read to the 23rd Meeting of the A.A.A.S., New York, 1956.

[10]L. W. Simmons, *The Role of the Aged in Primitive Society*. (New Haven: Yale University Press, 1945, p. 177).

[11]P. E. Slater, "Personality Structure in Old Age," *Correlates of Anxiety*. Unpublished report from the Age Center in New England, 1958.

[12]There is ambivalence in this asexual view of old people, as many jokes show. For example, there is the story of an old man in his seventies who married a girl of eighteen. He consulted his doctor about how he could be most sure of producing an heir. The doctor, embarrassed, suggested that, as she was just a girl and might find it lonely living with him, they should take in a lodger. This would keep her cheerful and make her more likely to conceive. A short time later, the old man came to the doctor and said, "You were quite right, she's pregnant." The doctor offered congratulations and asked cautiously, "And how is the lodger?" "Fine," replied the old man. "She's pregnant too." The laughter that follows this joke is caused not only by surprise but by the unexpected upward revision of our opinion of the old man, when we realize that we were wrong in assuming him impotent.

[13]A. C. Kinsey, W. B. Pomeroy, C. E. Martin, *Sexual Behavior in the Human Male*. (Philadelphia: Saunders, 1948, p. 235).

SELECTED BIBLIOGRAPHY

A convincing illustration of how purportedly neutral scientific descriptions of mental change in old age can carry ageist oversight and bias can be seen by comparing David Guttman's anthropological classic "Aging Among the Highland Maya: A Comparative Study," *Journal of Personality and Social Psychology* (1967) and Kathleen M. Woodward, "Master Songs of Meditation: The Late poems of Eliot, Pound, Stevens and Williams" in Stuart F. Spicker, Kathleen M. Woodward, and David D. VanTassel, *AEHPG*. The same mental changes in old age are described by Guttman as cognitive decline and by Woodward as metamorphic cognitive growth. The limits of scientific theories of aging, as well as their tendency to carry hidden evaluative implications, are well described in Geri Berg and Sally Gadow, "Toward More Human Meanings of Aging: Ideals and Images from Philosophy of Art," also in *AEHPG*. A brief analysis of the sometimes value-laden hidden connotations of scientific language is given by Robert Kastenbaum in his editorial "From the Editor-Running Subjects: A Change in Editorial Policy," *IJAHD*, 1973. A philosophically sophistocated discussion of normative bias in current theories of aging is found in "Notes for a Radical Gerontology," *IJAHD*, 1978, by Victor Marshal and Joseph Tindale. The authors argue that current theories in social gerontology contain a conservative bias toward conformity of aging individuals to society, and propose an alternative perspective stressing a less conformist image of the elderly. The role of negative stereotypes about aging in hypothesis formation in gerontology is examined by Ethel Straus in "Social Myth as Hypothesis: The Case of the Family Relations of Old People," *G*, 1979.

Ethical aspects of the tension between observation and personal rights, such as the right to privacy, are examined in Wilbur H. Watson, "Resistances to Naturalistic Observation in a Geriatric Setting," *IJAHD*, 1979.

The persistence and subtlety of bias in perceptions, descriptions, and classifications of the elderly is examined in a way useful for philosophy of science, in Leo Miller's essay "Toward a Classification of Aging Behavior," *G*, 1979.

Ethical values presupposed by current research objectives and preoccupations in gerontology are analyzed in Roy Hamlin, "A Utility Theory of Old Age," *G*, 1967. Hamlin argues that current research in gerontology is controlled by an excessive loyalty to physiological change as the exclusive underlying explanation of behavior in old age. Ethical questions about the overall direction, goals, and methods of establishing priorities in gerontological research are discussed by Leonard Hayflick in his provocative essay "Quantity, Quality and Responsibility in Aging Research," *G*, 1971. The ethical basis and intellectual rationale for research on aging is explored in James Birren, "Research on Aging: A Frontier of Science and Social Gain," *G*, 1967. Birren discusses the ethical nature of the gerontologist's commitment to enhancing the quality of human life. The role of the humanities, including history and ethics, in providing knowledge of aging is supported by Joseph Freeman in "Humanism and the Humanities of Aging," *G*, 1977. The importance of philosophy and history of science for gerontology is explained by Eric Cassell in "On Educational Changes for the Field of Aging," *G*, 1972. Cassell argues that the ideal of scientific explanation as reductive analysis has thwarted our attempts to provide an adequate scientific theory of aging. The need for basic philosophical knowledge in the education of geriatric professionals, including knowledge of moral theory and the philosophy of the person, is explained by Naomi Brill in "Basic Knowledge for Work With the Aging," *G*, 1969. A similar view is expressed in "Concepts, Knowledge and Commitment: The Education of a Practicing Gerontologist," by Walter M. Beattie, Jr., *G*, 1969. Beattie stresses the need for an ethical theory of social and professional commitment in the education of gerontologists.

Problems in the logic of longitudinal research, as well as other problems in the philosophy of gerontological sciences, are summarized in James Birren, et al. "Research, Demonstration and Training: Issues in Methodology in Social Gerontology," *G*, 1972. Logical and empirical difficulties encountered in predicting behavior from longitudinal research are described and analyzed in Erdman Palmore and Vira Kivett, "Changes in Life Satisfaction: A Longitudinal Study of Persons Aged 46–70," *JG*, 1977. Carefully analyzed conceptual proposals for a logic of longitudinal research in gerontology are given by K. Warner Schaie in "External Validity in the Assessment of Intellectual Development in Adulthood," *JG*, 1978. Schaie proposes a highly relativized or "situational" concept of validity for tests of intellectual abilities in old age. The same theme is further explored by Schaie, with Rick J. Scheidt, in "A Taxonomy of Situations for an Elderly Population: Generating Situational Criteria," *JG*, 1978. Several main issues are explained with clarity and brevity in Paul Baltes, "The Logical Status of Age as an Experimental Variable: Comments on Some Methodological Issues," in K. Warner Schaie (ed.), *Theory and Methods of Research on Aging* (Morgantown, West Virginia: West Virginia University Press, 1964), where Baltes argues that only postdictive rather than inductive or predictive inferences are logically defensible in aging research. Analyses of the problems of longitudinal research are found in John Nesselroade and Hayne W. Resse, (eds.), *Life Span Developmental Psychology: Methodological Issues* (New York: Academic Press, 1973). See also P. Baltes, "Longitudinal and Cross-Sectional Sequences in the Study of Age and Generation Effects," *HD*, 1968 and James E. Birren, "Principles of Research on Aging," in James E. Birren, (ed.), *Handbook of Aging and the Individual* (Chicago: University of Chicago Press, 1959). A clear explanation and discussion of the central conceptual problems is given by Robert Butler in his "The Facade of Chronological Age," *American Journal of Psychiatry*, 1963. For more detailed discussions of the same problems, see Gordon F. Strieb, "Longitudinal Studies in Social Gerontology," in Richard H. William, Clark Tibbetts and Elma Donahue, *Processes of Aging II* (New York: Atherton Press, 1963) and H. E. Jones, "Problems of Method in Longitudinal Research," *Vita Humana*, 1958. Conceptual problems in the related normative concepts of validity and reliability are examined in Jack Botwinick, *Aging and Behavior* (New York: Springer, 1973, Chaps. 19 and 20). Some limits of statistical norms for describing old persons are discussed in "Aged Negroes: Their Cultural Departures from Statistical Stereotypes and Rural-Urban Differences: by Jacqueline Johnson Jackson, *G*, 1970. An extended analysis illustrating the kinds of factors that can undermine generalization in longitudinal research is given by Leonard Cain in "Aging and the Character of Our Times" *G*, 1968. The same methodological problems as well as ethical aspects of the use of human subjects in age-related scientific research and the relation of individual differences to laws of development are analyzed in D. B. Bromley, *The Psychology of Human Aging* (Baltimore: Pelican Books, 1966).

An analysis of the nature of scientific knowledge in relation to social gerontology is given by Robert C. Atchley in *The Social Forces in Later Life* (Belmont, Ca.: Wadsworth, 1972). See also "Emerging Principles and Concepts" by Wilma Donahue, in Wilma Donahue and Clark Tibbits (eds.), *The New Frontiers of Aging* (Ann Arbor, Mich.: University of Michigan Press, 1957). A useful overview of competing theories of aging in biology, sociology and psychology is given by Ewald W. Busse in "Theories of Aging," in

Ewald W. Busse and Eric Pfeiffer (eds.), *Behavior and Adaptation in Late Life*, 2nd ed. (Boston, Little, Brown, 1977). A similarly useful summary giving perspective on the recent history of the development of theories in social gerontology is found in Chapter 5,of Jon Hendricks and C. Davis Hendricks, *Aging in Mass Society* (Cambridge, Mass.: Winthrop, 1977). A general philosophical and historical perspective on the aims and progress of theories in gerontology is given by Robert Kastenbaum in "Gerontology's Search for Understanding," *G*, 1978. In this essay Kastenbaum criticizes the ideal of a "value-neutral" science of gerontology.

Several issues in philosophy of science, including discussions of the relations between observed facts and theories and the nature of conceptual revolutions in science, are discussed in the essays on ecological theories of aging in *G*, 1968. See especially the introductory essay by Alfred Lauton and Thomas Rich, "Ecology and Gerontology," where the limits of a purely empiricist gerontology are discussed. Conceptual problems in describing and explaining psychological behavior in old age are discussed in Marjorie Fiske Lowenthal, "Psycho Social Variations Across the Adult Life Span," *G*, 1975, and Bernice Neugarten, "Adult Personality: Toward a Psychology of the Life Cycle" in Edgar Vinacke (ed.), *Readings in General Psychology* (New York: American Book, 1968).

In James Birren's "Research on Aging: A Frontier of Science and Social Gain," *G*, 1971, just mentioned in connection with the underlying philosophy of research on aging, Birren defends the view that gerontology is necessarily a multidisciplinary field. This view is explained with clarity by George Saslo in "Opportunities and Obligations," *G*, 1968. An epistemological rationale for this multidisciplinary model is given by Barry Lebowitz in "The Management of Research on Aging: A Case Study in Science Policy," *G*, 1979. The multidisciplinary model is also supported in David Guttman, Frances Eyster, and Garland Lewis, "Improving the Care of the Aged Through Interdisciplinary Efforts," *G*, 1975, and in Theodore Krauss, Interdisciplinary Communication in the Fields of Geriatrics and Gerontology," *G*, 1972. The same model is criticized by Robert Kastenbuam in "Theories of Human Aging: The Search for a Conceptual Framework," in *The Journal of Social Issues,* Vol. 21, 1965. According to Kastenbaum, the multidisciplinary model leads only to an atomized collection of findings from disciplines with different methods and theories, which cannot give a single unified understanding of old age that should be the goal of a theory of aging. A similar view is defended by Michel Philibert in "The Emergence of Social Gerontology," which is in the same volume. Kastenbuam presents a "developmentalist" theory of aging that is meant to be more comprehensive than the theories of individual disciplines in "Is Old Age the End of Development?" in R. Kastenbaum (ed.), *New Thoughts on Old Age* (New York: Springer, 1964). Theories of aging are discussed from a philosophically interesting perspective in "Gerontology, A Relatively New Area of Social Science in France," by Anne-Marie Guillemard, *G,* 1975 and in "The Functional Context of Elderly Behavior," by George Robok and William Hoyer, *G,* 1977. Robok and Hoyer favor a pluralist theoretical framework that combines the explanatory principles of separate disciplines without attempting to reduce them to a single theory.

Several issues in philosophy of science, including the nature of theories and their conflicts, and the role of hypotheses, are discussed in Jaber F. Gubrium, "Toward a Socio-Environmental Theory of Aging," *G,* 1972. Logical features of the disengagement theory are critically examined by Arlie Russell Hochschild in "Disengagement Theory: A Logical, Empirical and Phenomenological Critique," in Jaber F. Gubrium (ed.), *Time, Roles, and Self in Old Age* (New York: Human Sciences Press, 1976). An outline for an "intentionalist" theory of aging, which stresses the autonomous, proactive dimension of the experience of aging, as opposed to changes wrought by the physical, psychological, or social causation impinging on the aging person, is developed by Marjorie Fiske Lowenthal in "Intentionality: Toward a Framework for the Study of Adaptation in Adulthood," *IJAD,* 1971. This essay, like much of Lowenthal's work, should be of special interest to philosophers interested in aging. A useful discussion of the general advantages of, and obstacles to, the explicit development of theories in gerontology is found in Bruce W. Lemon, Vern Gengtson and James Peterson, "An Exploration of the Activity Theory of Aging: Activity Types and Life Satisfaction Among In-Movers to a Retirement Community," *JG*, 1972. The need for a general theory of aging emphasizing the social context of the aging person's experience is described by Ruth Bennet in "Social Context—A Neglected Variable in Research on Aging," *IJAHD*, 1970. A discussion of theories of aging and a proposal for an alternative to the major theories is found in "Aging as Exchange: A Preface to Theory," by James Dowd, *JG*, 1975. A theme similar to Dowd's is developed in J. David Martin, "Power, Dependence and the Complaints of the Elderly: A Social Exchange Perspective," *IJAHD*, 1971. The methodologic assumptions and relative explanatory power of the activity and disengagement theories are examined, and an alternative theoretical perspective developed, in Jaber Gubrium's *The Myth of the Golden Years* (Springfield, Ill: Charles C Thomas, 1973). Several essays developing and defending still another theoretical framework for explaining behavior and experience in old age—the "life-span framework"—are presented in *Life Span Models of Psychological Aging: A White Elephant?*, edited by Paul Blates, in *G*, 1973. Differences and similarities of two broad conceptual schemes that control much research on aging, and their relative strengths and weaknesses, are analyzed by Leroy Duncan in "Ecology and Aging," in which he also defends an ecologic framework for theoretical explanations of aging. The ecologic framework is also defended by John Bruhn in "An Ecological Perspective of Aging," *G*, 1971.

INDEX